COLLEGE CRIME

A Statistical Study of Offenses on American Campuses

R. Barri Flowers

McFarland & Company, Inc., Publishers
Jefferson, North Carolina, and London

LIBRARY OF CONGRESS CATALOGUING-IN-PUBLICATION DATA

Flowers, R. Barri (Ronald Barri)
    College crime : a statistical study of offenses on American
campuses / R. Barri Flowers.
        p.   cm.
    Includes bibliographical references and index.

    ISBN 978-0-7864-4034-4
    softcover : 50# alkaline paper ∞

    1. College students — Crimes against — United States — Statistics.
2. Universities and colleges — Security measures — United States —
Statistics.   3. Campus violence — United States — Statistics.
I. Title.
HV6250.4.S78F66   2009
364.10973 — dc22   2009034200

British Library cataloguing data are available

Cover images ©2009 Shutterstock

Manufactured in the United States of America

*McFarland & Company, Inc., Publishers
    Box 611, Jefferson, North Carolina 28640
    www.mcfarlandpub.com*

To H. Loraine, Marjah Aljean,
and college student nieces Kendre and Keeare

and to Michigan State University students
and alumni and the memories of life on campus.

TABLE OF CONTENTS

PREFACE

Colleges and universities across the nation offer, for the most part, a safe and welcoming environment for young adults to make the transition from high school into adulthood and independence. The campus brings together people from many backgrounds, races, ethnicities, nationalities, cultures, and religions, which makes for a great melting pot of ideas, perspectives, and open minds. At the same time, many traditions are passed on from generation to generation, such as forming friendships, becoming members of fraternities and sororities and athletic teams, and having new sexual experiences. Though these are all normal aspects of becoming a college student, they also can bring about circumstances that lead to criminality and victimization.

Recent years have seen their fair share of negative attention cast on institutions of higher learning with the focus on such issues as underage drinking, drug abuse, shootings, sexual assaults, stalking, and hate crimes. Though many students are able to complete their studies with no major issues of personal safety or misconduct, few students are untouched by the problems of unlawful or risky behavior experienced by most schools. Alcohol and drug use on and around campus is high and is often associated with other forms of aberrant behavior, which may lead to serious or violent criminality.

Considered a rite of passage, drinking and experimenting with drugs are as much a part of college life as attending classes, studying, and socializing. Underage drinking, binge drinking, smoking marijuana, and other forms of drug abuse, such as nonmedical use of prescription drugs, often in combination, are routine in the lives of many students. In some instances, the onset of substance abuse began in high school or even earlier, before the alcohol and/or drug users brought their dangerous habits to the college setting. In other cases, college becomes a learning ground and setting where strong peer pressure and the desire to conform outweigh the risks associated with alcohol and drug use (negative effects on one's health and school performance, increased susceptibility for crime offending or victimization, and other detrimental behaviors).

College Crime explores the scope of underage drinking, binge drinking, and alcohol abuse on campus, as well as drug use and abuse and its implications. The relationship between alcohol, drugs, and criminality, such as murder, sexual assault, dating violence, stalking, and hate crime is examined. Attention is also given to other aspects of crime occurring on university and college campuses and surrounding areas, including the prevalence, patterns, characteristics, precursors, victims and offenders. Finally, the issues of campus safety and crime prevention and victim resources are addressed, along with current laws aimed at prevention, deterrence, and controlling campus crime.

I extend gratitude to H. Loraine, without whose superb computer skills I would be lost.

Chapter 1

UNDERAGE ALCOHOL USE

The use and abuse of alcohol by juveniles and young adults has proven to be a persistent problem in the United States. In spite of a steady decline in underage drinking in recent years, there continues to be a significant number of youth younger than twenty-one consuming alcohol. In many instances, this has been in the dangerous form of binge drinking or in conjunction with other drugs. Underage alcohol use has also been a key factor in automobile accidents and related fatalities, campus crime and victimization, suicide, and other high-risk behavior such as family violence. Drinking has been shown to affect school performance and lead to various health-related consequences including alcoholism, alcohol poisoning, and sexual activity resulting in unplanned pregnancies and sexually transmitted diseases. Efforts by a number of federal agencies, community-based organizations, and advocacy groups have confronted underage drinking with some success, but clearly much more needs to be done to curb alcohol use and abuse by this group.

Minimum Legal Drinking Age

In an effort to contain underage drinking and the negative consequences associated with it, the National Minimum Drinking Age Act was signed into law in 1984.[1] It raised the national minimum age for the purchase or public possession of alcoholic beverages to twenty-one. With the Federal Aid Highway Act, states that failed to enforce the minimum age requirement would receive ten percent less in annual highway funds.[2] According to the U.S. Department of Transportation, the act has led to the compliance of all states.[3] The law does not forbid the consumption of alcohol by persons under twenty-one, per se. Indeed, in most states underage drinking is allowed under certain circumstances, such as in private, with the supervision of parents or guardians, and for medical or religious purposes.[4]

Much of the evidence reveals that the higher legal minimum age for drinking has proven effective in reducing alcohol use by persons under twenty-one, as well as lowering the incidence of automobile accidents and fatalities, suicide, and alcohol-related offenses and arrests.[5] While some believe that lower legal minimum drinking ages in other countries may actually result in less alcohol-based issues than in the United States, research has not supported this. For instance, the 2003 European School Survey Project on Alcohol and Drugs (ESPAD) indicates that the rates of drunkenness and binge drinking involving fifteen and sixteen year olds in France, Italy, and the United States are comparable.[6]

Opponents of the minimum legal drinking age argue that it is too high and has done more harm than good. This includes a group of over 130 chancellors and presidents of colleges and universities across the United States, who contend that alcohol use and abuse by youth persists in spite of current drinking laws. The Amethyst Initiative, named for the purple gemstone amethyst, which in Ancient Greece was thought to protect against intoxication, calls for debate on the twenty-one-year-old minimum legal drinking age.[7] Overall, limiting the purchase of alcohol and public consumption capabilities of young people continues to enjoy wide support in the United States.

The Prevalence of College Drinking

The laws and other efforts aimed at preventing or decreasing underage drinking notwithstanding, alcohol use and abuse by this group and its ramifications remain a serious concern. Alcohol is easily the most frequently used type of drug by today's youth.[8] It is often used in excess as well as with other drugs, making the effects even more threatening.[9] According to a recent National Epidemiologic Survey on Alcohol and Related Conditions (NESARC), around 70 percent of young adults in the United States drank alcohol in the year prior to the survey.[10] This represented some nineteen million people. Around 46 percent reported their consumption of alcohol went beyond the recommended amount per day on at least one occasion in the last year, while 14.5 percent drank an average amount surpassing the recommended maximum per week.

College students are especially prone to drinking. Believed by many to be a rite of passage, the use of alcohol is as commonplace on campus as attending classes with students feeling constant pressure to maintain tradition and/or fit in. Consequently, many such students become problem drinkers, leading to further problems.

How pervasive is drinking on college campuses across the United States? The indicators are alarming. More than four out of every five college students consume alcohol.[11] A high percentage of these drinkers are underage. According to the National Survey on Drug Use and Health (NSDUH), between 2002 and 2005, 57.8 percent of full-time college students ages eighteen to twenty drank alcohol in the past month, 40.1 percent were binge drinkers, and 16.6 percent consumed alcohol heavily.[12] Male students were more likely than female students to have been alcohol-involved in all three categories.

The NSDUH reported that in 2005, full-time college students between the ages of eighteen and twenty-two were more likely than part-time students or non college students to have consumed alcohol in the past month, been binge drinkers, or heavy alcohol users.[13] In a Monitoring the Future National Survey (MTF), it was found that college students who drink alcohol often do so in larger quantities than their non college student counterparts.[14]

In a study by Paul Greenbaum and colleagues of college freshman drinking patterns, it was found that alcohol consumption tended to increase around spring break, Thanksgiving, Christmas, New Year's Day, and just after they began attending school.[15] The study found, however, that alcohol use by freshmen varied significantly within the school year, likely based on classes and other aspects of campus life and holidays.

College Binge Drinking

Many students engage in drinking binges as part of the college experience. Binge drinking is the most dangerous form of alcohol use by young adults with wide-ranging implications.[16] Defining what constitutes binge or heavy episodic drinking has varied from one source to another. The NSDUH defines binge drinking as consuming five or more drinks during one occasion on at least one day within the last thirty days.[17] Heavy use of alcohol is defined as consuming five or more drinks on the same occasion on five days or more during the last thirty days. All heavy users of alcohol are considered binge drinkers.

The National Institute on Alcohol Abuse and Alcoholism's (NIAAA) National Advisory Council defines binge drinking as "a pattern of drinking alcohol that brings blood alcohol concentration (BAC) to 0.08 gram-percent or above. For a typical adult, this pattern corresponds to consuming 5 or more drinks (male), or 4 or more drinks (female), in about 2 hours."[18] Others require a longer span of alcohol abuse in order to refer to it as binge drinking. For instance, some clinicians define binging as two or more days "during which time a person repeatedly becomes intoxicated and gives up his or her usual activities and obligations in order to become intoxicated."[19]

The seriousness of binge drinking amongst youth is reflected in the data. While underage drinking is against the law, persons under age twenty account for 11 percent of all the alcohol consumption in the United States.[20] Over 90 percent of this alcohol is consumed through binge drinking.[21]

Studies show that about two of every five college students have been involved in binge drinking on at least one occasion in the past two weeks.[22] Some researchers have reported that many college binge drinkers' use of alcohol far exceeds five drinks on one occasion. A disturbing example is "the practice of attempting to drink 21 shots within the first hour starting at midnight of one's 21st birthday, which has resulted in alcohol poisonings."[23]

A correlation has been shown between college binge drinking or heavy alcohol usage and the college environment. In the Harvard School of Public Health College Alcohol Study (CAS), more than 50,000 students were surveyed from 120 colleges between 1993 and 2001.[24] The study found that binge drinkers were more likely to have academic troubles, social issues, high-risk sexual behavior, dangerous driving situations, alcohol-related injuries or overdose, and involvement with illegal drugs. The CAS also noted the second hand effects of problem drinkers to the campus environment, such as disrupting studies, sexual assaults, and vandalism.

Some researchers have suggested that many college students are erroneously labeled as binge drinkers. For instance, in a study by Dennis Thombs and associates of the nighttime blood alcohol concentration (BAC) of students at Kent State during a full semester, the BAC of the students was found on average to be much lower than what would be considered intoxication.[25] This could indicate that there is less problem drinking among college students than currently believed.

Trends in Underage College Drinking

Trends suggest that underage college binge and heavy drinking has remained relatively stable in recent years. The NSDUH reported that from 2002 to 2005, a yearly average of 40.1 percent of the full-time students ages eighteen to twenty were involved in binge drinking, while 16.6 percent consumed heavy amounts of alcohol. Nearly six in ten underage students consumed alcohol annually over the span (see Figure 1.1).

As seen in Figure 1.2, from 2002 to 2005, underage binge drinking for full-time college students increased with age. Nearly 44 percent of the twenty year olds were binge drinkers compared to almost 37 percent of the eighteen-year-olds. The pattern was true as well for heavy alcohol users and alcohol use within the past month. Heavy alcohol use was nearly 5 percent higher among twenty year olds than eighteen-year-olds, while almost 11 percent more twenty year olds consumed alcohol in the past month than eighteen-year-olds.

Underage full-time male college students were more likely than underage females attending college full-time to binge drink, consume alcohol heavily, and use alcohol within the past month during the three year span (see Figure 1.3). Almost half the males surveyed were binge drinkers; while nearly twice as many male students were heavy drinkers as female students.

The 2007 National Survey on Drug Use and Health indicates that full-time college students have consistently been more likely than part-time students or non students to be current users of alcohol, binge drink, and drink heavily in recent years.[26] As shown in Figure 1.4, between

Figure 1.1
Past Month, Binge, and Heavy Alcohol Use Among
Full-Time College Students Ages 18 to 20, By Year: 2002–2005

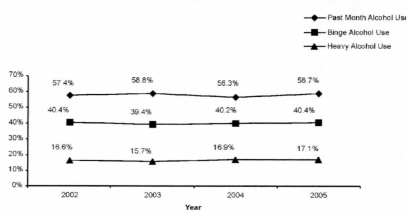

SOURCE: National Survey on Drug Use and Health, "Underage Alcohol Use Among Full-Time College Students," *NSDUH Report* 31 (2006).

Figure 1.2
Past Month, Binge, and Heavy Alcohol Use Among
Full-Time College Students Ages 18 to 20, by Age: 2002–2005

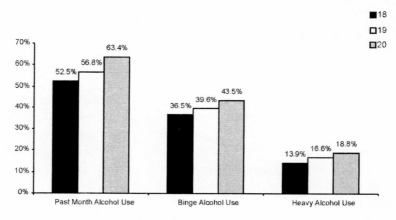

SOURCE: National Survey on Drug Use and Health, "Underage Alcohol Use Among Full-Time College Students," *NSDUH Report* 31 (2006).

Figure 1.3
Past Month, Binge, and Heavy Alcohol Use Among
Full-Time College Students Ages 18 to 20, by Gender: 2002–2005

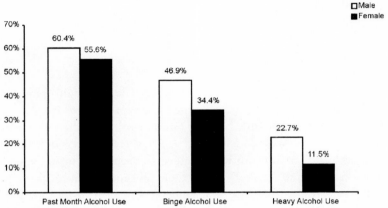

SOURCE: National Survey on Drug Use and Health, "Underage Alcohol Use Among Full-Time College Students," *NSDUH Report* 31 (2006).

Figure 1.4
Heavy Alcohol Use Among Adults Aged 18 to 22,
by College Enrollment: 2002–2007

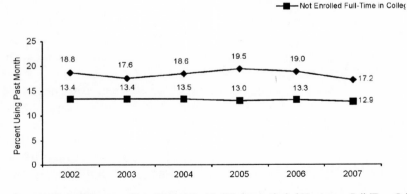

SOURCE: National Survey on Drug Use and Health, "Underage Alcohol Use Among Full-Time College Students," *NSDUH Report* 31 (2006).

9

2002 and 2007, heavy consumption of alcohol by full-time students ages eighteen to twenty-two was higher every year than for persons not enrolled full-time. Both groups showed a slight decline in heavy alcohol use during the span.

Onset of Underage Drinking

Though it is clear that entry into college and the resulting pressures and drinking environment play a major role in underage alcohol use by students, most who drink became familiar with alcohol well before attending college. According to the NIAAA, three-quarters of 12th grade students, over two-thirds of 10th graders, and around four in ten eighth graders have drunk alcohol during their lifetime beyond a few sips.[27] Forty-five percent of high school seniors, 34 percent of 10th grade students, and 17 percent of eighth grade students reported drinking alcohol within the past month. Three in ten seniors reported heavy episodic high school drinking, just over that number were intoxicated, and nearly three in four drank alcohol in the past year.[28]

Other research has supported these findings. The 2007 Youth Risk Behavior Survey (YRBS) reported that over the past thirty days, 45 percent of high school students drank some alcohol, 26 percent were binge drinkers, 11 percent drove while drinking, and 29 percent were in a car with a driver who had consumed alcohol.[29] Similarly, according to the Monitoring the Future Survey, in 2007, 72 percent of 12th grade students had tasted alcohol and 44 percent had done so within the past month; while 39 percent of eighth grade students drank alcohol, with 16 percent drinking in the last month.[30]

Some studies have shown that the onset of underage drinking begins even earlier. In a recent review of national and state surveys on children and alcohol use, it was found that 10 percent of students in the fourth grade had drank more than a sip of alcohol, with 7 percent having a drink in the last year.[31] The surveys revealed that underage alcohol usage increased with age, actually doubling between fourth and sixth graders. One survey reported that among sixth graders, 62 percent of boys and 58 percent of girls had ever tried alcohol.[32]

10

Underage binge drinking has been even more disturbing. The NIAAA found that 29 percent of students in the 12th grade, 22 percent in the 10th grade, and 11 percent of those in eighth grade have been binge drinkers.[33] The NSDUH reported that in 2007, 19 percent of youth twelve to twenty years of age were involved in binge drinking.[34] Males were more likely than females in this age group to be binge drinkers or heavy drinkers, while current alcohol use rates were similar. Binge drinking by high schoolers has been linked to such issues as cigarette smoking, poor grades, dating violence, and substance abuse.[35]

Underage drinkers' access to alcohol typically comes from their parents, adults purchasing it for them, and through social functions where alcohol is present. The ease in which alcohol is made available to minors is often the precursor to underage college drinking.

Trends in Underage Drinking

Recent trends have shown underage student drinking to be on the decline. The 2008 MTF report revealed that drinking within the past month for eighth graders has declined 37 percent and 33 percent for 10th graders since 1991 when the monitoring began. The rate of alcohol use in the past month by 12th grade students was the lowest it has been since the tracking started in 1975. From 2005 to 2008, lifetime prevalence rates of alcohol use by 12th graders fell 3.2 percent, 4.9 percent for 10th grade students, and 2.1 percent by eighth graders.[36]

Similarly, the YRBS reported that between 1993 and 2007, the prevalence of alcohol use by high school students in grades nine through twelve decreased in lifetime alcohol use, current use, episodic heavy drinking, and drinking alcohol on school property (see Figure 1.5). Drinking alcohol at some point in life fell nearly 6 percent over the span, while episodic heavy drinking dropped 4 percent, current alcohol use 3.3 percent, and drinking on school property 2.2 percent.

The PRIDE Surveys Report supports these findings. From 2006-07 and 2007-08, any alcohol use by junior high school students fell 4.3 percent, high school students fell 3 percent, and high school seniors fell 2.4 percent.[37] Comparatively, the 2007 NSDUH reported that between

Figure 1.5
Trends in the Prevalence of Alcohol Use,
National YRBS: 1993–2007

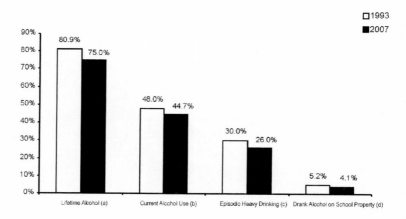

ª Consumed at least onee drink of alcohol on at least one day over lifetime.
ᵇ Consumed at least one drink of alcohol on at least one day within the 30 days prior to the survey.
ᶜ Consumed five or more alcoholic drinks in a row two hours on at least one day prior to the survey.
ᵈ Consumed at least one drink of alcohol on at least one day within the 30 days prior to the survey.

SOURCE: Adapted from the National Center for Chronic Disease Prevention and Health Promotion, *Trends in the Prevalence of Alcohol Use, National YRBS: 1993–2007*, http://www.cdc.gov/Healthy Youth/yrbs/trends.htm.

2002 and 2007, drinking over the past month for persons ages twelve to seventeen declined nearly 2 percent.[38]

In spite of these trends, the numbers of underage and college bound youth who drink alcohol remains a serious concern.

College Drinking, Consequences, and Criminality

Underage and/or excessive college drinking can bring about a host of problems for the drinker and others. These include serious health implications, drunk driving related accidents and deaths, and alcohol dependence.[39] According to the NIAAA's Task Force on College Drinking and other studies, consuming alcohol is responsible for more than 1,700 college student fatalities each year, while around 600,000 are unintentionally injured as a result of intoxication annually.[40] Alcohol-related health issues affect more than 150,000 students yearly, while nearly 2 percent of students report attempting suicide in the past year while under the influence of alcohol or drugs.[41]

Drinking alcohol can also result in criminal behavior and victimization. Almost 700,000 students between eighteen and twenty-four years of age are assaulted by a student under the influence of alcohol annually. More than 400,000 of the student perpetrators are younger than twenty-one.[42]

Sexual abuse on campus is often alcohol-related. Over 97,000 students eighteen to twenty-four are sexually assaulted or victims of date rape each year by a perpetrator who had been drinking. Around half the victims are under the age of twenty-one.[43] In addition, over 100,000 students in this age group report having had sexual relations while being too intoxicated to know if it was consensual.[44]

Vandalism is another common form of criminality in college settings tied to alcohol use and abuse. More than one out of every ten students who drink admit to damaging property while intoxicated.[45]

It is estimated that 100,000 college students eighteen to twenty-four years of age are arrested for alcohol-related offenses, including driving under the influence and public drunkenness.[46] Around 5 percent of students at four-year colleges have contact with the police or campus security due to drinking alcohol.[47]

According to *Alcohol and Drugs on American College Campuses*, in 2002 more than two-thirds of student respondents reported being the victims of physical violence shortly after having consumed alcohol or drugs.[48] Over one-third reported receiving threats of physical violence, and nearly half had been the victims of theft where force was used or threat of force after drinking or using drugs.

Another study of alcohol-related issues experienced by college students found that the percentage who had negative experiences varied according to their living arrangements. Those who lived in fraternity or sorority houses or residence halls where alcohol use was permitted were more likely than those who lived off campus or dormitories where alcohol was not allowed to have experienced such things serious arguments, assaults, and unwanted sexual advances.[49]

Reducing the Incidence of Underage Drinking

The prevention and reduction of underage drinking on college campuses across the country has gained traction in recent years with a number of initiatives. These include colleges providing alcohol-free residences, banning beer kegs and self-serving alcohol at campus parties, prohibiting the marketing or sale of alcoholic beverages at colleges and universities, and teaching students stress coping mechanisms other than drinking alcohol or using drugs. Studies have shown that these strategies have proven effective in lowering the incidence of binge drinking on campus and underage heavy episodic drinking.[50]

Other strategies have been successfully applied to the college drinkers and underage drinkers in general, such as:

- Enforcing minimum legal drinking age laws more seriously.
- Greater emphasis on enforcement of zero-tolerance laws.
- Raising prices on alcohol, usually through increasing taxes.
- Keeping a limit on the number of places locally that sell liquor, such as bars.
- Better training and procedures for personnel who serve or sell alcohol to prevent selling to underage drinkers or persons intoxicated.

Some research has indicated that there is a relationship between increased prices of alcohol and decreased consumption by underage and college drinkers who are generally more cash strapped than older drinkers.[51]

The federal government, advocacy groups, and the alcohol beverage industry are also tackling the problem of underage drinking. With the enactment of the Consolidated Appropriation Act of 2004, the Interagency Coordinating Committee on the Prevention of Underage Drinking (ICCPUD) was established.[52] Led by the Substance Abuse and Mental Health Services Administration (SAMHSA), the agency includes those representing the National Institute on Alcohol Abuse and Alcoholism, Office of Safe and Drug Free Schools, Office of the Surgeon

General, and the Office of Juvenile Justice and Delinquency Prevention.[53] (See also Chapter 2.)

Advocacy groups involved with the committee include Mothers Against Drunk Driving, Students Against Destructive Decisions, and National Liquor Law Enforcement Association; with the alcohol beverage industry represented by such groups as the Beer Wholesalers Association and Distilled Spirits Council of the United States.[54]

Chapter 2

DRUG USE

Drug use among college students has been on the decline since 1980, when 56 percent of students had used some type of illicit drug in the previous twelve months. While this is a positive sign and an indication that educational and preventative measures have had a positive effect, use and abuse of illegal and prescription drugs remains a serious issue for students attending colleges and universities around the country. Currently around 35 percent of college students are illegal drug users, with the percentage higher when adding the increasing number of students who misuse prescription drugs. Alcohol is the "drug" of choice for college students, with more than 80 percent drinking at least on one occasion. Most student drug users also drink alcohol, with many students being underage drinkers (see Chapter 1). Drug use for many college students began prior to entering college. Substance abuse not only affects health, school performance, and functioning properly within the college environment, but is often associated with other high-risk behaviors such as drug dealing, dating violence, sexual assault, stalking, hate crime, and homicide. Federal legislation has been enacted to address campus drug offenses and other crimes, which school administrators and educators have responded to with varying degrees of success. The onus, however, often falls on the shoulders of students to reject drug use and its serious implications.

Prevalence of Drug Use by College Students

Drug use and abuse among college students is fairly high in spite of various measures of deterrence including addiction, laws, arrest, and prosecution. The pressures to conform to standards of behavior as part of the college life are often greater in getting students to try illicit drugs or continue to use than never using drugs or discontinuing use. Though statistics on college student drug use are inconsistent or incomplete, most indicate that prevalence rates and trends on drug use remain steadily significant and, as such, are cause for concern.

What are illicit drugs? The National Survey on Drug Use and Health (NSDUH) defines illicit drugs as "marijuana/hashish, cocaine (including crack), inhalants, hallucinogens, heroin, or prescription-type drugs used nonmedically."[1] An example of a prescription stimulant often misused in methamphetamine. Illegal drug use includes abuse of nonprescription stimulants such as diet pills and stay-awake pills. Amongst illicit drugs that are popular with college students and other young adults are "club drugs" such as ecstasy (MDMA), GHB, methamphetamine, Rohypnol, and Ketamine — which are often used at night-long parties called "raves" or "trances," dance clubs, or bars. Alcohol also tends to be included in data on drug use among college students. While only underage drinking is considered illegal, alcohol use by students of any age often goes hand in hand with illegal drug use and increases the chances for involvement in other illegal activities such as assault and vandalism.[2]

According to the National Institute on Drug Abuse's *Monitoring the Future (MTF) National Survey Results on Drug Use, 1975–2007: Volume II, College Students and Adults Ages 19–45, 2007,* the lifetime prevalence of use for illicit drugs by full-time college students in 2007 was 50.5 percent. The drug use rate of prevalence for all full-time students for any illicit drug excluding marijuana was nearly half that at 25.3 percent (see Table 2.1). Male students were more likely to have ever used illegal drugs than female students at 53.2 percent compared to 49.4 percent. Male college students were more than twice as likely as female college students to have used hallucinogens and inhalants in their lifetime. Female students had a higher lifetime prevalence of methamphetamine and alcohol-related use than male students.

The MTF shows that the annual prevalence of any illicit drug use by full-time college students in 2007 was 35 percent (see Table 2.2). This prevalence rate dropped to 17.3 percent for any illicit drug other than marijuana, which had a nearly 32 percent annual prevalence of use. Male full-time college students had a higher annual rate of prevalence for any illicit drug use than female full-time students at 38 percent versus 33.1 percent. For illicit drugs other than marijuana, male students' yearly rate of drug use was 19 percent compared to 16.3 percent for female students. The prevalence of annual marijuana use for male students was nearly 36 percent versus just over 29 percent for female students. Full-time male students were more than twice as likely to use hallucinogens and heroin yearly as females.

Table 2.1
Lifetime Prevalence of Drug Use by
Full-Time College Students, by Gender, 2007

	Total	Males	Females
Any illicit drug[a]	50.5%	52.3%	49.4%
Any illicit drug[a] other than marijuana	25.3	26.5	24.6
Marijuana	47.5	51.7	44.9
Inhalants	6.3	9.4	4.5
Hallucinogens	9.1	13.5	6.4
LSD	3.3	5.4	2.0
Hallucinogens other than LSD	8.5	12.4	6.2
Ecstasy (MDMA)	5.4	5.3	5.5
Cocaine	8.5	9.6	7.8
Crack	1.3	1.7	1.1
Other cocaine	8.0	7.8	8.1
Heroin	0.5	0.7	0.4
With a needle	0.1	[b]	0.2
Without a needle	0.4	0.3	0.5
Narcotics other than heroin	14.1	15.6	13.2
Amphetamines, adjusted	11.2	12.3	10.6
Methamphetamine	1.9	1.7	2.1
Crystal methamphetamine (ice)	1.3	1.2	1.3
Sedatives (barbiturates)	5.9	7.3	5.0
Tranquilizers	9.1	9.5	8.8
Alcohol	83.1	82.3	83.6
Been drunk	71.6	67.8	74.1
Flavored alcoholic beverage	80.6	77.6	82.4
Steroids	0.6	1.3	0.2

[a]"Any illicit drug" includes use of marijuana, hallucinogens, cocaine, heroin or other narcotics, amphetamines, sedatives (barbiturates), or tranquilizers not under a doctor's orders.
[b]Prevalence rate of less than 0.05%.

SOURCE: Adapted from U.S. Department of Health and Human Services, *Monitoring the Future National Survey Results on Drug Use, 1975–2007: Volume II, College Students and Adults Age 19–45, 2007* (Bethesda, MD: National Institute on Drug Abuse, 2008), p. 240.

Other data on illicit drug use by college students suggests a slightly higher percentage of yearly involvement. The NSDUH report on past year illicit drug use by college students from 2002 to 2004 found the rate of drug use for full-time students to be 37.5 percent and part-time

Figure 2.1
Illicit Drug Use Among College Students,
by Enrollment Status and Gender, 2002–2004

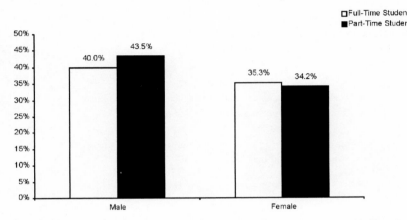

SOURCE: Adapted from U.S. Department of Health and Human Services, *National Survey on Drug Use and Health, The NSDUH Report: College Enrollment Status and Past Year Illicit Drug Use Among Young Adults: 2002, 2003, and 2004.*

students 38.5 percent.[3] Figure 2.1 shows a breakdown of college student illicit drug use by enrollment status and gender during the three years. Part-time male students had the highest rate of past year illicit drug use at 43.5 percent with full-time male students at a rate of 40 percent. By comparison, female full-time students had a higher rate of drug use at 35.3 percent than part-time students at 34.2 percent.

Past year illicit drug use was more likely to occur when college students were living away from a parent or other relative than living with a parent or another relative, regardless of whether the student was attending college full-time or part-time. Between 2002 and 2004, 41.7 percent of full-time students living away from home had used illegal drugs in the past twelve months versus 34.1 percent of students living at home; while 42.2 percent of part-time students living apart from a parent or other relative had used illicit drugs within the last year compared to 36.9 percent of part-time students who lived with a parent or another relative.

Similar to the MTF survey, the NSDUH findings reveal that marijuana had the highest rate of past year use by college students at around 32 percent for full-time and part-time students, followed by nonmedical use of prescription drugs at 13.4 percent for part-time students and 11.8 percent for full-time students. Hallucinogens and cocaine were the next most commonly used drugs by college students followed by stimulants and inhalants, with methamphetamine and crack cocaine the least commonly used illicit drugs used by full- and part-time students (Figure 2.2).

Table 2.2
Annual Prevalence of Drug Use by Full-Time
College Students, by Gender, 2007

	Total	Males	Females
Any illicit drug[a]	35.0%	38.0%	33.1%
Any illicit drug[a] other than marijuana	17.3	19.0	16.3
Marijuana	31.8	35.8	29.4
Inhalants	1.5	2.3	1.1
Hallucinogens	4.9	7.7	3.1
Cocaine	5.4	6.3	4.9
Heroin	0.2	0.3	0.1
Narcotics other than heroin	7.7	8.7	7.1
Amphetamines, adjusted	6.9	8.1	6.2
Sedatives (barbiturates)	3.6	4.2	3.2
Tranquilizers	5.5	6.2	5.1

[a]"Any illicit drug" includes use of marijuana, hallucinogens, cocaine, heroin or other narcotics, amphetamines, sedatives (barbiturates), or tranquilizers not under a doctor's orders.

SOURCE: Adapted from U.S. Department of Health and Human Services, *Monitoring the Future National Survey Results on Drug Use, 1975–2007: Volume II, College Students and Adults Age 19–45, 2007* (Bethesda, MD: National Institute on Drug Abuse, 2008), p. 241.

The MTF findings for thirty day prevalence of use for any illicit drugs, illicit drugs other than marijuana, and marijuana use by full-time college students in 2007 can be seen in Table 2.3. The prevalence of students who had used an illicit drug in the past thirty days was just over 19 percent, with nearly 23 percent of male students and just over 17 percent of female students having used an illegal drug in the past month. The prevalence rate of illicit drug use dropped to slightly more than 8 percent when not including marijuana use; whereas the rate of prevalence for marijuana use in the prior thirty days was higher for male full-time students at just over 20 percent than for total student illicit drug use. Amphetamines had the second highest rate of thirty day prevalence of use among illicit drugs after marijuana by male and female college students.

20

Figure 2.2
College Students' Past Year Illicit Drug Use,
by Enrollment Status and Type of Drug, 2002–2004

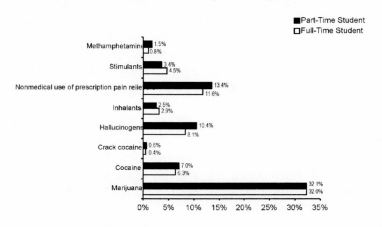

SOURCE: Adapted from U.S. Department of Health and Human Services, *National Survey on Drug Use and Health, The NSDUH Report: College Enrollment Status and Past Year Illicit Drug Use Among Young Adults: 2002, 2003, and 2004* (Rockville, MD: Office of Applied Studies, 2005), p. 3.

Table 2.3
Thirty Day Prevalence of Illicit Drug Use by Full-Time
College Students, by Type of Drug and Gender, 2007

	Total	*Males*	*Females*
Any illicit drug[a]	19.3%	22.7%	17.1%
Any illicit drug[a] other than marijuana	8.1	9.5	7.2
Marijuana	16.8	20.2	14.8
Inhalants	0.1	[b]	0.2
Hallucinogens	1.3	2.2	0.8
Cocaine	1.7	1.8	1.7
Heroin	0.1	0.3	0.1
Narcotics other than heroin	2.2	3.2	1.7
Amphetamines, adjusted	3.1	2.8	3.2
Sedatives (barbiturates)	1.4	1.0	1.6
Tranquilizers	1.8	1.6	1.9

[a]"Any illicit drug" includes use of marijuana, hallucinogens, cocaine, heroin or other narcotics, amphetamines, sedatives (barbiturates), or tranquilizers not under a doctor's orders.
[b]Prevalence rate of less than 0.05%.

SOURCE: Adapted from U.S. Department of Health and Human Services, *Monitoring the Future National Survey Results on Drug Use, 1975–2007: Volume II, College Students and Adults Age 19–45, 2007* (Bethesda, MD: National Institute on Drug Abuse, 2008), p. 242.

Trends in Drug Use Among College Students

The MTF long-term trends reveal a sharp drop in drug use by college students. As shown in Table 2.4, in 1980, the lifetime prevalence of any illicit drug use by college students in the United States was 69.4 percent. This number was down to 50.5 percent in 2007. The lifetime prevalence of college student drug use has remained fairly steady since 1991, when it was at 50.4 percent. For illicit drugs other than marijuana, the student rate of prevalence for ever using fell from 42.2 percent in 1980 to 25.3 in 2007. Nearly two-thirds of college students had a lifetime prevalence of using marijuana in 1980, compared to 47.5 percent in 2007; whereas the rate of cocaine use dropped nearly two-thirds over the span. Ever using inhalants, hallucinogens, and tranquilizers also showed steep declines between 1980 and 2007. However, the lifetime prevalence of narcotics use other than heroin rose from 8.9 percent in 1980 to 14.1 percent in 2007.

Table 2.4
Trends in Lifetime Prevalence of Illicit Drug Use
by College Students, 1980–2007

	1980	1991	2000	2007
Any illicit druga	69.4%	50.4%	53.7%	50.5%
Any illicit druga other than marijuana	42.2	25.8	25.8	25.3
Marijuana	65.0	46.3	51.2	47.5
Inhalants	10.2	14.4	12.9	6.3
Hallucinogens	15.0	11.3	14.4	9.1
Cocaine	22.0	9.4	9.1	8.5
Narcotics other than heroin	8.9	7.3	8.9	14.1
Tranquilizers	15.2	6.8	8.8	9.1

a"Any illicit drug" includes use of marijuana, hallucinogens, cocaine, heroin or other narcotics, amphetamines, sedatives (barbiturates), methaqualone (until 1990), or tranquilizers not under a doctor's orders.

SOURCE: Adapted from U.S. Department of Health and Human Services, *Monitoring the Future National Survey Results on Drug Use, 1975–2007: Volume II, College Students and Adults Age 19–45, 2007* (Bethesda, MD: National Institute on Drug Abuse, 2008), pp. 255–56.

Long-term trends in the annual prevalence rate for college students' use of illicit drugs also reveal a significant drop (see Figure 2.3). In 1980, the yearly prevalence of any illicit drug use by college students was 56.2 percent, compared to 35 percent in 2007. While the number of annual illicit drug users has remained steady since the mid 1990s, there was a

1.1 percent increase in annual college student illicit drug use between 2006 and 2007.[4] The annual prevalence rate of illicit drug use other than marijuana by students was down almost half from 1980 when it was at 32.3 percent to 2007 at 17.3 percent. Similarly, the annual prevalence of marijuana use was at 51.2 percent in 1980, dropping to 31.8 percent in 2007. However, the yearly use of marijuana by college students between 2006 and 2007 rose by 1.6 percent.[5] Short-term annual trends also reveal a slight year-to-year increase in students' use of cocaine other than crack, amphetamines, and barbiturates.[6]

Figure 2.3
Trends in Annual Prevalence of Illicit Drug Use
by College Students, 1980–2007

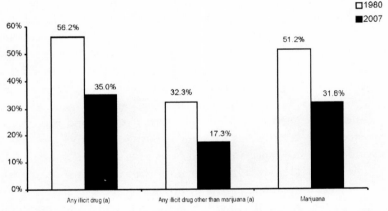

[a]"Any illicit drug" includes use of marijuana, hallucinogens, cocaine, heroin or other narcotics, amphetamines, sedatives (barbiturates), methaqualone (until 1990), or tranquilizers not under a doctor's order.

SOURCE: Adapted from U.S. Department of Health and Human Services, *Monitoring the Future National Survey Results on Drug Use, 1975–2007: Volume II, College Students and Adults Age 19–45, 2007* (Bethesda, MD: National Institute on Drug Abuse, 2005), pp. 258.

Trends in thirty day prevalence of illicit drug use by college students are consistent with lifetime and annual prevalence rates in the overall decline in drug use.[7] Between 1980 and 2007, any illicit drug use by students in the past thirty days went from 38.4 percent to 19.3 percent. For illicit drug use other than marijuana, the thirty day prevalence went from 20.7 percent in 1980 to 8.1 in 2007. The rate of prevalence for students using marijuana during the span fell by more than half, with significant declines as well in use of inhalants and cocaine. The thirty day prevalence showed an increase in the use of narcotics other than heroin by students between 1980 and 2007.[8]

Onset of Drug Use by College Students

Though many college students begin using drugs and alcohol after entering college, most college students who use alcohol or drugs had already been initiated to these or other substances prior to enrolling in institutions of higher learning, increasing their chances for a continuation of drinking or abuse of drugs. In a study of behavioral risks between high school and college, Kim Fromme and colleagues found that alcohol and marijuana use increased during the transition from the last three months of high school through the end of their first year in college.[9] Similarly, Kenneth Sher and Patricia Rutledge's study of more than 3,000 college students found there was a high rate of continuity in drinking patterns between high school and the first term of college.[10] Binge drinking in college was found to be strongly associated with the accessibility of alcoholic beverages in high school.[11] Other studies and surveys have supported these conclusions in demonstrating a positive relationship between college substance abuse and prior drug or alcohol use.[12]

The NSDUH gives a breakdown on the average age of first time use for illicit drugs among past year initiates in 2007, as shown in Figure 2.4. The mean age of initial use was under eighteen for marijuana, inhalants, and PCP, with the average age of PCP initiates 16.4, inhalants 17.1, and onset of marijuana use 17.6. First time users of LSD were 18.3 years of age on average. Most college students at four year institutions begin their studies at age eighteen or nineteen.

Most initiates of illicit drugs within the previous twelve months first used marijuana (see Figure 2.5), accounting for more than 56 percent of initial drug use. Nearly one in five initiates used pain relievers, while more than one in ten first used inhalants. Tranquilizers or stimulants were the first drug of over one in ten drug users. Less than five percent of drug users initiated with hallucinogens, sedatives, or cocaine.

Figure 2.4
Mean Age at First Use for Illicit Drugs Among Past Year
Initiates Age 12 to 49, by Type of Drug, 2007

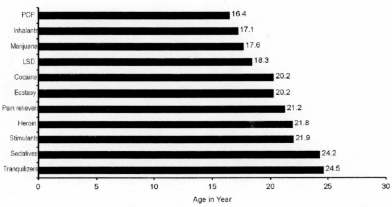

SOURCE: National Survey on Drug Use and Health, "Underage Alcohol Use Among Full-Time College Students," *NSDUH Report* 31 (2006).

Figure 2.5
Drugs Used When Initiating Illicit Drug Use Among
Past Year Initiates of Illicit Drugs, Age 12 and Older, 2007

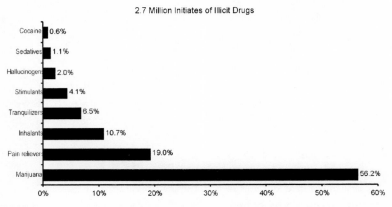

SOURCE: National Survey on Drug Use and Health, "Underage Alcohol Use Among Full-Time College Students," *NSDUH Report* 31 (2006).

High school drug use and its potential effect on college drug use is reflected by the extent of substance abuse among high school seniors and 10th grade students. The MTF survey of high school students reveals that in 2008, the lifetime prevalence of any illicit drug use by 12th graders was 47.4 percent and 10th graders 34.1 percent. For illicit drugs other than marijuana, the prevalence rate of ever using was 24.9 percent by 12th grade students and 15.9 percent by 10th grade students. When inhalants were included with any illicit drug, the rates of lifetime prevalence among 12th graders and 10th graders were 49.3 percent and 38.7 percent, respectively. The lifetime prevalence of marijuana or hashish use was 42.6 percent among 12th graders and 29.9 percent for 10th graders.

The annual prevalence of drug use in 2008 by high school 12th grade and 10th grade students and can be seen in Figure 2.6. Among 12th graders, 36.6 percent reported any illicit drug use in the previous twelve months, while 26.9 percent of 10th graders had used an illicit drug in the past year. For illicit drugs other than marijuana, the annual prevalence rate for 12th grade students and 10th graders was 18.3 percent and 11.3 percent, respectively. When any illicit drug included inhalants, the yearly rate of prevalence for 12th grade students was 37.3 percent and for 10th grade students 28.8 percent. The annual prevalence of marijuana or hashish use was 32.4 percent for 12th graders and 23.9 percent for 10th graders.

Though trends generally show drug use among high schoolers to be on the decline, MTF survey results of long-term trends reveal an increase in drug use by high school seniors (see Figure 2.7). Between 1991 and 2007, the annual prevalence of any illicit drug use by 12th graders increased from 29.4 percent to 35.9 percent. Increases during the span can also be seen for any illicit drug use other than marijuana, any illicit use of drugs including inhalants, and marijuana or hashish. However, all of the 2007 figures for drug use among high school seniors were down from 1997, when each peaked over the sixteen-year trend.

Data for 2008 indicate that stimulant drug use such as amphetamines, methamphetamines, cocaine, and crack among high school students continue a pattern of decline in the annual prevalence of use.[13] However, the use of marijuana by high school students showed a slight increase in 2008 and use of prescription drugs for nonmedical purposes by high

Figure 2.6
Annual Prevalence of Illicit Drug Use
by 12th and 10th Grade Students, 2008

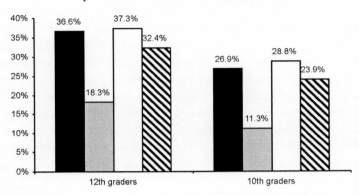

SOURCE: Adapted from University of Michigan News Service, "Various Stimulant Drugs Show Continuing Gradual Declines Among Teens in 2008, Most Illicit Drugs Hold Steady," (December 11, 2008), http://monitoringthefuture.org/data/08data.html#2008data-drugs. *See also* U.S. Department of Hleath and Human Services, *Monitoring the Future National Survey.*

Figure 2.7
Trends in Annual Prevalence of Illicit Drug Use
by High School Seniors, 1997–2007

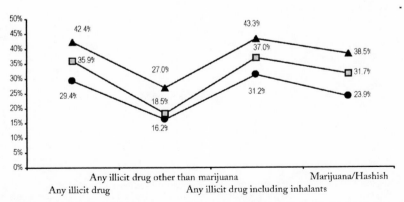

SOURCE: Adapted from U.S. Department of Health and Human Services, *Monitoring the Future National Survey Results on Drug Use: 1975–2007: Volume I, Secondary School Students, 2007* (Bethesda, MD: National Institute on Drug Abuse, 2008), p. 213.

schoolers has risen; while a number of other drugs used by high schoolers remained steady, including LSD, PCP, heroin, other narcotics such as Vicodin and OxyContin, and club drugs like Rohypnol and GHB.[14]

The easy access high school students have to many drugs serves as a forerunner to their continual availability as these students make the transition to college. Table 2.5 shows the accessibility to high school seniors of drugs in 2008. Nearly 84 percent of 12th graders believed they could easily obtain marijuana and more than 92 percent felt they could get alcohol with no problem. Other drugs believed to be easily obtainable include amphetamines at nearly 48 percent, cocaine at over 42 percent, cocaine powder and sedatives at almost 39 percent, and some other hallucinogens at around 43 percent. The troubling message is clear: many 12th grade drug users (and college students) as well as other secondary school students involved with alcohol and drugs find it relatively simple to get what they want, in spite of preventative measures, drug-related laws, and a general trend in society against drug use.

Table 2.5
Availability of Drugs as Perceived
by 12th Grade Students, 2008

Percentage saying "fairly easy" or "very easy" to get	
Marijuana	83.9
Amyl/butyl nitrites	16.9
LSD	28.5
Some other hallucinogen	42.8
PCP	20.6
Ecstasy (MDMA)	41.9
Cocaine	42.4
Crack	35.2
Cocaine powder	38.9
Heroin	25.4
Some other narcotic (including methadone)	34.9
Amphetamines	47.9
Crystal meth. (ice)	23.3
Sedatives (barbiturates)	38.8
Tranquilizers	22.4
Alcohol	92.2
Steroids	35.2

SOURCE: Adapted from University of Michigan News Service, "Various Stimulant Drugs Show Continuing Gradual Declines Among Teens in 2008, Most Illicit Drugs Hold Steady," (December 11, 2008), http://monitoringthefuture.org/data/08data.html#2008data-drugs. *See also* U.S. Department of Health and Human Services, *Monitoring the Future National Survey Results on Adolescent Drug Use: Overview of Key Findings, 2008* (Bethesda, MD: National Institute on Drug Abuse, 2009).

The MTF survey found that the majority of high school drug users plan to complete four years of college, a strong predictive measure of transitioning into college drug use. However, college-bound students had lower rates of illegal drug use than high schoolers who had no plans to attend college, suggesting a relationship between drug use and higher educational aspirations.[15]

Marijuana Use

Marijuana use is widespread among college students and more commonly used than any other illicit drug. The peer pressures faced by students to fit into the campus environment and party atmosphere of most colleges often includes the use of alcohol and drugs, with marijuana (typically referred to as "pot," "grass," or "weed") the drug of choice. Among full-time college students, more than one in two male students and nearly one in two female students have used marijuana in their lifetime; while nearly four in ten male students and almost three in ten female students have smoked marijuana in the past year. Within the past month, more than one in five full-time male students and over one in six full-time female students has used marijuana.[16]

The implications of marijuana use by college students and other young adults can be far reaching. In a study of heavy marijuana users, or those who had smoked marijuana at least twenty-seven of the prior thirty days, it was found that this impaired a number of vital skills including memory, attention span, learning, and organization.[17] In another study that measured the occurrence of cannabis use disorders (CUD) among first year college students, it found that for students who had used cannabis five times or more within the last year, 10 percent met the Diagnostic and Statistical Manual of Mental Disorders (DSM)-IV clinical definition of cannabis dependence, while 14.5 percent fell under the definition of cannabis abuse.[18] Students who used cannabis at least five times in the past twelve months were seen as in danger of CUD. Nearly one-fourth of these students placed themselves in danger physically while under marijuana influence and more than 40 percent had problems with concentration. More than one in ten marijuana users continued using in spite of it causing problems to arise with family and friends.

Studies have found marijuana use to be related to depression, personality disorders, memory loss, anxiety, and respiratory issues.[19] One study concluded that the effects of marijuana on the brain can lead to increasing deterioration of important life skills, associating marijuana use with "reduced capacity for self-reinforcement, a group of psychological skills that enable individuals to maintain confidence and persevere in the pursuit of goals."[20]

Marijuana use by college students also often exposes them to other dangerous drugs. According to the National Institute of Justice's Community Epidemiology Work Group, which studies trends in drug use and its patterns, marijuana is regularly mixed with other drugs like crack cocaine and PCP, in many instances without the marijuana user's knowledge.[21] Users of marijuana also frequently combine the drug with alcohol. Any such combinations increase the hazards presented by substance abuse.[22]

Club Drugs

Club drugs are "a pharmacologically heterogeneous group of psychoactive compounds" that are often a big part of the college life and the high-risk behaviors of many college students and young adults.[23] These drugs include ecstasy (MDMA), GHB (gamma hydroxybutyrate), roofies (Rohypnol), Special K (Ketamine), methamphetamine (meth), and acid (LSD) and are often used and abused by youth at all-night dance parties known as raves, and at nightclubs or bars. These club drugs are promoted by dealers and users as harmless and "producing psychedelic and stimulant effects, giving users energy, stamina, and feelings of euphoria."[24]

The reality is that they can lead to a myriad of serious physical, psychological, economic, and other problems for college students, including affecting school performance, substance abuse, other law violations, and high-risk sexual activity.

The most popular club drugs are described as follows:

- *Ecstasy*— a synthetic, psychoactive drug that acts as a stimulant and hallucinogen. Taken as a pill or powder. Street names include X, XTC, Adam, and hug drug.
- *GHB*— an anabolic steroid that has euphoric and sedative effects. Taken orally as a liquid or capsule, it is sometimes used as a substitute to ecstasy or speed. Street names include G, liquid X, liquid ecstasy, and grievous bodily harm.
- *Ketamine*— a depressant with anesthetic and dissociative effects. In liquid and powder forms, it can be consumed, injected, smoked, or snorted. Street names include K, kit kat, Special K, and vitamin K.
- *Methamphetamine*— a stimulant, highly addictive, with euphoric effects and an instant high. It can be smoked, snorted, ingested, and injected. Street names include chalk, ice, speed, and poor man's cocaine.
- *Rohypnol*— a sedative with hypnotic effects. Usually taken in pill form, it can also be snorted or injected, and is sometimes used with alcohol, marijuana, or heroin. Street names include roofies, ruffles, forget pill, and Mexican valium.

Apart from recreational use by college students, some club drugs such as GHB, Rohypnol, and Ketamine are used as date rape drugs on college campuses and such popular gathering places as fraternity houses and nightclubs.[25] Rapists and other sexual predators use such drugs "because they act rapidly, reduce inhibition, relax voluntary muscles, and cause the victim to have lasting amnesia for events that occur under the influence of the drug."[26] See more discussion on sexual assault, date rape drugs, and dating violence in Chapters 4 and 5. The 2007 NSDUH reported that approximately 12.4 million persons age twelve and older in the United States have tried ecstasy at least once during their lifetime.[27] An estimated 2.1 persons were past year users of ecstasy and about 503,000 past month users.[28] According to the Substance Abuse and Mental Health Services Administration, around 15 percent of persons between eighteen and twenty-five have ever used ecstasy and 24 percent have used ecstasy or another hallucinogen. About 11 percent of youth have a lifetime prevalence of methamphetamine use or other illegal stimulants.[29]

In a study of club drugs use by college students attending two state universities, Jeffrey Simons and associates found that 18 percent of the sample of 831 students had ever used club drugs.[30] Of these students, nearly 23 percent reported use of such drug seven to twelve times or more within the last year. The researchers found a positive relationship between the use of club drugs and marijuana use.[31] Other studies have supported this contention and also associated club drug use with drinking alcohol.[32]

Using club drugs separate from other drugs or in combination can have serious health consequences, including death. According to the Drug Abuse Warning Network, in 2006 an estimated 1,742,887 visits to the emergency room (ER) in the United States involved substance abuse.[33] Of these, 16,749 trips to the ER were related to ecstasy, 1,084 to GHB, and 270 to Ketamine. Ecstasy can cause an increase in the heart rate, muscle tension, blurred vision, along with such psychological problems as depression, severe anxiety, and confusion.[34] Rohypnol in higher doses can result in loss of consciousness, amnesia, and problems with muscle control, along with other severe effects when used with alcohol.[35] GHB's sedative effects can lead to coma, seizures, trouble breathing, and overdose.[36] Ketamine can lead to a heart attack or stroke, hallucinations, paranoia, impaired perception, and withdrawal syndrome.[37] When more than one illicit drug is used, or used with prescription drugs or alcohol, the risks to one's health and well-being increase precipitously.[38]

Prescription Drugs

The nonmedical use of prescription drugs by college students is a growing concern on campuses across the country. Researchers have found that abuse of prescription medications is more common than any other illegal drug use aside from marijuana.[39] In a 2004 MTF survey, it was estimated that 7.4 percent of students enrolled in college used Vicodin, a prescription painkiller, for nonmedical purposes that year, an increase over the 6.9 percent using the drug in 2002.[40] A comparable rise was found in the use of other opioid medications, sedatives, and stimulants.

As many as one in four students at some colleges have reported abusing prescription stimulants.[41] According to a 2001 survey of 10,904 students attending 119 institutions of higher learning across the country, 4 percent reported use of a stimulant without a prescription on at least one occasion within the prior year.[42] The survey also found:

- Males abused Ritalin, Dexedrine, and Adderall twice as often as females.
- White students abused stimulant medication more often than African American or Asian students.
- Fraternity or sorority members were more likely to abuse stimulants than non members.
- Abusers of prescription stimulants had a higher incidence of smoking cigarettes, using marijuana, cocaine and ecstasy, and problem drinking.

Other data also shows alarming numbers of students misusing prescription drugs. In a survey of 9,161 undergraduate students conducted at a large college in the Midwest, around 9 percent had used prescription pain medication on one occasion or more without a physician's consent.[43] Sixteen percent said they had ever abused prescription drugs. More than half of this group had gotten the drugs from friends, with nearly one in five obtaining prescription drugs from family members.

In a 2005 web-based survey of 3,638 full-time undergraduate college students at a public four year university, use of prescription stimulants for nonmedical purposes was compared to other drug use and related problems. Students who used prescription stimulants for nonmedical purposes had a greater likelihood than users of other drugs to have been polydrug users. It was concluded that most nonmedical prescription stimulant users are polydrug users and, as such, needed to be screened for possible drug abuse or addiction.[44]

Why do college students misuse prescription drugs? According to a former researcher with the National Institute on Drug Abuse's Division of Epidemiology, Services and Prevention Research, "Students abuse prescription drugs to get high, to self-medicate for pain episodes, to help concentrate during exam time, and to try to relieve stress."[45] Some evidence suggests that many college students falsely believe that using medically prescribed drugs is harmless, irrespective of whom the drug was prescribed for; or they are "brain steroids" that are safe and "help maximize performance with minimal risk."[46] However, "a drug or dose that a doctor orders for one person is not necessarily appropriate for another, and prescription abusers are potentially taking a serious risk."[47] Misuse of prescription drugs can result in physical dependence or addiction, an irregular heartbeat, withdrawal symptoms, high blood pressure, and other harmful effects, including death. The dangers of prescription drug abuse multiply when such drugs are used with other illicit drugs and/or alcohol.[48]

It was reported by the University of Maryland's Center for Substance Abuse Research that students who believe prescription drugs to be "relatively harmless" are ten times as likely to misuse such drugs as students who perceive prescription drugs to be "extremely harmful."[49] Other research indicates that college freshman students regard the misuse of prescription pain killers and stimulants to be a somewhat riskier proposition than using marijuana or having five alcoholic drinks each weekend, while feeling that nonmedical use of prescription drugs is not as risky as using cocaine.[50] College students who are seen as "sensation seekers" have been found to be more likely to abuse prescription drugs than other students.[51]

College Drug Offenses and Crime Data

Official crime data on drug use among university and college students is limited in scope and precision, while often combined with information on secondary and elementary schools or general crime statistics. It is also incomplete due to the number of participating law enforcement agencies, limitations in the Department of Education (ED) crime statistics, and definitional issues. This notwithstanding, some indication of the incidence of drug use on college campuses or involving college students can be seen in official data when combined with student surveys as explored earlier.

In the Federal Bureau of Investigation's National Incident-Based Reporting System Data on crime in schools and colleges, offense categories include drug and narcotic violations and drug equipment violations. As seen in Table 2.6, between 2000 and 2004, there were a reported

47,108 drug or narcotic violations and 11,412 drug equipment violations at schools and colleges in the United States. In 2004, there were 12,222 reported drug or narcotic violations at schools or colleges compared to 10,685 in 2003 and a low of 6,477 in 2000. The total of 2,859 drug equipment violations in 2004 was nearly double that of the 1,431 in 2000.

Table 2.6
Number of Drug-Related Offenses in Schools,
by Type of Offense, 2000–2004

	2000	2001	2002	2003	2004	5-Year Total
Drug/Narcotic Violations	6,477	8,879	8,845	10,685	12,222	47,108
Drug Equipment Violations	1,431	2,237	2,310	2,575	2,859	11,412

Adapted from U.S. Department of Justice, Federal Bureau of Investigation, School Violence, *Crime in Schools and Colleges: A Study of Offenders and Arrestees Reported via National Incident-Based Reporting System Data* (October 2007) http://www.fbi.gov/ucr/schoolviolence/2007/appendixa.htm.

According to the ED, in 2007 there were 23,197 drug arrests and 49,098 liquor law violations at institutions of higher education (see Table 2.7). Drug arrests and liquor law violations occurred most often at public schools of four years or more, followed by private colleges of four or more years, and public two year institutions. Between 2005 and 2007, drug arrests were fairly steady, with a slight increase between 2006 and 2007, whereas liquor law violations declined from year to year, but were still more than twice as high in 2007 as drug arrests. As substance abuse by college students often involves alcohol use, it increases the high-risk associated circumstances of drug use.

Indicative of the serious nature of drug use and related behaviors on college campuses was the 2008 drug bust at San Diego State University. In an operation dubbed Operation Sudden Fall, a six month undercover investigation by the Drug Enforcement Administration (DEA) led to the arrest of seventy-five students and twenty-one others on various drug-related charges.[52] There were more than 130 drug seizures made by authorities and evidence of extensive drug dealing involving members of fraternities. Evidence confiscated by the DEA included fifty pounds of marijuana, forty-eight hydroponic marijuana plants, four pounds of cocaine, 350 ecstasy pills, methamphetamine, mushrooms, and illegal prescription drugs, along with a shotgun, three semiautomatic pistols, and $60,000 in cash. Afterward, a DEA spokesperson praised the university for tackling a problem that "is rampant on U.S. campuses."[53]

Table 2.7
Drug Arrests and Liquor Law Violations
on University and College Campuses, 2005–2007

	2005	2006	2007
Drug Arrests			
Public, 4-year or above	15,204	15,216	15,525
Private nonprofit, 4-year or above	3,708	4,025	4,030
Private for profit, 4-year or above	327	141	152
Public, 2-year	2,954	2,312	2,450
Private nonprofit, 2-year	91	109	85
Private for profit, 2-year	146	198	357
Public, less-than-2-year	413	336	322
Private nonprofit, less-than-2-year	10	12	17
Private for profit, less-than-2-year	447	443	259
Total	23,300	22,792	23,197
Liquor Law Violations			
Public, 4-year or above	38,599	38,625	37,557
Private nonprofit, 4-year or above	9,344	8,427	7,871
Private for profit, 4-year or above	108	98	100
Public, 2-year	2,809	3,227	2,879
Private nonprofit, 2-year	115	95	53
Private for profit, 2-year	115	133	346
Public, less-than-2-year	70	65	105
Private nonprofit, less-than-2-year	7	14	6
Private for profit, less-than-2-year	215	140	181
Total	51,382	50,824	49,098

SOURCE: U.S. Department of Education, Campus Security, "Data on Campus Crime: Summary Crime Statistics for 2005–07," http://www.ed.gov/admins/lead/safety/campus.html.

The problem of drug use and abuse in the college community is also reflected in the official statistics on drug and alcohol involved criminality and student victimization such as dating violence, sexual assault, stalking, hate crime, aggravated assault, property crime, and murder.[54] In most of these offenses, substance abuse has been shown to often be a precursor or motivator.[55]

Combating Drug Use on Campus

Efforts to curtail and prevent drug abuse on campus and related offenses have been led by the federal government through legislation. The Drug-Free Schools and Campuses Act (DFSCA) of 1989 (also called the Drug-Free Schools and Communities Act) required under Part 86, the Drug and Alcohol Abuse Prevention Regulations (Education Department General Administrative Regulations [EDGAR]), that in order for institutions of higher education to qualify for federal funds, schools must provide, at the very least, the following to students and personnel[56]:

- Conduct principles that expressly prohibit possessing, using, or distributing illegal drugs or alcohol on campus grounds or related to college activities.
- Describe the appropriate legal penalties under Federal, State, or local law regarding illegally possessing or distributing illicit drugs or alcohol.
- Describe the health perils related to drinking alcohol and using illicit drugs.
- Make known the availability and whereabouts of alcohol or drug counseling, treatment, rehabilitation, and/or reentry programs.
- Put in explicit terms sanctions that will be imposed of college students and personnel by the school in accordance with the laws, including expulsion from college or employment termination and turning the case over to proper law enforcement authorities.
- Conduct biennial review of its program's effectiveness must be carried out by institutions.

The Student Right-to-Know and Campus Security Act was passed in 1990 and addressed disclosure of campus crime and security measures to the student body of colleges and universities across the country.[57] Specifically, Title II of the Act, Crime Awareness and Campus Security Act, required all institutions of higher education that received federal funds to publish an annual report on criminality that occurred on and near campus, including criminal homicide, sex crimes, property offenses, and drug and liquor law violations.[58] The Act also required colleges to divulge campus security measures in place and develop better crime prevention policies (see also Chapter 4).

Other means for assessing and preventing campus drug use include data gathering, such as the Monitoring the Future surveys, The National Survey on Drug Use and Health, The National College Health Assessment, and the Core Institute's Core Alcohol and Drug Survey. These important research programs can be instrumental in understanding the nature of drug and alcohol abuse among college students and other young adults and developing strategies to contend with it.

The burden for controlling student drug use rests to a large degree on college administrators in implementing policies that discourage substance abuse and can be enforced by campus and local law enforcement, counselors, residence hall personnel, and students themselves; while providing other outlets for dealing with stress, peer pressure, and breaking away from long and risky college traditions.

Chapter 3

MURDER

Though school-related shootings and homicides have been relatively rare on college campuses, particularly in relation to more common types of offenses such as sexual assault, stalking, and vandalism, in recent years there have been a number of high profile school murders that have put a greater focus on this crime and doing much more to make the college environment safer for students and faculty. The 1986 rape-murder of a nineteen-year-old college student in her residence hall room led to the enactment of the Clery Act (see also Chapter 4), which required colleges and universities to report crime statistics to the Department of Education along with the almost sixteen million students attending some 4,200 institutions of higher education. The easy access of firearms, substance abuse, and the freedom of entry and exit for potential killers at most colleges make students vulnerable to such lethal acts of violence. This is especially true in conjunction with other dangerous issues that typically place many students in high-risk situations, such as dating violence, sexual predators, stalking, and hate crime. Most students will complete their studies successfully without ever encountering a potentially deadly attack. But the fact that conditions are present that could lead to such victimization makes it an important topic to explore.

Violent Crimes on Campus

The incidence of violent crimes, including murder, on university and college campuses across the country, has declined in recent years. Yet campus violence remains a serious issue for students, faculty, personnel, and visitors to institutions of higher education. According to the Department of Justice, there are approximately 7.9 million students, ages eighteen to twenty-four, enrolled full-time or part-time in a university or college in the United States.[1] Around 526,000 of these students are victims of violent crimes each year.[2] In more than 128,000 of the victimizations, a weapon is used or there is serious injury sustained by the victim. Most crimes of violence against college students occur off campus, including the victimization of students living on campus, with roughly 85 percent of them taking place off school property. Comparatively, about 95 percent of violent victimizations of students living off campus occurred away from campus.[3]

Other facts of college violence and victimization include[4]:

- Male students are nearly twice as likely as female students to be victims of violence in general.
- Female students are more than four times as likely as male students to be victims of rape or sexual assaults.
- White students have the highest rate of violent crime victimization, followed by Hispanic and African American students.
- Apart from rape or sexual assault, around six in ten crimes of violence against college students are committed by strangers.
- Almost one in ten crimes of violence against college students involves the presence of a firearm.
- Around four in ten student violent victimizations are perpetrated by offenders under the influence of alcohol or drugs.
- About one in eighteen violent crime student victimizations are perpetrated by a gang member.
- Nearly three in four violent student victimizations off campus take place at night.

Trends reveal that rates of violent crime against students have fallen. In a National Crime Victimization Survey (NCVS) on the violent victimization of college students, it was reported that between 1995 and 2002, the rate of total violent crime and serious violent crime victimization dropped 53.7 percent and 43.8 percent, respectively (see Figure 3.1). Overall, college students were victimized at a lower rate than nonstudents in the same age group.

As shown in Table 3.1, almost one in four violent victimizations of college students from 1995 to 2002 occurred in an open area, on the street, or public transportation. This represents almost 116,000 victimizations annually. More than 18 percent of victimizations (or more than

87,000 each year) were perpetrated in a commercial place, and around 17 percent (or almost 82,000 annually) took place at or near the home of the victim's friend, relative, or neighbor. Over one in four student violent victimizations (or around 123,000 every year) happened at or near the victim's residence or in school. Nearly six in ten on campus crimes of violence transpired during the daytime, compared to about one in four off campus victimizations.

Figure 3.1
Violent Victimization Rates of College Students, 1995–2002

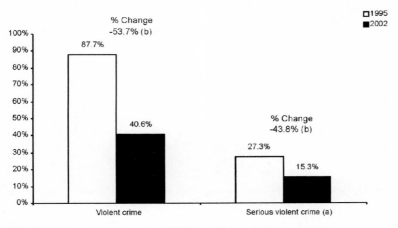

ªSerious violent crime includes rape/sexual assault, robbery, and aggravated assault.
ᵇThe difference from 1995 to 2002 is at the 95%-significance level.

SOURCE: Adapted from U.S. Department of Justice, Bureau of Justice Statistics Special Report, *Violent Victimization of College Students, 1995–2002* (Washington, DC: Office of Justice Programs, 2005), p. 2.

College students are most likely to be daytime victims of violence while working and nighttime victims during leisure time away from home or residence hall (see Table 3.2). During the seven year span, the NCVS found that more than one in five violent student victimizations between the hours of 6 A.M. and 6 P.M. occurred with the victim at work; with over three in ten daytime victimizations taking place during the student's leisure activity away from home or other activities while at home. Between the hours of 6 P.M. and 6 A.M., nearly half of all violent crime victimizations occurred while the victim engaged in leisure activity outside the home, with almost 12 percent of victimizations perpetrated when the victim was en route to or from another place.

Table 3.1
Violent Victimization of College Students,
by Location and Time of Crime, 1995–2002

Location characteristics	Average annual number	Percent of all crimes
Location of incident		
Open area/on street/public transportation	115,990	24.2%
Commercial place	87,420	18.2
In/at/near home of friend/relative/neighbor	81,940	17.1
Victim's home	51,580	10.8
Parking lot/garage	42,880	9.0
Near victim's home	38,270	8.0
School	32,750	6.8
Other	28,330	5.9
Off campus		
Day (6 A.M.— 6 P.M.)	112,930	25.5%
Night (6 P.M.— 6 A.M.)	319,260	72.0
On campus		
Day (6 A.M.— 6 P.M.)	18,160	56.1%
Night (6 P.M.— 6 A.M.)	12,480	38.5

SOURCE: U.S. Department of Justice, Bureau of Justice Statistics Special Report, *Violent Victimization of College Students, 1995–2002* (Washington, DC: Office of Justice Programs, 2005), p. 5.

Only around 35 percent of college students report violent crime victimization to the police, as seen in Table 3.3. The reasons most often given for not reporting include believing it to be a private matter, seeing the offense as minor, or they reported the crime to someone else. Of course, for the crime of murder, and in some instances attempted murder, the victim is unable to report the crime or identify the assailant.

Homicides in Schools

The data on homicides at colleges and universities in the United States is conflicting and often combined with statistics on pre-college schools or murders in areas close to institutions of higher learning. This is understandable to some degree, as recent mass murder school shootings at colleges and high schools have shown them to be equally vulnerable and cast a shadow on the relationship between homicidal tendencies and education as a whole. Furthermore, though colleges are required by law to keep accurate data on violent crimes and report this to the Department of Education, they are not required to share the information with the Federal Bureau of Investigation's (FBI) Uniform Crime Reporting program, the most comprehensive source of statistical data on violent crime in the United States.[5] As such, it is unclear precisely how many homicides take place on college campuses or involving college students on or off campus.

Table 3.2
Student Activity at Time of Violent Victimization,[a]
by Time of Day, 1995–2002

Activity at time of victimization	*Percent of all violence*
Day (6 A.M. — 6 P.M.)	100.0%
Working	21.4
To/from work	2.4
To/from school	7.2
To/from other place	10.0
Shopping/errands	5.4
Attending school	6.2
Leisure activity away from home	15.5
Sleeping	0.5[b]
Other activities at home	15.5
Other	7.7
Do not know activity	0.6[b]
Night (6 P.M. — 6 A.M.)	100.0%
Working	7.6
To/from work	3.1
To/from school	1.1[b]
To/from other place	11.8
Shopping/errands	2.3
Attending school	0.7[b]
Leisure activity away from home	48.7
Sleeping	2.3
Other activities at home	9.5
Other	6.4
Do not know activity	0.1[b]

[a]Excludes those who did not know the time when the violent victimization occurred.
[b]Based on 10 or fewer sample cases.

SOURCE: Adapted from U.S. Department of Justice, Bureau of Justice Statistics Special Report, *Violent Victimization of College Students, 1995–2002* (Washington, DC: Office of Justice Programs, 2005), p. 6.

Overall there were 16,929 murders in this country in 2007, according to the FBI. This represented 5.6 murders per 100,000 inhabitants and was a 2.3 percent increase over homicides in 2003. Of these, there were 4,176 murder victims between the college age years of seventeen and twenty-four, with 3,758 persons under the age of twenty-two as homicide victims in 2007.[6] Firearms were the weapon of choice most often by offenders in taking the lives of 3,463 college age murder victims, followed by knives/cutting instruments, personal weapons such as fists, and blunt objects (see Figure 3.2).

Table 3.3
Reasons for Students Not Reporting
Violent Victimization to Police, 1995–2002

Reasons for not reporting	Percent of all violence
Reported	35.2%
Not reported	
Private or personal matter	30.7
Minor crime/no loss	24.7
Reported to another official	8.5
Fear of reprisal	2.5
Protect offender	3.1
Not clear a crime occurred	4.2
Lack of proof	4.5
Inconvenient	2.5
Police will not bother	2.4
Child offender	0.6
Police inefficient	0.5
Police bias	0.2
Property unrecoverable	—[a]
Other reason given	15.7

[a]Less than .05%.

SOURCE: Adapted from U.S. Department of Justice, Bureau of Justice Statistics Special Report, *Violent Victimization of College Students, 1995–2002* (Washington, DC: Office of Justice Programs, 2005), p. 6.

The available information on school- and college-related murders indicates that the number of students killed is fairly low compared to other types of school crime. Data from the FBI's National Incident-Based Reporting System (NIBRS) for school, college, and university crimes against persons between 2000 and 2004 can be seen in Table 3.4. There were thirty-seven murders in educational institutions reported during the five-year span, with the number peaking at fourteen in 2002 and falling to five in 2003 before rising to eight murders in 2004. Only two negligent manslaughters were reported for the period with none in 2004. By comparison to these figures, there were 129,675 total simple assaults reported for the five years, 15,298 aggravated assaults, 489 sexual assaults with a weapon, and 35,715 incidents of intimidation among other crimes against persons. Also, far more prevalent on school and college campuses than homicides are many crimes that fall under the categories of crimes against property and crimes against society, including destruction of property, larceny-theft, and drug violations.[7] Because the NIBRS data is based in part on a limited number of law enforcement agencies reporting UCR statistics in the NIBRS system, actual figures for personal crimes at schools and colleges is likely higher. But the information does give us some perspective on the relative breakdown on such offenses in relationship to one another.

Figure 3.2
Weapons Used to Murder College Age Students, 2007

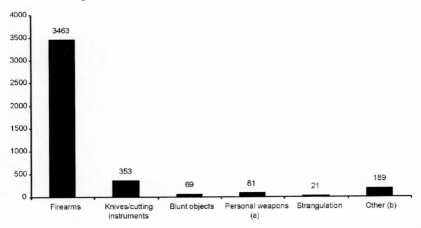

[a]Includes hands, fists, feet, and pushed.
[b]Includes poison, explosives, fire, narcotics, asphyxiation, drowning, and weapons not stated.

SOURCE: Derived from U.S. Department of Justice, Federal Bureau of Investigation, *Crime in the United States 2007* (Washington, DC: Criminal Justice Information Services Division, 2008), http://www.fbi.gov/ucr/cius2007/offenses/expanded_information/data/shrtable_08.html.

Other crime statistics on murder and negligent manslaughter on college and university campuses or involving college students show higher numbers (see Table 3.5). According to the Department of Education's (ED) data on campus crime, there were sixty-four murders at all post-secondary institutions receiving federal funding in 2007, more than twice the total from 2006 and 2005 combined. There were 117 homicides reported during the three-year span. Among institution sectors, the vast majority of murders occurred at public colleges of four years or more, followed by private, non-profit schools of four years or above. Eight negligent manslaughters at college were reported for 2007, well down from the thirty-three in 2005. Most of the cases of negligent manslaughter occurred at public colleges and private, non-profit colleges of four or more years.

Table 3.4
Number of Offenses of Crimes Against Persons in Schools, by Offense, 2000–2005

Year of Incident

Offense	2000	2001	2002	2003	2004	5-year total
Simple Assault	16,898	23,614	26,587	29,015	33,561	129,675
Intimidation	5,154	8,340	6,792	7,164	8,265	35,715
Aggravated Assault	2,417	2,920	3,092	3,235	3,634	15,298
Forcible Fondling	1,148	1,479	1,745	1,736	2,085	8,193
Forcible Rape	241	301	320	359	441	1,662
Kidnapping/Abduction	153	200	230	278	307	1,168
Forcible Sodomy	74	107	108	123	130	542
Sexual Assault With An Object	75	74	101	111	128	489
Statutory Rape	28	32	45	74	101	280
Murder & Nonnegligent Manslaughter	2	8	14	5	8	37
Incest	0	5	9	5	0	19
Negligent Manslaughter	1	0	0	1	0	2

SOURCE: Adapted from U.S. Department of Justice, Federal Bureau of Investigation, School Violence, Crime in Schools and Colleges: A Study of Offenders and Arrestees Reported via National Incident-Based Reporting System Data, http://www.fbi.gov/ucr/schoolviolence/2007/appendixa.htm

Recent more expansive homicide statistics on college students reflect the sobering realities of murder at higher institutions of learning in this country.

For instance, in the School Violence Resource Center fact sheet, "Murders Involving the College Population," it reported that according to the Office of Postsecondary Education, in 2000, there were 395 murders that involved college students on campus or off campus (including possibly such places as fraternities/sororities and popular student hangouts).[8] This represented a 29 percent increase over the total of 306 murders in 1999 and the school murder rate almost doubling (see Figure 3.3).[9]

Table 3.5
Murder and Negligent Manslaughter
at Postsecondary Institutions, 2005–2007

	2005	2006	2007
Murder			
Public, 4-year or above	11	12	49
Private nonprofit, 4-year or above	11	9	12
Private for profit, 4-year or above	0	0	0
Public, 2-year	6	1	1
Private nonprofit, 2-year	0	0	0
Private for profit, 2-year	0	0	1
Public, less-than-2-year	0	1	0
Private nonprofit, less-than-2-year	0	0	0
Private for profit, less-than-2-year	0	2	1
Total	28	25	64
Negligent Manslaughter			
Public, 4-year or above	7	0	4
Private nonprofit, 4-year or above	25	0	3
Private for profit, 4-year or above	0	0	0
Public, 2-year	0	0	1
Private nonprofit, 2-year	0	0	0
Private for profit, 2-year	0	0	0
Public, less-than-2-year	1	0	0
Private nonprofit, less-than-2-year	0	0	0
Private for profit, less-than-2-year	0	0	0
Total	33	0	8

SOURCE: Adapted from U.S. Department of Education, The Campus Security Data Analysis Cutting Tool, Office of Postsecondary Education, "Data on Campus Crime: Criminal Offenses," http://www.ed.gov/admins/lead/safety/campus.html

The ED reported that in 2001 there were 859 murders occurring on or in the vicinity of university and college campuses nationwide.[10] While data suggests the number of murdered postsecondary students has fallen considerably as of 2009, many college students remain at risk for becoming victims of homicide or other violent crimes as conditions persist in the campus environment for such victimization.

Figure 3.3
College Population-Involved Murders, 1999–2000

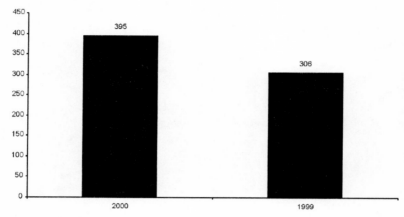

SOURCE: Derived from U.S. Department of Education, Office of Postsecondary Education, http://www.ed.gov/about/offices/list/ope/reports.html.

The National Center for Education Statistics, Institute of Education Services, and Bureau of Justice Statistics jointly provide complementary data on school-associated violent deaths, defining them as "homicide, suicide, legal intervention (involving a law enforcement officer), or unintentional firearm-related death in which the fatal injury occurred on the campus of a functioning elementary or secondary school in the United States."[11] According to their *Indicators of School Crime and Safety: 2007*, between July 1, 2005, and June 30, 2006, thirty-five school-associated violent deaths occurred at elementary or secondary schools. Such "at school" deaths include violent deaths of students, school staff and non-students taking place while the "victim was on the way to or from regular sessions at school, or ... attending or traveling to or from an official school-sponsored event."[12] (See Figure 3.4.)

Table 3.6 shows the number of school-related homicides between 1992–93 and 2005–06 in the United States. The total of twenty-six homicides in 2005–06 was down from thirty-nine in 2004–05 and nearly half as few as the forty-seven school-associated murders which peaked in 1992–93 and was matched during the period of 1997–98.

In spite of a recent sharp decline in homicides involving school, college and university students and improved security and reporting procedures at institutions, the plethora of illegal (or misused legal or licensed) firearms available, along with alcohol and drug abuse, and unbalanced individuals who have shown a propensity for targeting college and secondary students for mass or single killings, illustrate the continuing threat to all students.

Figure 3.4
School-Associated Violent Deaths, 2005–2006

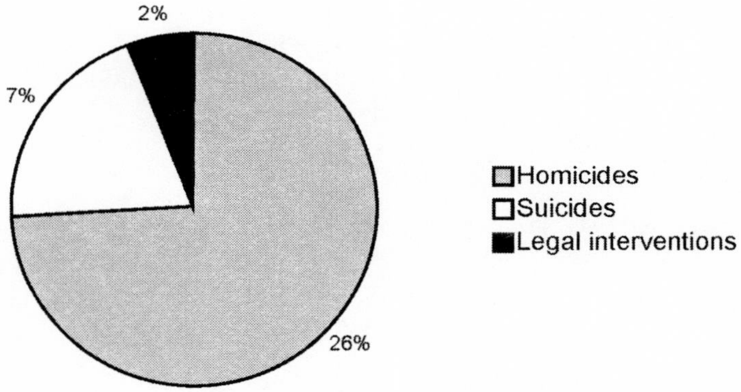

SOURCE: Derived from U.S. Department of Education, National Center for Education Statistics, *Indicators of School Crime and Safety: 2007* (Washington, DC: Institute of Education Sciences, 2007), p. 69.

School Shootings

A number of deadly mass or spree shootings have occurred in colleges and high schools in recent years, putting greater focus on the vulnerability of students across the United States to random or premeditated attacks and the need for better identification of potential perpetrators and safety measures on campuses. The term *school shooting* has generally referred to firearm violence that takes place in a school setting that can include universities, colleges, high schools, middle schools and other institutions of education.

The perpetrators often have an association with the school, or someone in attendance or employment there, and tend to target either one or more individuals in particular or multiple people who may have no connection with the shooter or shooters other than being at the institution at the wrong day and time. Today school shootings are considered to be domestic acts of terrorism and the assailants often have an agenda tied to targeting victims or shooting rampage. Substance abuse tends to play a big role in the process that leads to a school shooting, along with access to weaponry and a troubled history such as family violence, bullying, and relationship issues.[13]

Table 3.6
Number of School-Related Violent Deaths
of Students, Staff, and Nonstudents, 1992–2006

Year	Homicides	Total[a]
1992–93	47	57
1993–94	38	48
1994–95	39	48
1995–96	46	53
1996–97	45	48
1997–98	47	57
1998–99	38	47
1999–2000	24	36
2000–01	24	30
2001–02	26	37
2002–03	25	35
2003–04	31	36
2004–05	39	50
2005–06	26	35

[a]Includes suicides, legal interventions, and unintentional deaths.

SOURCE: Adapted from U.S. Department of Education, National Center for Education Statistics, *Indicators of School Crime and Safety: 2007* (Washington, DC: Institute of Education Sciences, 2007), p. 69.

Examples of notable school shootings in the United States include[14]:

- On October 27, 2008, two students were shot to death and a nonstudent wounded at the University of Central Arkansas in Conway, Arkansas. The four men charged with the murders and attempted murder were waiting to go to trial as of January 2009.
- On February 14, 2008, Steven Kazmierczak, twenty-seven, stepped inside a packed lecture hall at Northern Illinois University in DeKalb, Illinois, and opened fire, killing five and injur-

ing eighteen before fatally shooting himself. The former graduate student at the school was heavily armed with a Remington
870 shotgun, along with a 9mm Glock, 9mm Sig Sauer, and .380
Hi-Point handguns to perpetrate the attack.

- On February 8, 2008, Latina Williams, twenty-three, entered a
classroom at Louisiana Technical College in Baton Rouge,
Louisiana, where the nursing student used a .357 revolver to shoot
to death two people before committing suicide.

- On April 16, 2007, Seung-Hui Cho, a twenty-three-year-old
undergraduate student, went on a shooting rampage at Virginia
Polytechnic Institute and State University in Blacksburg, Virginia, killing thirty-two and wounding seventeen others before
taking his own life. Cho used a 9mm semi-automatic Glock 19
handgun and a .22-caliber Walther P22 semi-automatic handgun in the attacks in what became the deadliest single shooter
school or off campus mass murder in American history.

- On October 2, 2006, Charles Roberts, thirty-two, went inside
the West Nickel Mines School in Bart Township, Lancaster
County, Pennsylvania, a one-room Amish schoolhouse, heavily-
armed, where he killed five girls and injured four others before
killing himself. His weapons included a 12-gauge shotgun, .30–06
bolt-action rifle, and 9mm handgun.

- On April 20, 1999, Eric Harris, eighteen, and Dylan Klebold, seventeen, entered Columbine High School in Littleton, Colorado,
heavily armed with weapons including .a Hi-Point 995 Carbine,
9mm TEC-DC9 semi-automatic handgun, and a double bar-
reled sawed-off shotgun. The two students went on a shooting
rampage, killing thirteen, including twelve students, and wounding twenty-three others before taking their own lives. It was the
fourth deadliest shooting at a school in United States history.

- On May 21, 1998, Kip Kinkel, fourteen, was well-armed with a
9mm Glock handgun, Ruger .22 pistol, and a .22 semiautomatic
rifle, as he entered Thurston High School in Springfield, Oregon, and opened fire, killing two students and wounding twenty-
five. Earlier that day, he had committed parricide in murdering
his mother and father.

- On March 24, 1998, Mitchell Johnson, thirteen, and Andrew Goldman, eleven, were wearing camouflage as they opened fire on students and teachers from the woods outside Westside Middle School in Jonesboro, Arkansas, killing five and wounding ten. The perpetrators' firearms included a Universal M1 Carbine, a Ruger rifle, and several handguns.
- On August 1, 1966, Charles Whitman, twenty-five, carried out a massacre at the University of Texas in Austin, Texas. The architectural engineering student made his way to the observation deck in the thirty-two story Tower Building. Heavily armed with a sawed off shotgun, Remington 700 6mm bolt-action hunting rifle, Remington 35-caliber pump rifle, .357 Magnum pistol and other weapons, he killed fifteen and wounded thirty-two others before being shot to death by police. Earlier Whitman had also murdered his wife and mother.[15]

Aside from these incidences of mass casualties on school campuses, there have been many other instances of school shootings over the years, often with fatalities.[16] Moreover, there have been a number of planned school attacks recently that have been averted, including a Columbine-like massacre planned in 2001 by a student at De Anza College in Cupertino, California.[17]

Risk factors commonly associated with school shooters are:

- Severe depression or other mental problems.
- History of anger issues.
- Built-up resentment toward others.
- Social rejection.
- A history of substance abuse.
- A strong interest in firearms or explosives.
- Accessibility of firearms or other weapons.
- Victim of child physical or sexual abuse.
- Experienced family violence.
- Disciplinary issues at home.
- School problems such as truancy, suspensions, or being expelled.
- History of cruelty to animals.
- Obsessed with hate or antigovernment groups.

- Membership in a gang or antisocial group.
- Involvement with a satanic cult.
- A fascination with violent games, books, movies, or other violent entertainment.
- Suicidal thought.
- Affixes blame for problems in life to others.

Researchers have found that, contrary to popular belief, most school shooters are not loners, but rather *joiners*, "whose attempts at social integration fail so that they let their thinking and even ... plans be known, sometimes frequently over long periods of time. The shootings seem ... an attempt to adjust their social standing and image, from 'loser' to 'master of violence.'"[18]

The majority of school shooters are male, reflecting the gender dynamics of violent crime in general.[19] Most shooters have a purpose to their acts of homicidal violence, whether real or perceived. The motivation is often triggered by revenge or getting back at someone, a group, or an institution (or those representing such) that the perpetrator(s) blames for having wronged them in some manner such as alienation, bullying, and persecution.[20]

Firearms and School Homicides

The strong relationship between firearms and homicides on school and college campuses has been documented in statistics and studies. According to the NIBRS data, from 2000 to 2004, guns were used in school violence 3,461 times (see Figure 3.5). Handguns accounted for 58 percent of the firearms used, followed by unknown or other types of firearms. Rifles were used more often than shotguns in crime on campus. Some researchers have looked at firearms as a "growing menace" at colleges and universities[21]; while others have examined the correlation between lethal campus violence and alcohol use and firearms.[22]

Studies have found that six to seven percent of college students carry some type of weapon at school.[23] One study reported that guns constituted 14 percent of the weapons in students' possession.[24] In a survey of 130 colleges from around the United States that involved 26,920 students, with respect to owning a firearm and drinking, 3.5 percent of the respondents reported having a gun on campus.[25] Students age twenty-one and over were more likely to own firearms than younger students. Around 40 percent of the student respondents were binge drinkers or had consumed five drinks or more of alcohol in a row during the two weeks prior to the survey. These students were more likely to have owned a firearm than non binge drinkers.

Figure 3.5
Type of Firearms Used in School Violence, 2000–2004

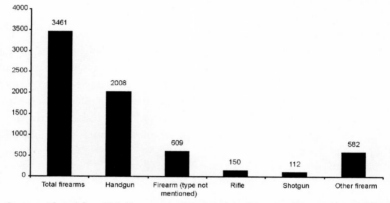

SOURCE: Adapted from U.S. Department of Justice, Federal Bureau of Investigation, School Violence, *Crime in Schools and Colleges: A Study of Offenders and Arrestees Reported via National Incident-Based Reporting System Data*, http://www.fbi.gov/ucrschoolviolence/2007/analyses.htm.

Other information yielded by the survey includes[26]:

- Two out of three student gun owners lived off campus.
- Students having guns were more likely than not to be in fraternities or sororities.
- Students owning guns more often were married or in a relationship than not.
- Cocaine or crack use was more likely among students owning guns than those who did not.
- Students with alcohol-related conduct such as DUI were more than twice as likely to possess firearms as students without alcohol-associated behaviors.

- Ownership of guns was higher among students hurt as a result of alcohol-involved fights compared to students uninjured or injured due to other circumstances.
- Students who owned guns more often attended rural colleges instead of urban colleges.

The study also found that college students who own guns are most likely to be male, white, go to public colleges, and attend schools in the South and West.[27] The correlation between lethal weapons, substance abuse, and various acts of violence has been shown in research to be significant, including homicide, domestic violence, dating violence, sexual assault, and suicide.[28]

In spite of the fact that homicides represent only a small fraction of overall school violence, most fatal school violence tends to involve firearms that can be used by perpetrators to commit single victim crimes or those involving mass casualties.[29] This has led to debate on more gun control laws to limit the accessibility of firearms to high risk persons versus more legal ownership of guns by college students and faculty to protect themselves.[30] Efforts to allow licensed gun owners to carry concealed firearms on college campuses have had mixed results. Bills recently introduced by sixteen states for carrying concealed weapons on campus all failed to pass. However, three states were introducing such legislation again.[31] As of February 2009, eleven public universities allowed concealed weapons to be carried on campus.[32] The majority of college students appear to prefer that guns are not allowed on campus as a means for increasing violence and fatalities. According to one report, 94 percent of students are against firearms on campus, legal or not, reflecting the realities of the potential for gun violence when tied in with gun accessibility on and off school grounds.[33]

Causes of School-Related Homicides and Other Violent Crimes

Experts have explored the reasons behind school violence such as murder and aggravated assault. There is no one reason attributed to campus violent criminality, but rather a number of issues that often go hand in hand. These include offender alcohol or drug use, pent-up hostilities, desire for vengeance aimed at someone in particular, a group, or the school itself, mental issues such as depression, and access to firearms and other weapons that can exacerbate the urge or willingness to commit violence.[34]

Some believe that school violence in today's times is largely a reflection of perpetrators who think only in terms of themselves or what is satisfying for the individual rather than the community or society as a whole. As a sociologist contended, "'If it feels good for me, then it's all right.' There's just not the same sense of responsibility that upholds what is good for everybody. There's not a sense of right and wrong."[35]

Others associate violent crimes on campus with the violent culture we live in that includes constant violence on TV, in movies, video games, books, and the Internet.[36] With violence being so accepted on so many levels as part of our society, some people may come to believe that violence is a natural response to anger in real life situations. The pressures in school life such as studies, dating, peer group acceptance, being away from home, competition, bullying, substance abuse, and other factors may make some students even more susceptible to committing violent acts such as murder and suicide. Studies have also linked school violence to child abuse, domestic violence, peer violence, and a cycle of violence.[37]

Such issues can be even more deeply rooted in school mass murderers, along with possessing serious mental problems such as severe depression, schizophrenia, and paranoia.[38] One criminologist characterized mass murderers as having "a serious psychiatric disturbance,"[39] while in a study of mass killers and serial murderers, nearly all the killers were classified as insane.[40] However, others who study mass murderers assert that though these individuals may lack "normal psychosocial and emotional responses, they typically are not mentally ill."[41] Instead, they argue that such killers tend to be fully aware of their actions, often planning in advance, and are motivated by hatred, frustration, vengeance, hopelessness, humiliation, rage, suicidal tendencies, and a desire to kill as many as possible.[42]

The media appears to play a big role in campus mass murders, along with copycatting previous school shootings, which are often tied together, as a result of extensive coverage and giving the killer or killers the type of infamy that could never occur on a worldwide stage with a single shooting incident or another less dramatic or violent means of expressing frustrations.[43]

Protecting Students from Violent Crime on Campus

Currently all the existing laws against homicide and other acts of violence are applicable for preventing school violence and protecting students on and off campus. With a greater focus on campus crimes in recent years, more emphasis has been put on making the school environment safer for students and faculty alike, as well as being better informed on school violence and campus crime data, and providing improved services and response from campus law enforcement for victims of crime.

A key piece of federal legislation addressing violent crimes and student safety on college campuses is the Student Right-to-Know and Campus Security Act of 1990.[44] In Title II of the Act, Crime Awareness and Campus Security Act, all institutions of higher learning receiving federal student aid are required to release school security policies and publish annually a report containing specific college crime statistics on and off campus.[45] The crime categories of these statistics include:

- Criminal homicide (murder/nonnegligent manslaughter and negligent manslaughter)
- Sex offense (forcible sex offenses, including rape and non forcible sex offenses)
- Robbery
- Aggravated assault
- Burglary
- Motor vehicle theft
- Arson
- Hate crime (see Chapter 7)

The Act also requires colleges and universities to report on incidences of substance abuse and firearms-related incidences that led to an arrest or disciplinary referral, including:

- Liquor law violations
- Drug law violations
- Illegal weapons possession

The report must include not only crime data from within official campus grounds, but areas neighboring the campus that typically involve frequent use by students, such as public sidewalks, streets, and parking garages; as well as on campus properties that may be run by a third party (for example, a food vendor).

In 1998, the Act was renamed the Jeanne Clery Disclosure of Campus Security Policy and Campus Crime Statistics Act (referred to as the Clery Act).[46] Amendments to the Act in 2008 under the Higher Education Opportunity Act required institutions to issue an immediate notification to students, faculty, and employees of any known danger , criminality, or emergency on campus.[47] The Act also expanded hate crime statistics to include such offenses as intimidation and assault, while another provision was aimed at protecting whistleblowers from any retaliatory response.[48]

Institutions failing to comply with the requirements risk a fine or loss of eligibility to receive federal funds.[49] The majority of schools have submitted their report on campus security annually in accordance with the Act to the U.S. Department of Education, with over two-thirds of colleges and universities including crime data amongst the information.[50] However, a recent report from the General Accounting Office (GAO) indicated that some schools had problems understanding the reporting requirements.[51] Definitions of certain crimes have also been inconsistent from school to school, affecting the accuracy of crime statistics submitted. The GAO found that only 37 percent of the colleges studied were in full compliance with the reporting requirements.[52]

Protecting college students from deadly attacks and other acts of violence on campus is primarily the responsibility of campus and local law enforcement. Campus security is required under the Act to maintain a public crime log of all criminal offenses that take place within their jurisdiction or are reported to them, as well as disclose measures in place for protecting students from criminal victimization.[53] According to the Bureau of Justice Statistics Special Report, *Campus Law Enforcement, 2004–05*, almost three-quarters of the law enforcement agencies serving four year institutions with at least 2,500 students had sworn law enforcement personnel.[54] This gave them full arrest powers. During the 2004 to 2005 school year, two in three campus law enforcement agencies included armed patrol officers. More than 90 percent of agencies had an emergency preparedness plan in writing, while nearly 60 percent of law enforcement agencies took part in emergency preparedness excerises.[55]

In addition to campus and local law enforcement, colleges and universities must rely on student patrols and residence hall safety personnel to help identify potential threats and ensure student safety from crime and violence.[56] College students are also subject to following a code of conduct in attending institutions of higher education, being aware of campus crime data and security, as well as taking personal responsibility to protect themselves from victimization such as locking doors and being aware of one's surroundings, day and night.

Chapter 4

SEXUAL ASSAULT

Teenagers and young adults face not only increased exposure to alcohol and drug use and their implications, but sexual violence. Though students attending colleges and universities throughout the United States are generally safe from harm, often in the company of friends or involved in the routines of school and campus life, they are also at risk for becoming victims of sexual assault, including forcible rape and other nonconsensual sex acts. A plethora of research has surfaced in recent years as a result of the incidence of rapes and other crimes on college campuses and a lack of appropriate response from school administrators, campus security, and others there to ensure student safety.

Young women are especially vulnerable to college sexual victimization, be it stranger rape, date rape, acquaintance rape, or other types of sexual mistreatment. Young men are far more likely to be the perpetrators of sexual violence than victims, though male victimization does occur. The convergence of a college environment that is conducive to socializing, underage drinking, binge drinking, drug use, parties, dating, and sexual experimenting only increases the danger for sexual victimization. Sex crimes, including forcible rape and sexual abuse, are against the law everywhere in this country. Legislation has also been passed by Congress to address issues of student rights, campus security policies, and access to crime data from colleges and universities. However, lack of clarity on what constitutes certain crimes such as sexual assault and stalking, underreporting, institutional shortcomings, and even student peer pressure contribute to continued risk for sexual victimization and its consequences.

Defining Sexual Assault and Rape

The terms rape and sexual assault have often been used interchangeably in recent years, along with sexual abuse, in defining forced or unwanted sexual relations between two or more people, without respect to gender specificity or other limitations. For instance, the U.S. Department of Justice's Bureau of Justice Statistics defines rape as:

> Forced sexual intercourse including both psychological coercion as well as physical force. Forced sexual intercourse means vaginal, anal or oral penetration by the offender(s). This category also includes incidents where the penetration is from a foreign object such as a bottle. Includes attempted rapes, male as well as female victims and both heterosexual and homosexual rape. Attempted rape includes verbal threats of rape.[1]

This is in stark contrast to earlier times when rape was seen as a sexual offense against adult females and perpetrated by adult males only.[2] The word "rape" originates from the Latin *rapere*, meaning to "steal, seize, or carry away."[3] In common law, rape was defined as "the unlawful carnal knowledge of a female by force and against her will."[4] Sexual penetration, no matter how slight, was enough to represent a criminal offense, assuming the other elements were there. A resistance standard was established "for the victim in order to distinguish forcible carnal knowledge (rape) from consensual carnal knowledge (fornication and adultery)."[5]

Traditional definitions of rape were problematic in their narrow parameters, gender-based, societal and interpretational aspects, as noted by Kaare Svalastoga:

> Rape is commonly defined as enforced coitus. But this very definition suggests that there is more to the offense than the use of force alone. This must be so, since no society has equipped itself with the means of measuring the amount of force applied in the act of coitus. Hence rape, like any other crime, carries a heavy social component. The act itself is not a sufficient [criterion]. The act must be interpreted as rape by the female actee, and her interpretation must be similarly evaluated by a number of officials and agencies before the official designation of "rape" can be legitimately applied.[6]

Since the 1970s, rape reform laws have been passed on the federal level and in states, expanding the definition of rape to be a gender-neutral offense, where females and males could be victims and offenders, as well as encompassing a broader range of acts to constitute rape, sexual abuse, or sexual assault. These include[7]:

- Sexual penetration acts aside from penis penetration of the vagina.
- Differentiating kinds of sexual abuse based on degree of force or threat thereof used.

- Threats in addition to force are seen as a way to compel the victim to submit to crime.
- Taking advantage of a victim who is incapacitated, such as under the influence of alcohol or drugs, or mentally ill.

State laws vary in their precise definitions of rape and sexual assault, with some states including a broad range of sex crimes under one grouping, denoting different degrees of severity; while other states define sex crimes as various offenses without degrees present.[8] The Illinois Criminal Sexual Assault Act is often viewed as a national model in its definition of criminal sexual assault as (1) an act of sexual penetration by the use of force or threat of force; or (2) an act of sexual penetration and the accused knew that the victim was unable to understand the nature of the act or was unable to give knowing consent.[9]

The statute defines aggravated criminal sexual assault as criminal sexual assault under aggravating circumstances such as "with a dangerous weapon; or when there is bodily harm; or when the accused threatens the life of the victim or another; or in the commission of another felony; or the accused delivered any controlled substance to the victim, including use of rape drugs to the victim."[10]

This definition notwithstanding, given the lack of uniformity in state definitions of sexual assault, including the U.S. territories and District of Columbia, the federal definitions become all the more important to set a true national standard. The U.S. Criminal Code defining rape and other kinds of sexual assault excludes labeling victims in gender-specific terms and the word "rape," while not requiring victims to refer to the incident as a rape as a condition for constituting a criminal offense.[11]

The Federal Code defines sexual abuse as when a person knowingly:

> causes another person to engage in a sexual act by threatening or placing that other person in fear (other than by threatening or placing that other person in fear that any person will be subjected to death, serious bodily injury, or kidnapping); or ... engages in a sexual act with another person if that other person is ... incapable of appraising the nature of the conduct; or ... physically incapable of declining participation in, or communicating unwillingness to engage in, that sexual act.[12]

The U.S. Code's definitions of aggravated sexual assault (or forcible rape) are when a person:

By force or threat ... knowingly causes another person to engage in a sexual act by using force against that other person; or ... by threatening or placing that other person in fear that any person will be subjected to death, serious bodily injury, or kidnapping; or attempts to do so (or) by other means ... knowingly renders another person unconscious and thereby engages in a sexual act with that other person; or ... administers to another person by force or threat of force, or without the knowledge or permission of that person, a drug, intoxicant, or other similar substance and thereby ... substantially impairs the ability of that other person to appraise or control conduct; and ... engages in a sexual act with that other person; or attempts to do so.[13]

Federal law requires institutions of higher education to differentiate between forcible and nonforcible sex offenses in their own definitions of sexual assaults perpetrated against students.[14] The Federal Bureau of Investigation's *Uniform Crime Reports* classifies forcible sex crimes as forcible rape, forcible sodomy, sexual assault with an object, and forcible fondling. Nonforcible sex crimes include incest and statutory rape.[15]

Within the context of criminal sexual assault definitions are subtypes of sexual assaults or nonconsensual or enforced sexual (genital, anal, or oral) acts through physical penetration or use of a foreign object, such as acquaintance rape, date rape, and marital rape.

The Extent of College Sexual Assaults

Overall, recent data suggest that sexual assaults in the United States are on the decline. In a Bureau of Justice Statistics (BJS) report on violent victimization of college students from 1995 to 2002, rapes or sexual assaults had dropped by more than 23 percent.[16] However, the incidence of rapes and other sexual offenses remains high. In 2006, there were 260,940 rapes, attempted rapes, or sexual assaults in this country, according to the Justice Department's National Crime Victimization Survey (NCVS). Incidents and victimizations were higher for rapes than attempted rapes or sexual assaults, which included threats (see Table 4.1).

Approximately every two minutes, a person is sexually assaulted in this country. Nearly eighteen million women have been rape or attempted rape victims; while one in six women will be the victim of a sexual assault in her lifetime. Comparatively, one in thirty-three men will ever face rape or attempted rape victimization.[17]

Table 4.1
Number of Rape/Sexual Assault Incidents
and Victimizations, 2006

Type of Crime	Incidents	Victimizations	Ratio
Rape/Sexual assault	255,630	260,940	1.02
Rape/Attempted rape	187,010	192,320	1.03
Rape	113,290	116,600	1.03
Attempted rape[a]	73,720	75,720	1.03
Sexual assault[b]	68,620	68,620	1.00

[a]Includes verbal threats of rape.
[b]Includes threats.

SOURCE: Adapted from U.S. Department of Justice, Bureau of Justice Statistics, "Criminal Victimization in the United States, 2006 Statistical Tables," (June 30, 2008), http://www.ojp.usdoj.gov/bjs/pub/pdf/cvus0602.pdf

College age persons are especially at risk for sexual assault victimization. Statistics show that most rape victims are between the ages of eighteen and twenty-four. This group, representing most females in college, is four times more likely than any other to be the victim of a sexual assault.[18] Furthermore, some research indicates that young women attending college have a greater risk of becoming sexual assault victims than comparably aged women in the population at large.[19] One in five female college students are raped while attending college; while over one in four female students have reported incidents that could be legally defined as rape or attempted rape.[20]

Though many continue to associate rape victimization with offenders who are strangers, the reality is that most rapists are not strangers to their victims. Studies reveal that between 78 percent and 97.8 percent of rapes are committed by persons the victims know.[21] This is reflected in the BJS findings, in which nearly eight in ten rape or sexual assaults of college students were perpetrated by someone known to them (see Figure 4.1).

Often the rapist is a current or former boyfriend. The likelihood that an actual rape will occur rather than attempted rape that was not completed increases the more intimately involved the female is with the male.[22] In many incidents, college women were victimized by another student, with stalking, sexual harassment, and other partner violence often precursors for sexual assault.[23]

Figure 4.1
Rape/Sexual Assault Victimization of College Students by
Offender Characteristics and Relationship to Victim, 1995–2002

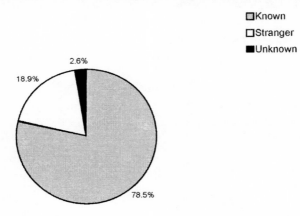

□ Known
□ Stranger
■ Unknown

2.6%

18.9%

78.5%

NOTE: Unknown is based on 10 or less sample cases.
SOURCE: Adapted from U.S. Department of Justice, Bureau of Justice Statistics Special Report, *Violent Victimization of College Students, 1995–2002* (Washington, DC: Office of Justice Programs, 2005), p. 4.

In an influential National College Women Sexual Victimization (NCWSV) study of 4,446 females in college, funded by the National Institute of Justice, it was found that 2.8 percent had been the victims of a completed or attempted rape during the present school year.[24] Nearly 23 percent of the victims had been raped multiple times. The researchers estimated that given the victimization rate of 35.3 per 1,000 female students, on a college campus where 10,000 women were enrolled; there could be in excess of 350 rapes per year.

According to the study, approximately 20 to 25 percent of college females will be the victims of an attempted or completed rape during their college years. This finding was supported by another study of over 6,000 college women attending thirty-two universities and colleges, in which 27 percent of students reported experiencing completed or attempted rape at some point in their lives.[25]

Other research gives further evidence of the high incidence of sexual assaults among college females, with studies yielding a prevalence rate of sexual assault victimization at between 14 and 27.5 percent.[26] In the Campus Sexual Assault (CSA) study, the authors surveyed 5,446 female undergraduates and 1,375 male undergraduates from two universities. Nearly 14 percent of the female students had been sexually assaulted on at least one occasion since they began attending college. Almost 29 percent of the female undergraduates reported being the victims of an attempted or actual sexual assault prior to or since starting college.[27]

In a smaller survey of 635 college students, Charlene Muehlenhard and Melaney Linton found that nearly 80 percent of the female students and almost 60 percent of the male students reported experiencing some type of sexual aggression.[28] Fourteen percent of the female students had been the victims of nonconsensual sexual relations. A study by the U.S. Centers for Disease Control and Prevention found that 20 percent of the female college students reported being the victims of forcible rape during their lifetimes.[29]

Other findings on college students and sexual assaults include[30]:

- Nearly 60 percent of on campus completed rapes occurred in the victim's dorm room or apartment.
- Three in ten on campus rapes occurred in other living space.
- Off campus rapes occur most often in residences.
- Off campus sexual assaults are more common than on campus ones.
- Most college sexual assaults occur in the evening.
- In almost eight in ten incidents of rape, the victim and offender were the same race.
- Around seven in ten rapists were classmates or friends.
- Most sexually victimized female students seek to take protective measures during the occurrence.
- Attempted sexual contact without force has the highest nonrape or attempted rape rate of sexual victimization.
- Stalking is a form of sexual victimization.

- Only about four in ten institutions report crime statistics to fit criterion mandated by law.[31]

The devastating effects of sexual assault on victims are many, such as[32]:

- Twenty-five to 45 percent of rape victims experience trauma other than genital.
- Around one in five rape victims experience genital trauma.
- As many as 40 percent of rape victims contract a sexually transmitted disease.
- Approximately 32,000 pregnancies occur as a result of rapes in the United States each year.
- Substance abuse is much higher among rape victims than non-rape victims.
- Most victims suffer from depression, lack of concentration, and insomnia.
- The majority of victims undergo chronic physical or mental issues.
- Almost one-third of rape victims suffer from post-traumatic stress disorder in relation to the rape at some stage in life.
- Victims of rape are thirteen times as likely to attempt suicide as persons who are not crime victims.
- Rape victims are six times more likely to attempt suicide as other crime victims.
- Rape costs more annually for victims than any other crime.

Underreported Sexual Assaults

Even with the disturbing statistics on sexual assault victimizations of females attending colleges and universities, most such sexual assaults are believed to be vastly unreported. The NCVS found that among violent offenses, rape or sexual assault is reported the least to law enforcement; whereas attempted rapes are the most likely type of crime victimization to be unreported.[33] Less than 5 percent of completed or attempted college student rapes are reported to campus or law enforcement authorities; though around two-thirds of victims tell someone about the assault, most often a close friend.[34] One study found that while 97 percent of the rape victims confided to someone about the victimization, virtually none reported it to the police or other law enforcement.[35] Another study found that while one in four females in college reported at least one rape encounter that would be legally defined as attempted or completed rape, the closer the victim was to her perpetrator, the least likely she was to report the sexual assault.[36] As such, date and acquaintance rapes are reported less often than stranger rapes, which constitute only a fraction of the rapes and other sexual assaults occurring on campus grounds.[37]

Reasons most often given by college student sexual assault victims for not reporting the crime include:

- Did not consider the incident serious enough.
- Preferred that family or friends did not know about incident.
- Unsure if a crime was committed or intended.
- Insufficient proof of a crime.
- Fearful of retaliation by offender or someone else.

One of the main reasons attributed to the low rate of reporting college rapes is a misperception by female student victims on what constitutes rape and sexual assault. A number of studies have found that most females who experience rape or attempted rape that meets the legal threshold of a crime do not define it as a sexual assault.[38] In the NCWSV study, only 46.5 percent of the incidents identified as completed rapes were regarded as rape by the victims.[39] A study by Mary Koss and colleagues of college students found that just 27 percent of the female victims believed the legally defined sexual assault to be a rape.[40]

Not recognizing the acts of attempted or completed rape as criminal sexual assaults, and therefore not reporting, can have serious consequences with respect to victim safety from a repeat attack or assaulting other college women, health considerations, and the underestimation of the magnitude of campus sexual assaults.

Lower reporting rates of college sexual assaults have also been associated with alcohol and/or drug use by perpetrators and/or victims, in which victims may be reluctant to come forward due to fearing detection of alcohol or drugs in their system, possibly resulting in disciplinary actions.[41] On campus sexual assaults are more likely to be reported than off campus victimizations, and most often to campus law enforcement.[42]

There is some indication that too often inadequate response on the part of university and college personnel, including resident advisors and faculty, to student complaints of sexual victimization may play a role in low reporting by victims[43]; as well as their reluctance to get involved in the criminal justice system for fear of further victimization or a perception of racial bias.[44]

Even when a rape is reported, there is only around a 50 percent chance that an arrest will be made. However, when considering unreported rapes, just 6 percent or so of rapists will ever serve any time behind bars, illustrating the implications in the lack of reporting sexual assaults.[45]

Correlates of College Sexual Assaults

Substance Abuse

Alcohol and drug use among college students are a common part of campus life, traditions, and socializing. They are also positively associated with college sexual assaults, with both victims and offenders who use and abuse these substances at high-risk for involvement in sexual criminality and victimization. Drugs and alcohol can lower inhibitions and defenses, while also leading to confusion, misunderstandings, and loss of control or consciousness on the part of the victim, any of which could lead to a sexual assault.

Research shows that more than half the college student sexual assault victims and offenders were consuming alcohol before the victimization occurred.[46] In a study of rape among college students, Mary Koss found that 74 percent of the rape offenders and 55 percent of the rape victims had been under the influence of alcohol when the assault took place.[47] Similarly, in the NCWSV study, 69 percent of the perpetrators and 43 percent of the victims had consumed alcohol.[48] In one study of college undergraduates who had been victims of a sexual assault or attempted one, more than half the females had drank alcohol. Of these, 60 percent said that they had impaired judgment to some degree as a result of alcohol use.[49]

A report from the Commission on Substance Abuse at Colleges and Universities actually showed that 90 percent of rapes at college took place with either the victim or perpetrator intoxicated.[50] A study by Dennis Greene and Rachel Navarro found that heavy use of alcohol by college female students was predictive of a later sexual victimization during the length of a school year; while Meichun Mohler-Kuo and colleagues found heavy episodic drinking to be the greatest predictor of rape while intoxicated, forced physically, or caused by threats.[51]

Use of drugs other than alcohol has shown a strong correlation as well to college sexual assaults. The Harvard College Alcohol Study found student drug use to be related to an increased risk of being raped.[52] One study found drug use to be a factor in more than 60 percent of sexual assault victimizations, with around 5 percent of the victims testing positive for so-called date rape drugs. A little more than 4 percent of victims were unaware they had been drugged, while approximately 35 percent had voluntarily used drugs, causing them to be impaired when the sexual assault occurred.[53] College students' misuse of prescription drugs and illicit drugs are seen as increasing their risks for sexual assault victimization and other types of violence.[54]

Fraternities and Sororities

The likelihood of college females being sexually assaulted increases in relation to involvement with fraternities and sororities, and often in conjunction with alcohol or drug use. In one study, sorority sisters were found to have been the victims of a substantially higher occurrence of attempted rape than college female students as a whole. Nearly half of these victimizations were perpetrated at fraternities.[55] According to the CSA study, more than one-fourth of sexually assaulted college women who were incapacitated reported that the perpetrator was a member of a fraternity when the assault occurred.[56] The victims were largely under the influence of alcohol or intoxicated before the incident.

In Leandra Lackie and Anton de Man's study of college male students, they found membership into a fraternity to be a predictor of sexual aggression.[57] Based on the results of questionnaires to 1,500 female college students, M. P. Frintner and L. Rubinson found that of the women who had been victims of a sexual assault, they pointed to members of fraternities and school sports teams as their attackers in numbers disproportionate to the perpetrators' percentage of the school population.[58]

Other studies have yielded similar findings. In T. J. Brown and associates study of male college students at a largely white university in the Midwest, membership in a fraternity, traditional attitudes toward females, and watching contact sports were found to be strongly predictive of sexual aggression toward females.[59] Scot Boeringer found, in examining the relationship between sexual assault and being in a fraternity or on an athletic team, that members of these groups were more likely to have attitudes supporting rape than students who were not members.[60]

Gang rapes on and around college campuses have been shown to be disproportionately perpetrated by fraternity members. In one study, members of fraternities were identified as the rapists in 55 percent of reported student gang rape victimizations.[61] Another study found that in twenty-two out of twenty-four documented cases of college gang rape, the assailants were either fraternity members or on intercollegiate sports teams.[62]

Previous Sexual Assault Victimization and Offending

College students who are involved in sexual assaults as either victims or perpetrators have often continued a pattern of victimization and/or offending that began prior to attending college. Studies have shown that previous sexually aggressive and assaultive behavior, as well as sexual victimization, is amongst the most significant predictor of sexual violence and victimization. In the NCWSV study, around 10 percent of the student respondents reported they were raped before the beginning of the current academic year, while nearly 11 percent were victims of attempted rape.[63] Similarly, in the CSA study, almost 16 percent of the students had been sexually assaulted prior to attending college, with 11.3 percent the victims of a completed sexual assault and 10.1 percent victimized by an attempted sexual assault.[64]

Violent victimization during the adolescent years has been seen as more predictive of victimization as a college student than being victimized in childhood.[65] Young women who were victims of a physical assault during adolescence face a higher risk of being victimized again as first year students and in succeeding years than students who have not been victimized. In a study by Kimberly Hanson and Christine Gidcyz, it was found that adolescent females who were victims of an attempted or completed rape were twice as likely to be sexually assaulted while in college.[66] Research suggests that females who were victims of a physical assault stood a much greater chance of becoming victims of a sexual assault in the same year.[67]

College females who were victims of a partner sexual assault prior to entering college are particularly at risk for sexual victimization as students. In a longitudinal study of women in college by Melissa Himelein, it was found that those who had been sexually assaulted by someone they were dating before beginning college had a much higher possibility of being sexually assaulted while in college.[68] The earlier victimization was the greatest predictor of a college sexual assault. Similar findings were made in Christine Gidcyz and colleagues' longitudinal study on sexual assault incidences.[69]

Prior alcohol use and abuse by females entering college have also been shown to be significant correlates of high school and college sexual assaults. In a study of nearly 1,100 female undergraduate students at four New England institutions of higher education, one in four had been sexually assaulted by someone known to them, since the age of sixteen, with over half the victims under the influence of alcohol at the time.[70] Another study of the transition between high school and college for female students found that among continuing drinkers entering college, nearly six in ten increased their drinking as first year students and therefore increased their risk of being sexually assaulted.[71] Other studies have related an early initiation of alcohol drinking and frequency in consumption with a higher risk of sexual assault while incapacitated.[72]

Researchers have also have linked young adult sexual victimization with other drug use, childhood sexual abuse, other forms of violence, a cycle of sexual and physical victimization, as well as depression, low self-esteem, and related issues that could increase their susceptibility for becoming the victim of a sexual assault again.[73]

Male college students who were perpetrators of sexual assaults prior to entering college are also at higher risk to re-offend as college students. Many criminologists and experts on sexual violence against women contend that "growing up in a traditionally patriarchal environment that objectifies women contributes to the likelihood of college males committing the crime of rape."[74] Studies have shown a correlation between male sexual aggression and an ideology fostering rape and other sexual assaults.[75] Martha Burt held that three attitudinal factors are prognostic of myths supportive of rape: (1) sex role stereotyping, (2) adversarial sexual beliefs, and (3) acceptance of interpersonal violence.[76]

Previous sexual victimization has been associated with males becoming sexual offenders. The Justice Department found that young offenders incarcerated for sexual assaults were more likely to report being victims of child sexual or physical abuse than any other type of inmate.[77] In a study of recurrently violent youthful offenders, Jeanne Cyriaque concluded that a history characterized by sexual and physical violence within the family was a strong predictor of juvenile killers and sex offenders.[78]

Date Rape

Within the context of campus sexual assaults are rape or attempted rape that occurs in a dating situation. As such, date rape is defined as rape in general, or forced sexual relations upon a person who the victim is romantically involved with as in a boyfriend or ex-partner. The crime also includes rape in which the victim is incapacitated or otherwise unable to give consent. Date rape is an aspect of dating violence, which is discussed at length in Chapter 5.

Acquaintance rape (in which the victim and offender are acquainted on some level) and date rape are common forms of sexual assault in the college environment, along with other rape involving perpetrators the victims are acquainted with. Nine in ten victims of college sexual assaults knew the assailant. Gang rapes, where the victim is sexually assaulted by multiple offenders (and is often acquainted with one or more of their attackers) has also proven to be an issue on campus, though the rate of such attacks is lower than sexual assaults by single assailants.[79]

According to the NCWSV, nearly one in every four completed single-offender rapes of college females was perpetrated by a current or ex-boyfriend.[80] Though sexual assaults by college professors are relatively low, some cases have been reported and it needs further study.[81] The same is true where it concerns high school teachers and sexual assaults of students.

A number of studies have explored the scope of date rape on college campuses or involving college students. In a *MS* magazine survey of college students, one in four reported being the victims of rape or attempted rape.[82] The perpetrators were described as dates in almost six out of ten incidents. In Eugene Kanin and Stanley Parcell's study of college sexual aggression, 20 to 25 percent of the female students were victims of date rape, with more than 25 percent of the male students admitting to forceful sexual relations, causing the victim distress.[83] In a study of the likelihood of college men to rape or attempt sexual intercourse by force, the researchers found that 60 percent of students indicated hypothetically that they would rape or use force to gain sexual relations under the right circumstances.[84]

As with other types of campus sexual assaults, alcohol or drugs often play a role in date rape, increasing the likelihood of perpetration and victimization. Further telling findings on the dynamics of college date rape include[85]:

- Insufficient communication in dating situations can result in sexual victimization.
- High school dating violence is often a precursor of college date rape and other sexual assaults.
- More than eight in ten college rapists do not view their actions as rape.
- More than one in ten males used physical restraint in forcing the female into sexual relations.
- Four out of every ten female rape victims do not disclose the victimization to anyone.

Date Rape Drugs

Date rape drugs, such as Rohypnol, Ketamine, ecstasy, and gamma-hydroxy butyrate (GHB), are a means used by males to sedate college women for sexual assaults. They are colorless, with no taste or odor to alert the potential victim. The effects of these drugs can render the victim unconscious and/or helpless to resist a rapist or even remember that the rape occurred. Often used with alcohol, but also alone or with water or nonalcoholic beverages, date rape drugs make college women especially vulnerable to sexual predators — especially at campus parties, fraternities, and bars, where fun and mistrust can turn into a nightmare. The most popular of these drugs are as follows:

- *GHB* affects the central nervous system as a potent depressant. It is usually administered as a clear liquid, but can also be in tablet form or as white crystalline powder.
- *Rohypnol,* often referred to as "roofies" or the "forget pill, is a powerful sedative, typically given in tablet form, but can also be in powder or liquid.
- *Ketamine,* also called "Special K" is a dissociative general anesthetic that can be administered as a liquid, powder, or tablet.
- *Ecstasy* is a highly toxic stimulant and hallucinogenic drug usually taken as a small tablet or capsule, or powder, but it can also be in liquid form.

Just how prevalent is the use of date rape drugs in the college environment? This is unclear, given the low rate of reporting college sexual assaults overall and often the lack of knowledge by victims that a crime even occurred. The CSA study found that just over 5 percent of their female undergraduates were given drugs that were nonconsensual or unknowledgeable to the victims. However, less than 1 percent of the students reported being victims of sexual assault after receiving such a drug without their consent or awareness.[86] This suggests that the vast majority of alcohol- and drug-related college sexual assaults are not drug facilitated sexual assaults (or those that occur when victims are incapacitated as a result of being given a drug without knowledge or consent, thereby making the sexual relations unwanted). This notwithstanding, it is very likely that there are still more females in college who are at risk for being given date rape drugs and sexually victimized than the data indicates.

Typologies of Rapists

More than fifty types of rapists have been identified by criminologists.[87] Many offenders fit into multiple classifications. In Paul Gebhard and his colleagues' analysis of sex offenders, rapists (referred to as "heterosexual aggressors") were broken down into six types[88]:

- *Assaultive rapists*— the most common type of rape offenders, characterized by hostile and sadistic feelings towards women.
- *Amoral delinquents*— the second most common type of rapists, who are bent on achieving sexual objectives.
- *Drunken variety*— rape offenders who are as common as amoral delinquents.
- *Explosive variety*— rapists with psychotic tendencies and a history that often belies the propensity to rape.
- *Double-standard variety*— rape offenders who divide females into good ones, to be treated with respect, and bad ones, who are not treated respectfully.
- *Other types*— a combination of the other types of rapists, along with mental defectives and psychotics.

Nicholas Groth, Ann Burgess, and Lynda Holmstrom advanced that three components are present in almost every case of forcible rape: (1) power, (2) anger, and (3) sexuality; while concluding that rape "is the sexual expression of aggression rather than the aggressive expression of sexuality. Although rape is a sexual crime, it is not sexually motivated."[89]

Power rapists make up 55 percent of all rapists. Their crimes are usually premeditated, recurring, and derive from fantasies and exposure to pornography. The power rapist will often use weapons to achieve his objective and keep the advantage over the victim. Power rapists are further divided into: (1) power-assertive rapists, and (2) power-reassurance rapists.[90]

- *Power-assertive rapists* typically feel powerless, with the sexual assault an expression of masculinity, command, and dominance, along with feelings of entitlement.
- *Power-reassurance rapists* sexually assault their victims primarily for reassurance of their masculinity and sexual adequacy.

Anger rapists are the second most common type of rapists, comprising around 40 percent. These sex offenders tend to be more impulsive, spontaneous, and dangerous than power rapists. Their crimes are often episodic and not premeditated. Subtypes of anger rapists are (1) anger-retaliation rapists, and (2) anger-excitation rapists.

- *Anger-retaliation rapists* tend to commit rapes as a result of their hostility towards females. The assault is meant to degrade, hurt, and humiliate the victim as a retaliatory response to women the rapists believe have hurt or wronged them.
- *Anger-excitation rapists* associate anger with sexual arousal. These offenders derive excitement and pleasure from their victims' pain and suffering and the rapist's own aggression and violence, which is eroticized through their conduct.

Sociologists Diana Scully and Joseph Marolla separate rapists into admitters and deniers.[91] Admitters acknowledge the forced sexual relations with their victims, defining it as rape; while deniers, even when admitting that there was sexual contact, do not look upon their behavior as rape.

Confronting Campus Sexual Assaults

In response to the problem of sexual assaults plaguing colleges and universities across the country, Congress enacted legislation aimed at requiring institutions of higher education to become more transparent in reporting campus crime, as well as developing strategies to prevent sexual assaults and reacting appropriately to the needs of students who have been victimized.

The Student Right-to-Know and Campus Security Act was passed in 1990, requiring the public disclosure of campus crime statistics, including specific sex offenses, and policies in place toward crime prevention and security on campus.[92] A 1998 amendment renamed a section of the Higher Education Act the Jeanne Clery Disclosure of Campus Security Policy and Campus Crime Statistics Act (referred to as the Clery Act). It was named in memory of Jeanne Ann Clery, a nineteen-year-old college freshman, who was raped and murdered in her dormitory room.[93]

The Campus Sexual Assault Victims' Bill of Rights of 1992 requires colleges and universities to establish policies in crime prevention and afford victims of sexual assault certain rights, such as assisting in notifying law enforcement. It was amended in 1998, expanding requirements, including the categories of criminality to be reported.[94]

Other key legislation includes[95]:

- The Campus Sex Crimes Prevention Act of 2000 requires collecting and disclosing information about convicted registered sex offenders who are enrolled at or employed by institutions of higher education.
- National Campus Safety Awareness Month of 2008. Congress unanimously approved a resolution in support of Security on Campus, Inc. and its designation of September as National Campus Safety Awareness Month in drawing further attention to campus safety.
- The Higher Education Opportunity Act of 2008 includes provisions for emergency response and notification to the Clery Act, along with protection for whistleblowers.

In addition, between 1990 and 2000, campus crime statistics reporting laws were passed in fourteen states, with other states enacting related legislation in providing student protection and safety measures.[96]

More than eight out of ten colleges and universities, in accordance with the law, submit a security report annually to the U.S. Department of Education. Crime statistics are included by over two-thirds of the schools. However, less than four in ten schools' reporting of crime statistics are in full compliance with the Clery Act.[97] Moreover, campus security for many students continues to be tenuous at best with the particulars of the college environment — including frequent alcohol and drug use, sexual predators hiding in plain view, and the tendency to trust those who may not have one's best interests at heart — putting students in high-risk situations.

Chapter 5

DATING VIOLENCE

An important aspect of reaching young adulthood is entering the dating stage of life. This is a natural experience for college and high school students throughout the country. Unfortunately, many students find themselves involved in dating situations that result in violence either as perpetrators or victims. Dating violence is all too common on campuses these days with males typically the aggressors and females the victims, particularly for the more severe forms of relationship violence. Same-sex dating also can lead to violent encounters. Dating violence comes in many forms, including date rape, battering, intimidation, sexual harassment, and verbal abuse. It is a branch of domestic violence, where there is often a pattern of abusive behavior and cycle of mistreatment. Intimate or relationship violence is amongst the most underreported type of offense affecting young adults and teenagers in the United States, making it more difficult to stop, and prevent such violence. Substance abuse often plays a key role in student dating violence, along with inadequate education about identifying the problem, and campus security and resources.

What Is Dating Violence?

Dating violence can encompass various acts of physical aggression, intimidation, and emotional abuse. As such, definitions of dating violence have focused on both narrow and broad ranges of violent behavior and victimization. In *Kids Who Commit Adult Crimes*, dating violence is defined as "a means used by the perpetrator to control and dominate the victim through intimidation, threats, and physical, emotional, sexual, and verbal abuse."[1] The Dating Violence Resource Center's definition is "controlling, abusive, and aggressive behavior in a romantic relationship. It occurs in both heterosexual and homosexual relationships and can include verbal, emotional, physical, or sexual abuse, or a combination of these."[2]

The Women's Resource Center defines dating violence as "a type of intimate partner violence, also called domestic violence, in which the violence occurs when two people know each other and have been involved in a relationship.... The violence can also be financial, spiritual, verbal, emotional, or sexual. Dating violence occurs in both straight and gay/lesbian relationships."[3]

Dating violence has been described as ranging "from a single violent act (such as sexual assault) to an ongoing and continuous pattern of victimization and mistreatment. The definition of dating violence must be elastic to allow it to fit the wide variety of relationship situations out there."[4] Many researchers have defined dating violence in terms of physical violence only while excluding sexual violence[5]; whereas others have emphasized the sexual aspects of dating violence.[6] Some have put emotional abuse on an equal footing with physical and sexual abuse in the definition.[7]

What these definitions have in common are the dynamics of violence within the framework of dating or a romantic involvement either currently or previously between two people. The aggressor's violence is seen as a means of imposing his or her "will on the object of the violence by releasing frustrations, jealousies, or other pent up negative energy and lashing out at the victim."[8] See more detailed discussion on date rape and stalking, two components of dating violence, in Chapters 4 and 6, respectively.

College Dating Violence

Dating violence can affect young adults from all walks of life and backgrounds, as it knows no boundaries in who may be an aggressor and who is targeted. It is especially prevalent amongst college students with a confluence of environment, drinking, drugs, attitudes, vulnerabilities, and high-risk situations contributing to this form of domestic violence which can lead to a synthesis of health, psychological, and even financial ramifications.

College dating violence can include physical, sexual, and emotional kinds of victimization such as:

- Angering
- Attempted rape
- Biting
- Belittling
- Brandishing a weapon
- Brawling
- Bullying
- Calling names
- Drugging
- Frightening
- Hitting
- Humiliating
- Intimidation
- Killing
- Punching
- Screaming at
- Sexually assaulting
- Shooting
- Shouting profanities at
- Slapping
- Stalking
- Targeting
- Threatening
- Wrestling

These types of dating or relationship violence are certainly not mutually exclusive. Offenders typically perpetrate one in conjunction with others, such as physical and sexual violence or physical, sexual, and emotional violence. As noted by the National Center for Victims of Crime's report, *Dating Violence on Campus*, "dating violence victims often suffer multiple incidents as part of a continuum of violence and abuse used to coerce and control them."[9]

Unfortunately for many students entering the college environment or perhaps are overwhelmed by trying to multitask, recognizing the various kinds of dating violence can be difficult as they may lack the knowledge or experience to understand what is healthy and normal in a dating experience or relationship. Campus traditions and pressures to conform, join sororities, fraternities, and other social groups, attend parties, experiment sexually, and drink alcohol or use drugs only adds to the problem and often plays to the advantage of the perpetrator.

The Prevalence of College Dating Violence

Dating violence among college students is widespread in this society. A number of studies have documented the severity and range of the problem. According to the Dating Violence Resource Center, 32 percent of college students were victims of dating violence by a former partner, while 21 percent have experienced violence from a current mate.[10] The Centers for Disease Control reported that one-third of those in dating relationships will experience at least one episode of violence over the length of the involvement.[11] Other estimates of campus violence have fallen between 20 percent and 30 percent.[12]

In a survey by Christine Forke and colleagues of 910 college undergrads, 407 of the students or 44.7 percent, reported experiencing violence in a relationship while in college or prior to.[13] More than 42 percent were the victims of the dating violence and 17.1 percent the perpetrators. Emotional violence occurred more often before entering college, whereas sexual and emotional violence were equally likely during college.

The literature is replete with research documenting the prevalence of date rape as part of the specter of dating violence. In one national study of female college students, 27.5 percent revealed being the victims of rape or attempted rape on at least one occasion since the age of fourteen.[14] Only 5 percent of these were ever reported to the authorities. In another study, more than half the female college students sampled at a large university reported experiencing unwanted sex of some type.[15] Forty-three percent were victimized by someone they were involved with in a steady relationship, and 12 percent of the victimizations were perpetrated by casual dates.

A survey by Mary Koss of 6,159 female college students revealed that one quarter of the students were victims of rape or attempted rape. Eighty-four percent of the rapists were described as acquaintances and 57 percent as dates.[16] In an earlier study, Eugene Kanin and Stanley Parcell found that 83 percent of female college students were the victims of male sexual aggression.[17] Sixty-one percent had been sexually assaulted since entering college, while 24 percent had been date raped. See further discussion on date rape in Chapter 4.

Other data on college dating violence reveal the following:

- Between 39 percent and 54 percent of persons victimized by dating violence continue to be in abusive relationships.[18]
- Thirteen percent of college females in one year reported being stalked.[19]
- Forty-two percent of the female students were stalked by boyfriends or an ex-mate.[20]
- One in four women in the United States have been the victims of a physical assault or rape by a significant other.[21]
- Almost one-third of college students admit to physically abusing someone they were dating within the last year.[22]
- Up to one-fourth of female college students were victims of a sexual assault during their college years.[23]
- Over half of male college students report committing one or more sexual assaults while in college.[24]
- Around 90 percent of college sexual assault victims know their perpetrator.[25]
- Male students are more likely to commit sexual acts of aggression, while female students are more likely to commit physical violence.[26]
- Half of the college victims of dating violence report it to someone.[27]
- Females between twenty and twenty-four have the greatest risk for nonfatal victimization in intimate relationships.[28]
- Female students tend to report dating violence victimization more than male students.[29]
- Two in ten students report dating violence to law enforcement.[30]
- There are laws against dating violence in all fifty states and the District of Columbia.[31]

The degree and type of college dating violence corresponds with the nature of the relationship between victim and perpetrator. Researchers have found that between 47 percent and 86 percent of dating violence occurred when the couple was "going steady," or in a relationship.[32] In other findings, the rate of male violence in dating relationships was highest in the most serious attachments[33]; rising as the level of commitment grew.[34]

Studies indicate that many female and male students consider physical or sexual aggression in a dating relationship to be normal behavior.[35] This may be due to sex role expectations and inadequate physical, emotional, sexual, and social development. In some instances, the dating violence is a progression of the domestic violence and/or child abuse experienced by one or both parties.[36]

Underreporting of Campus Dating Violence

In spite of the high rate of reported dating violence on college and university campuses across the country, many experts believe that it is vastly underreported, illustrating the true scope of violence affecting students involved in dating relationships.[37] About one in two cases of dating violence go unreported to even a close family member or relative.[38] According to *The Sexual Victimization of College Women*, less than 5 percent of actual rapes or attempted rapes of female college students are reported to the police.[39] The study did find that two-thirds of the victims told of the sexual assault to someone, often a friend. Another study supports this finding, as nearly nine in ten college student rapes or sexual assaults went unreported to law enforcement.[40] Similarly, more than eight out of ten stalking episodes are not brought to the attention of campus police or local law enforcement.[41] However, more than nine out of ten stalking victims do disclose this to a non professional, such as a friend.

Aside from the police, students are also reluctant to report their sexual victimization to other professionals, such as medical practitioners, counselors, or school administration.[42] Victims of college dating violence are typically unwilling to report the victimization for reasons that include:

- Belief that violence is normal in a relationship
- Denial
- Embarrassment
- Fear of the perpetrator
- No one will believe
- Not realizing a crime has been committed
- Peer pressure
- Protecting the perpetrator
- Private matter
- School environment is not conducive
- Self-blame
- Sex role
- Social stigma
- Traditional sex role expectations
- Unimportant
- Under the influence of alcohol or drugs

Research has shown that the two reasons most often given for reluctance to report dating violence are fear of offender reprisal and "lack of faith in the criminal justice and institutional disciplinary systems."[43]

High School Dating Violence

A strong predictor of college dating violence appears to be the maltreatment that students experienced while in high school. Studies have shown a correlation between victimization or offending prior to college and while in college or beyond high school.[44] In a study at a university in North Carolina, two-thirds of the participants reported they had been physically or sexually abused by a significant other during high school.[45] Forke and associates found that amongst the college undergraduates surveyed, there was a higher rate of relationship violence for both victims and perpetrators prior to attending college than while in attendance.[46]

The dynamics of high school dating violence are similar to college dating violence. High schoolers also tend to be involved in dating that can result in physical, sexual, psychological, and verbal abuse. Victims and offenders may be caught in a cycle of violence that began at home or through a peer group and comes from misguided love, jealousy, domination, obsession, and ignorance.[47]

The consequences for victims can include sustained abuse, a pattern of victimization, serious injury, high-risk sexual behavior, delinquency, disruption of normal development, low self-esteem, mental illness, substance abuse, and suicide. Perpetrators may also face such issues, and an escalation of violent behavior in the current relationship or a future one which could possibly spread to other crimes of violence.

The Prevalence of High School Dating Violence

High school dating violence is a serious problem, much like relationship violence on the college level. In a review of studies on high school dating violence, it was found that prevalence rates involving nonsexual violence varied from 9 percent to 65 percent, dependent upon if threats, along with verbal and emotional abuse were included.[48] Other findings have estimated physical and sexual abuse of high school students to be between 10 percent and 25 percent.[49]

The 2007 Youth Risk Behavior Survey reported that 10 percent of adolescents in the United States were the victims of physical violence inflicted by a romantic mate during the past year[50]; whereas in the National Longitudinal Study of Adolescent Health, as many as three in ten teens reported being the victims of psychological or verbal relationship abuse.[51]

In a six-month survey of 500 females between the ages of fifteen and twenty-four, 60 percent reported they were currently in an abusive relationship.[52] Nearly all those surveyed had experienced dating violence during their lifetime.

Other sobering statistics on high school dating violence are as follows[53]:

- One in eleven teens has been the victim of physical dating violence.
- One in four teenagers are victims of physical, sexual, emotional, or verbal abuse each year.

- One in three females will be physically abused by a boyfriend before reaching the age of eighteen.
- Four in ten female teens know someone their own age who has been abused by a boyfriend.
- Around one-third of all female rape victims are between twelve and seventeen years of age.
- Seventy percent of adolescent girls abused in a dating relationship report sustaining an injury.
- The rates of substance abuse are twice as high in teenage girls who report being victims of physical and sexual dating violence than those who do not.
- Teenagers in same sex or bisexual relationships face equal risk for involvement in dating violence as those in heterosexual relationships.[54]
- Teenagers involved in abusive dating relationships are at high-risk to continue being victims or offenders in their future dating involvements.

Much of high school dating violence goes unreported or underreported for the same reasons as college dating violence, pointing toward the seriousness in addressing this aspect of domestic violence which is often a prelude for intimate violence amongst college students.

Gender and Dating Violence

Although much of the data on dating violence among college students and high schoolers focuses largely on male inflicted violence and female victimization in heterosexual relationships, some studies indicate that male and female aggressors and victims in dating violence are in equal proportion.[55] Other studies have found a higher rate of female offending in dating relationships than male offending.[56] Female dating violence is more often seen as defensive in intent. Studies show than males tend to inflict more severe violence than females in the dating relationship; whereas females are more likely to be victims of physical dating violence, as well as sexual violence and suffer more serious injuries as a result of the dating violence.[57]

Recent studies of college students and dating violence have yielded mixed results. In Forke and colleagues survey, nearly twice as many female undergraduates (53 percent) as male (27.2 percent) reported being victims of dating violence.[58] However, in a study by Rohini Luthra and Christine Gidycz of college dating violence, 25 percent of the females admitted to being violent to a partner, compared to 10 percent of the males.[59] When using multivariate logistic regression analysis to predict dating violence by gender, the researchers suggest violence of college women at 83 percent with male violence at just 30 percent.

In one study of dating violence, it was reported that 37 percent of the males and 35 percent of the females perpetrated some type of physical violence, whereas 39 percent of the males and 32 percent of the females were the victims of dating violence.[60] A survey by Martin Fiebert and Denise Gonzalez of 978 college women over a five-year span revealed that nearly three in ten reported physically abusing a male romantic mate.[61] Of these, the reasons most given for the violence were (1) insensitivity to her needs, and (2) wished to gain his attention. Abuse by the male partner was amongst the least reasons given.

Among high school students, studies have also shown a roughly equal rate of male and female aggression in dating involvements. In a 2007 survey of more than 1,200 high school students from Long Island, New York, 66 percent of males and 65 percent of females who were in physically violent relationships reported there was mutual aggression.[62] A national survey reported that 22 percent of the adolescent females and 21 percent of the adolescent males were victims of physical or psychological dating abuse.[63] A second nationwide study found that 32 percent of the adolescents reported physical or psychological victimization in a dating relationship, with the numbers virtually the same across gender lines.[64] This notwithstanding, studies show that heterosexual teenage females are disproportionately likely to be victims of sexual and emotional maltreatment and suffer injuries than heterosexual teenage males.[65]

The research is more scant on same-sex or bisexual dating violence, but suggests a similar pattern of involvement as heterosexual adolescents and young adults. In a National Longitudinal Study of Adolescent Health survey of adolescents involved in same-sex dating relationships, 28 percent of female respondents and 24 percent of male respondents reported being victims of physical violence, while 26 percent of the females and 14.6 percent of the males were victims of psychological violence.[66] A study of lesbian, gay, bisexual, and transgender youth revealed that 43.6 percent of the males and 39.8 percent of the females had experienced some form of dating violence, such as physical, sexual, or emotional abuse.[67]

Why Does Dating Violence Occur?

Given its nature as aggression between persons who are dating or romantically involved, it goes against the grain of normal, healthy relationships. So why is dating violence so prevalent in our society? Most experts agree that there is no single explanation, but rather a number of factors and circumstances that come into play, often in conjunction with one another though any could trigger dating violence.

On its basic level, anger, jealousy, love, mistrust, low self-esteem, insecurity, and desire to dominate, intimidate, and control another's movement are all seen as key components for aggressive behavior and passivity in a relationship. Both the perpetrator and victim may find themselves entangled in these factors and experience mutual aggression. Oftentimes as the violence escalates, the victim becomes even more reluctant to report because of the conflicting pressures.

Substance abuse has also been shown to be strongly associated with the onset and continuation of dating violence.[68] Alcohol and drug use by the aggressor or victim can weaken inhibitions, encourage aggressive tendencies, and affect one's ability to resist victimization. According to the U.S. Department of Education's Core Alcohol and Drug Survey of almost 90,000 students across the nation, alcohol or drugs was a factor in 74 percent of campus sexual assaults.[69] The Harvard School of Public Health found that four in five college students who lived on campus but did not drink alcohol in excess, saw one or more of the consequences associated with drinking heavily, such as being an assault victim or receiving unwanted sexual overture.[70] Other studies have frequently found that alcohol and drug use among male and female high school students directly correlates with dating violence and mutual aggression.[71]

Date rape drugs such as Rohypnol and GHB are often used by an aggressor in college environments to render a victim helpless in the process of sexually assaulting them.[72] See more on this issue in Chapter 4.

Dating violence is also viewed as part of the larger picture of violence commonplace in society, such as child abuse, child sexual abuse, domestic violence, peer violence, sexual violence against women, and stranger violence. Exposure to these has been shown to correlate with involvement in dating violence.[73]

Some experts on dating violence have looked at gender and inequality in terms of power and resources as key indicators in relationship aggression.[74] Others posit that males in patriarchal cultures engage in violence to exercise and sustain power and control over females.[75]

Combating Dating Violence

With increasing focus on campus dating violence and other crimes affecting college students and teenagers, greater emphasis has been made in recent years to offer more protection and prevention strategies to ensure student safety. Currently there are laws in all fifty states and the District of Columbia against dating violence-related offenses such as domestic violence, sexual assault, and stalking. The term "dating violence" is seldom included in the statutes.

In thirty-five states, minors who are victims of dating violence can apply for protective orders against the perpetrator. However, age and language restrictions vary from state to state.[76]

Since 1990, there have been several key Federal laws passed in combating college campus crime and increasing student safety. These include:

- *Student Right-to-Know and Campus Security Act of 1990.* Requires schools to publish and dispense a yearly report on campus crimes, including certain sex offense categories, describe campus security policies, crime prevention actions, and crime reporting procedures.[77]
- *Campus Sexual Assault Victims' Bill of Rights of 1992.* Requires schools to establish and publish prevention policies regarding sex

crimes and measures for responding when such crimes occur, including medical, psychological, and legal help accessible for crime victims.[78]

- *Higher Education Amendments of 1998.* Increases campus crime statistics that schools are required to publicize to include manslaughter and arson, disclosure of disciplinary referrals for alcohol, drug, and weapons violations; expansion of hate crimes, broadening the definition of "campus" to include off campus fraternity/sorority houses, student apartments, and public property; and requires colleges to take measures aimed at reducing binge drinking.[79]

In spite of these legal steps taken, studies show that there is still inadequate training of campus security and residence hall staff in dealing with sexual assault victims, in particular; as well as insufficient education about dating violence and support services available for new, foreign, minority, and physically challenged students.[80]

When dating-related mistreatment does occur, there are 24-hour crisis hotlines and school help lines for aide and referrals, support groups, counseling services, shelters, university or college health centers, school resource officers, and community-based advocacy groups available for victims of dating violence.

Chapter 6

STALKING

Stalking is another persistent and serious crime affecting college students and young adults across America. It can encompass a number of facets and disturbing patterns of behavior, including repeated acts of following, watching, phoning, harassing, intimidating, and targeting a victim for an unnatural interest. In recent years, stalkers have also taken advantage of modern technology in electronics, such as computers and cell phones, to perpetrate cyberstalking. Stalking is a gender-neutral act, with offenders and victims male and female, though females are more likely to be targeted by stalkers. This type of offense can escalate into dating violence, domestic violence, sexual assault, physical assault, property damage, kidnapping, and even murder. It can also have a lasting psychological effect on victims, along with potential physical, sexual, educational, and social implications. Stalking is a crime in all fifty states, the District of Columbia, and U.S. Territories, though defining what constitutes stalking differs from state to state. Moreover, victims are often unsure if a crime is being committed, unwilling to come forward, or unable to stop the stalking before it becomes more than an irritant, making the problem that much more troublesome.

Defining Stalking

Stalking has a broad range of recurring and threatening behaviors that can be included in the definition. As there is no broad consensus on these, there are no uniform definitions of stalking.[1] For example, state definitions vary on the "element of victim fear and emotional distress, as well as the requisite intent of the stalker."[2] The Oregon statute on stalking is as follows:

> (1) A person commits the crime of stalking if:
> (a) The person knowingly alarms or coerces another person or a mem-

ber of that person's immediate family or household by engaging in repeated and unwanted contact with the other person;

(b) It is objectively reasonable for a person in the victim's situation to have been alarmed or coerced by the contact; and

(c) The repeated and unwanted contact causes the victim reasonable apprehension regarding the personal safety of the victim or a member of the victim's immediate family or household.[3]

The North Dakota law defines stalking as engaging in "in an intentional course of conduct directed at a specific person which frightens, intimidates, or harasses that person, and that serves no legitimate purpose. The course of conduct may be directed toward that person or a member of that person's immediate family and must cause a reasonable person to experience fear, intimidation, or harassment."[4]

In the National Crime Victimization Survey's (NCVS) *Stalking Victimization in the United States*, stalking is defined as "a course of conduct directed at a specific person that would cause a reasonable person to feel fear."[5] The Supplemental Victimization Survey (SVS), as part of the report, lists seven types of unwelcome behavior that fit the criterion for stalking:

- Making uninvited phone calls.
- Sending unsolicited or unwelcome letters or e-mails.
- Pursuing or spying on a person.
- Showing up without a justifiable reason.
- Waiting somewhere for the person.
- Leaving unwanted gifts or items.
- Spreading rumors or putting information about the person in a public site, the Internet, or through word of mouth.[6]

Other researchers on stalking have also defined it in terms consistent with these definitions or with a broader range in patterns of stalking actions. In *Stalking in America*, the authors define stalking as "a course of conduct directed at a specific person that involves repeated (two or more occasions) visual or physical proximity, nonconsensual communication, or verbal, written, or implied threats, or a combination thereof, that would cause a reasonable person fear."[7]

The National Violence Against Women (NVAW) Survey's definition of stalking is "a conduct directed at a specific person that involves repeated visual or physical proximity, nonconsensual communication, or verbal, written or implied threats, or a combination thereof, that would cause a reasonable person fear."[8] The Department of Public Safety at Idaho State University went even further in defining stalking behavior as extending beyond the primary victim to include "vandalism of victim's property, home, vehicle, workplace, or vandalism to the property, etc. of any friend or family member who helps him/her."[9]

Other examples of stalking include:

- Burglary
- Cyberstalking
- Defamation
- Objectifying
- Multiple offenders stalking
- Theft
- Trespassing
- Unwelcome touching

Stalking often begins as relatively harmless but annoying attention. If not dealt with or derailed early on, the stalking can progress into obsessive and dangerous behavior that becomes criminal and victimizes the target psychologically with potentially physical and fatal consequences as well.

A psychological definition of stalking was provided by Lambèr Royakkers:

> Stalking is a form of mental assault, in which the perpetrator repeatedly, unwantedly, and disruptively breaks into the life-world of the victim, with whom he (or she) has no relationship (or no longer has), with motives that are directly or indirectly traceable to the affective sphere. Moreover, the separated acts that make up the intrusion cannot by themselves cause the mental abuse, but do taken together (cumulative effect).[10]

The types of feelings stalking victims typically experience as a result of their victimization include:

- Anger
- Anxiety
- Depression
- Distrust
- Frustration

- Guilt
- Insecurity
- Insomnia
- Isolation
- Pity
- Vulnerability

These feelings often tend to motivate the stalker to further his or her pursuit of the victim for gratification and achieving the perpetrator's objectives.

The National Victim Assistance Academy summed up the dangers of stalkers and stalking as:

> less about surveillance of victims than it is about contact with them.... Stalkers, by their very nature, want more.... They want to be part of their victims' lives. And, if they cannot be a positive part of their victims' lives, they will settle for a negative connection.... It is this mind set that not only makes them "stalkers," but also makes them dangerous.[11]

The Magnitude of Stalking

How prevalent is stalking in our society? By most accounts, the problem is widespread in this country. According to a U.S. Department of Justice's Bureau of Justice Statistics (BJS) Special Report on stalking that was released in 2009, over a twelve month period between 2005 and 2006, it is estimated that 3.4 million persons ages eighteen and older were stalking victims in this country.[12] Of these, nearly half had experienced at least one uninvited offender contact per week, while more than one in ten victims reported being stalked for five or more years. Forty-six percent of the victims were afraid of what would occur next and around one in five feared being physically harmed.

When combining stalking with harassment (defined as meeting the requirements constituting stalking aside from those connected to inducing fear or the perpetration of other related offenses) during the twelve month span, approximately 5.9 million persons eighteen and older were identified as being victims of stalking or harassment in the United States. Amongst these, more than half were victims of behavior that fit the criterion for stalking.

As shown in Table 6.1, nearly two-thirds of the stalking victims experienced receiving unwanted phone calls or messages, while almost four in ten were victimized by the spreading of rumors. More than three in ten victims of stalking received unwanted letters and e-mails, were followed, or the stalker showed up at places. Nearly six in ten persons were harassment victims of unwanted phone calls and messages, and around three out of ten victims of harassment received unwanted letters of e-mail.

Table 6.1
Nature of Stalking and Harassment
Behaviors Experienced by Victims

		Percent of Victims	
	All	Stalking	Harassment
Unwanted phone calls and messages	62.5%	63.2%	57.2%
Unwanted letters and e-mail	30.1	30.6	29.4
Spreading rumors	29.1	35.7	19.9
Following or spying	24.5	34.3	10.6
Showing up at places	22.4	31.1	10.2
Waiting for victim	20.4	29.0	8.3
Leaving unwanted presents	9.1	12.2	4.8
Number of victims	5,857,030	3,424,100	2,432,930

NOTE: Details sum to more than 100% because multiple responses were permitted.

SOURCE: U.S. Department of Justice, Bureau of Justice Statistics Special Report, National Crime Victimization Survey: Stalking Victimization in the United States (Washington, DC: Office of Justice Programs, 2009), p. 2.

The BJS report also revealed the following:

- Women were more likely than men to be victims of stalking.
- Women and men were just as likely to be victims of harassment.
- Persons ages eighteen to nineteen had the highest rate of stalking victimization, followed by person ages twenty to twenty-four.
- About one in four stalking victims were victimized by cyberstalking, mostly through e-mail.
- Nearly four in ten stalking victims attributed the stalking to retaliation, anger, or spite.
- Almost seven in ten victims of stalking felt angry or annoyed at the onset of and as stalking progressed.

- Nearly six in ten stalking victimizations of females and more than six in ten of males were unreported to the police.
- Females were slightly more likely to report stalking victimizations than males.[13]

Table 6.2
Victim-Offender Relationship in Stalking and Harassment

Percent of Victims

	All	Stalking	Harassment
Total[a]	100%	100%	100%
Known, intimate	27.6%	30.3%	22.5%
Current intimate			
Spouse	4.3	5.6	1.8[b]
Boy/girlfriend	3.8	3.2	5.1
Former intimate			
Spouse	7.1%	8.4%	4.6%
Boy/girlfriend	12.4	13.1	11.0
Known, other	44.7%	45.1%	44.4%
Friend/roommate/neighbor	16.7	16.4	17.4
Known from work or school	10.1	9.9	10.6
Acquaintance	9.4	9.8	8.8
Relative	8.5	9.0	7.6
Stranger	10.6%	9.7%	12.5%
Unknown	16.9%	15.0%	20.6%
Number of victims	4,619,430	3,064,950	1,554,480

NOTE: Table excludes 0.5% of all victims, 0.3% of stalking victims, and 0.7% of harassment victims due to missing data. Detail may not sum to 100% due to rounding.

[a]Includes victims who could identify a single offender who was most responsible.
[b]Estimate based on 10 or fewer cases.

SOURCE: U.S. Department of Justice, Bureau of Justice Statistics Special Report, *National Crime Victimization Survey: Stalking Victimization in the United States* (Washington, DC: Office of Justice Programs, 2009), p. 4.

Other studies have also illustrated the scope of stalking nationwide, with the incidence varying. According to an earlier NVAW survey, *Stalking in America*, researchers Patricia Tjaden and Nancy Thoennes reported that more than one million women and nearly 400,000 men are the victims of stalking in the United States yearly.[14] When expanding the definition of stalking, the figures rose to six million women and almost a million and a half men as victims of stalking annually.[15] Over 8 percent of women and more than 2 percent of men in the country have been stalked over the course of their lives. This number jumps to 12 percent for stalked women and 4 percent of men stalked on an annual basis with the broader definition. Nearly eight in ten stalking victims are female, while almost nine in ten perpetrators are male. Over three-fourths of the women knew their stalker.

In reviewing national prevalence estimates on stalking from an Injury Control and Risk Survey, Kathleen Basile and colleagues found that approximately seven million women and two million men have been victims of stalking in the United States.[16] A meta-analysis of 175 studies of stalking by Brian Spitzberg and William Cupach revealed that between 60 percent and 80 percent of the stalking victims were female. Seventy percent of the victims knew their stalkers and over half of the acquaintanceship was of a romantic nature.[17]

Other revealing findings on the dynamics of stalking include[18]:

- More than eight in ten females stalked by a current or former intimate were also physically assaulted by person.
- More than three in ten females stalked by a current or former intimate were also sexually assaulted by the stalker.
- Around eight in ten stalking victims and offenders are white.
- Nearly three in ten female stalking victims received a protective order against the stalker.
- Over half of stalkers were in a previous intimate relationship with the victim.
- Eight in ten stalkers use more than one way to contact the victim.
- Two in three offenders stalk their victims at least once a week.
- One in three stalkers are repeat stalking offenders.
- One-seventh of stalkers were psychotic when the stalking occurred.
- Stalking is amongst the greatest risk factors for murdering women in violent relationships.[19]
- Substance abuse is amongst the strongest predictors of higher rates of stalking-related violence.[20]
- Eighty percent of stalking cases are precipitated by a defining occurrence, such as ending a relationship or loss of job.[21]
- Threats, jealousy, and ex-partner substance abuse were strong precursors of violence by stalkers.[22]

- Stalking victims are much more likely to experience anxiety, severe depression, sleeplessness, and social dysfunction than the population at large.[23]

Stalking of College Students

Stalking on college campuses around the country has proven to be particularly prevalent as the open and inviting environment, along with extensive use of the Internet has allowed stalkers to both hide in plain view and remain elusive or anonymous online. Stalking of college students is gender-neutral, though most studies indicate that females are much more likely to be the targets of stalkers, while males are far more likely to be the ones who stalk.[24] While stalkers on and around campus can be strangers or non-strangers, the literature shows a strong correlation between stalking and familiarity between victim and offender, often of a romantic nature.[25]

The attraction of colleges and universities for stalkers is everything that a typical campus offers: attractive surroundings, lush landscape, and a healthy supply of young, attractive and often naïve and inexperienced students. The California Coalition Against Sexual Assault (CALCASA) report, *Campus Stalking*, further describes what works to the stalker's advantage with respect to the college setting as perfect for targeting victims:

> It is easy to determine a student's schedule; it has a highly social atmosphere ... student movement through the campus is predictable and access to residences (and) academic buildings may be quite easy. One can easily find information about a selected student through the campus directory, including the student's address, telephone number, and e-mail address.[26]

How widespread is the problem of stalking on college campuses? In a phone survey that was co-sponsored by the National Institute of Justice and Bureau of Justice Statistics, of 4,446 female students from 223 universities and colleges nationwide, it was found that 13.1 percent, or more than one of every eight students, had been the victims of stalking since the school year started.[27] Over 80 percent of the students were acquainted with or had seen the stalker beforehand, while 30 percent of the victims reported suffering injuries. The stalking victimization averaged two months in length. The findings suggest that female college students may be twice as likely to be stalked as women in the population at large and more likely to be victimized than other subgroups within society. The survey also found that:

- Among known stalkers, 42.5 percent were a current or former boyfriend.
- Around one in ten known stalkers was an acquaintance.
- Female students were rarely stalked by a professor or graduate assistant.
- Around seven in ten students were stalking victims entirely on campus or victimized on and off campus grounds.
- Three in ten students were victims of stalking off campus only.
- Calling the victim by phone was the most common type of stalking behavior.
- Waiting for the victim somewhere was the second most common kind of stalking behavior.
- In 15.3 percent of the stalking incidents, the stalker threatened or tried to hurt the victim.
- Victims were more likely to be psychologically victimized than physically.
- More than one in ten stalking episodes involved forcible or attempted sexual contact.
- In almost three-quarters of the stalking incidents, victims took action in response to it.

Among other studies, a comparable six-month prevalence rate of 10.5 percent stalking victimization of women was reported in Elizabeth Mustaine and Richard Tewksbury's survey of 861 female students at nine colleges.[28] A lower annual rate of prevalence, between 1 and 6 percent of women stalked, was given by Tjaden and Thoennes, whose study used a narrower definition of stalking and was not focused on college students and the particulars of the campus environment that may make them more susceptible to stalking victimization.[29]

An empirical study by Beth Bjerregaard of stalking among college students at a public university revealed that 25 percent of female students and 11 percent of male students had been the victims of stalking in their lifetimes, while 6 percent were being stalked at present.[30] In two other studies of over six hundred undergraduates from two universities and stalking by current or former intimates, about 20 percent of the students reported being the victims of a stalking behavior by such a person.[31] The researchers referred to stalking as "intrusive contact," for such incidents as phone calls, following the victim, watching the target's residence, and threatening the person with physical harm. Female students were more likely than male students to have experienced intrusive contact. Twenty-five percent of victims reported fearing for their well-being.

In spite of these alarming figures, most experts on student victimization believe that stalking of college students is vastly underreported. According to *The Sexual Victimization of College Women* study, around 83 percent of the female stalking victims did not report this to law enforcement or campus police, though in more than nine out of ten stalking episodes, the victim did tell someone such as a family member or friend that they were being stalked.[32] The reasons most often given for not reporting the stalking victimization were the belief that the authorities would not take the allegation seriously or the victim was unaware that the unwelcome behavior was a criminal offense.

The Dynamics of Stalking College Students

Stalking on and near campus is a real concern that is illustrated by the prevalence of stalking victimization. It affects students of all ages, gender, sexual orientation, race, and nationality. There is a strong correlation between stalking and dating violence, both of which have become part of the college life and socializing processes.[33] (See Chapter 5.) In turn, a positive relationship also exists between stalking and substance abuse. The association is even greater when combined with having had a prior relationship with the stalker.[34]

Though females are disproportionately likely to be victims of college stalking, some female students are also the perpetrators of stalking. In a survey of 756 students at the University of Pennsylvania and Rutgers University, 42 percent of the stalking victims were male, well above the national average.[35] Some researchers have found that there are gender differences in perception of what defines stalking, which may partly account for the larger numbers in general for female victims of stalking.[36] There is also indication that males are less likely to report stalking victimization, though the rate of reporting is low for female victims.[37]

The consequences of stalking victimization of college students can be serious and lasting, affecting everything from health to school life to dating. Research on the dynamics of college stalking victimization has found that[38]:

- One in three students felt that stalking had a negative impact on other relationships.
- More than 16 percent of victims confronted their stalker.
- More than four in ten victims tried to avoid their stalker.
- Nine in ten student victims of sexual assault knew the offender.
- Sexual harassment is a common occurrence on campus.[39]
- More than three-quarters of victims of femicide had been stalked by their killer.[40]
- Less than 4 percent of stalking victims tried to get a restraining order against their stalker.
- Under 3 percent of victims went for counseling.
- Less than 2 percent of stalking victims filed criminal charges.
- Less than 1 percent of victims took a self-defense course.
- Almost four in ten stalking victims lost time from school or work because of the stalking.
- Native American students are at greater risk to become stalking victims than students in other racial groups.[41]

Professors may also be at risk for stalking victimization. One study found that college faculty may misinterpret student attention as a "harmless crush," or flattery instead of what actually could be an "obsessive fixation."[42] The relationship between the confined college campus structure, incoming students with limited experience in building healthy connections, and even "celebrity status" among some professors who may unwittingly or willfully encourage student interest were noted as elements that could result in student stalking of faculty. There is also evidence that college professors, for such reasons, are less likely to report stalking by students to school administration or campus or law enforcement authorities, which could only compound the problem in the greater context of stalking on college campuses.[43]

Typologies of Stalkers

Though stalkers can cross the spectrum in terms of background, motivations, personality traits, and deviant characteristics, criminologists and psychologists have developed various categories of stalkers based on motives, mentality, ways in which they operate, and other factors. In many instances, stalkers may overlap into different types, depending upon the definition applied and processes used in stalking their victims.

In its basic sense, stalkers can be put in three categories with respect to the nature of their connection to the victims or lack thereof as follows:

- *Intimate stalkers.* They are or have been intimately involved with the target of their stalking, such as a current or ex-spouse, romantic mate, or significant other.
- *Acquaintance stalkers.* They are acquainted with their victims in a non romantic way, such as friends, colleagues, or neighbors.
- *Stranger stalkers.* They have no intimate relationship or acquaintance with their victims beforehand.[44]

Some psychologists have broken stalkers down into two typologies: (1) psychotic and (2) nonpsychotic. Psychotic stalkers are seen as having such preexisting disorders as delusional disorder or schizophrenia. The majority of stalkers are believed to be nonpsychotic, but may suffer from such disorders as antisocial, narcissistic, paranoia, severe depression, or substance dependence.[45] Nonpsychotic stalkers' obsession over their target can be linked to psychological dynamics like anger, denial, jealousy, and resentment.[46]

Ronnie Harmon and colleagues classified stalkers in terms of (1) the kind of attachment, ardent or angry, and (2) the nature of prior relationship to victim.[47] In a study of seventy-four stalking cases, Michael

Zona and associates identified three particular kinds of stalkers as follows[48]:

- *Simple obsession stalkers.* Are or were intimately involved with the victim such as a spouse, girlfriend, or ex-romantic partner and often had a history of domestic violence or emotional abuse toward them. Rejection, low self-esteem, and a desire to regain power and control over the victim are often motivating factors for the stalking. Six in ten cases of stalking fall into this category and it is the most likely to lead to murder.

- *Love obsession stalkers.* May be casually acquainted with the victim or a total stranger. These types become fixated on their victims and seek out a personal relationship with them that is unwelcome. Such stalkers often fantasize about a romantic involvement between them that exists only in their heads. They typically have a low self-esteem and will turn to negative attachments such as aggressive behavior to try to gain the love of the person victimized.

- *Erotomania stalkers.* Are delusional and, most often, schizophrenic. They tend to convince themselves that an involvement between them and their victims already exists. Erotomaniacs often target celebrities or public figures in a desire to gain fame and a higher self-esteem. Though not usually violent, irrational and unpredictable behavior can still be threatening to their victims. This type of stalker constitutes less than 10 percent of all stalking cases.

In their study of stalkers, Paul Mullen and colleagues developed five categories of stalkers, which they noted were not altogether mutually exclusive[49]:

- *Rejected stalkers.* Primarily ex-intimates who are angered, jealous, and vengeful after being rejected by their victims. Most stalkers fit into this category and they are the most threatening to the object of their stalking.

- *Intimacy-seeking stalkers.* They include erotomaniacs, obsessive, and those with dark infatuations who have persistently pursued their victims, believing they were meant to be romantically involved. This type of stalker is the second most determined behind the rejected stalker.

- *Incompetent stalkers.* They are fixated on their victims and seek an intimate involvement with them, in spite of weak skills in socializing and courting. They are often narcissistic and repeat stalking offenders, but not generally threatening or violent.
- *Resentful stalkers.* Have a vendetta against their victims often associating with former oppressors or those who humiliated them. The stalking is intended to frighten and cause suffering. These stalkers tend to be the most obsessive and likely to use verbal threats against victims.
- *Predatory stalkers.* Sexual predators whose motivation is sexual gratification and control of their victims. These stalkers are sexual deviants with poor social skills and less than average intelligence. They are the least common type of stalker.

Cyberstalking

Cyberstalking is another category of stalking that has been increasingly employed by stalkers to pursue victims. In a U.S. Department of Justice report on cyberstalking, it is defined as "the use of the Internet, e-mail, or other telecommunication technologies to harass or stalk another person."[50]

Paul Bocij provides a more expansive definition of cyberstalking in his study of the subject as:

> A group of behaviors in which an individual, group of individuals or organization, uses information and communications technology to harass another individual, group of individuals or organization. Such behaviors may include, but are not limited to, the transmission of threats and false accusations, damage to data or equipment, identity theft, data theft, computer monitoring, the solicitation of minors for sexual purposes and any form of aggression.[51]

It has been further suggested that in order for cyberstalking to rise to the level of actual stalking, the behavior should be characterized to one degree or another as "malice, premeditation, repetition, distress, obsession, vendetta, no legitimate purpose, personally directed, disregarded warnings to stop, harassment, and threats."[52]

Cyberstalking is the virtual space equivalent of stalking in the physical world and can be just as victimizing psychologically to the person targeted. This form of stalking can also progress from cyberspace to actual stalking victimization and its potential violence or other hazards. Cyberstalkers tend to meet and target their victims via computers, e-mail, cell phones, instant chats, chat rooms, discussion boards, online groups, search engines, and such popular social networks as MySpace.

Victims of cyberstalking generally tend to be young (ages eighteen to thirty-two), female, vulnerable, and are often racial, ethnic, or religious minorities, gay or lesbian; or otherwise situated in society to catch the attention and obsession of the stalker. Most cyberstalker victims are familiar with their offender in one manner or another.

Stalking in cyberspace has evolved into one of the biggest threats for college students in this country. As colleges and universities are amongst the largest users of Internet technology, with more students taking advantage of the opportunity than ever, it is a cyberstalker's virtual playground. The anonymity of use by such stalkers, who often rely on multiple identifications and sources, and the difficulty in identifying them, makes it a real problem for victims and law enforcement. In some instances, the stalker may pretend to be the victim as a means to encourage others to stalk or harass the true victim. Other ways in which the cyberstalker strikes are listed below:

- Making false accusations.
- Gathering information on the target.
- Sending viruses in order to damage victim's computer.
- Seeking to meet in person.
- Trying to recruit others to stalk the victim as well.
- Using the victim's name to order items or services.[53]

Cyberstalkers, similar to stalkers in general, often have antisocial personalities, are obsessive-compulsive, manipulative, and deceiving, with a history of unsuccessful relationships.[54] They are motivated by a fixation on the victim and desire to have power over them, often as a result of a real or virtual relationship with the person.

107

How big is the issue of cyberstalking? According to the *Sexual Victimization in the United States* report, more than one in every four stalking victims in the United States are victimized by cyberstalkers. As shown in Table 6.3, nearly 83 percent of stalking victimizations involved e-mails and over 35 percent instant messaging. When electronic devices were used by stalkers, video or digital cameras were used most often along with listening devices or bugs.

Table 6.3
Involvement of Cyberstalking or
Electronic Monitoring in Stalking and Harassment

	Percent of Victims		
	All	Stalking	Harassment
Total	100%	100%	100%
No cyberstalking or electronic			
monitoring involved	72.7%	73.2%	72.1%
Any type of cyberstalking or			
electronic monitoring	26.6%	26.1%	27.4%
Cyberstalking	23.4	21.5	26.4
Electronic monitoring	6.0	7.8	3.4
Don't know	0.6	0.7	0.6
Percent of cyberstalking involving —[a]			
E-mail	82.6%	82.5%	82.7%
Instant messenger	28.7	35.1	20.7
Blogs or bulletin boards	12.5	12.3	12.8
Internet sites about victim	8.8	9.4	8.1
Chat rooms	4.0	4.4[c]	3.4[c]
Percent of electronic monitoring			
involving —[b]			
Computer spyware	44.1%	33.6%	81.0[c]
Video/digital cameras	10.3	46.3	19.3[c]
Listening devices/bugs	35.8	41.8	14.6
GPS	9.7[c]	10.9[c]	5.2[c]
Number	5,200,410	3,158,340	2,042,070

NOTE: Table excludes 8.8% of all victims, 7.8% of stalking victims, and 10.2% of harassment victims due to missing data. Details sum to more than 100% because multiple responses were permitted.

[a]Based on 1,217,680 total victims, 677,870 stalking victims, and 539,820 harassment victims who experienced cyberstalking.
[b]Based on 314,400 total victims, 244,880 stalking victims, and 69,530 harassment victims who experienced electronic monitoring.
[c]Estimate based on 10 or fewer samples.

SOURCE: U.S. Department of Justice, Bureau of Justice Statistics Special Report, *National Crime Victimization Survey: Stalking Victimization in the United States* (Washington, DC: Office of Justice Programs, 2009), p. 5.

For victims of harassment, more than one in four was a victim of cyberstalking or electronic monitoring with most victimizations through e-mail, followed by instant messaging. Nearly two in ten cases of harassment-related electronic monitoring involved the use of digital or video cameras.

The Justice Department suggests that "there may be potentially tens or even hundreds of thousands of victims of recent cyberstalking incidents in the United States."[55] Anecdotal evidence from police agencies supports the contention that cyberstalking is a growing concern. For instance, it was estimated by the Los Angeles District Attorney's office that approximately 20 percent of the cases in the Stalking Threat Assessment Unit involved e-mail or another means of electronic communications.[56]

Studies indicate that there is a high incidence of cyberstalking victimization, particularly when considering college students who have been stalked. In one study of sexual victimization among 4,446 female students in attendance at two and four year colleges, of 696 stalking incidents described, nearly 25 percent involved e-mail.[57] Similarly, in a study by Eileen Alexy and associates of 756 students from two colleges, almost 32 percent of the students who reported being victims of stalking had been victimized by cyberstalking.[58]

Other studies have also yielded results that indicate the scope of cyberstalking. A study by B. H. Spitzberg and G. Hoobler of 235 undergraduate students majoring in communications found that nearly one-third were the victims of some form of cyberstalking.[59] Rebecca Lee also found in a study of 556 female and male students enrolled at six universities that more than half the females were cyberstalking victims, with the perception of the incidents as stalking dependent upon other kinds of behavior that was exhibited aside from online communication.[60]

Cyberstalkers fit into one or more of the aforementioned typologies as stalkers in general. They have also been categorized as "love rats," or stalkers who "surf the web with the intention of starting relationships and may have several simultaneous relationships. The targets of a cyberstalker may know little about the person they are talking to (other than what they've convincingly been fed) and be unaware of a trail of other targets past and present."[61]

Applying the laws against stalking has been more problematic due to the nature of stalking in cyberspace and difficulty in going after cyberstalkers, particularly those with no known association with the victim in the real world.

Responding to Stalking

In response to the serious issue of stalking victimization, antistalking laws exist on the federal level, in all fifty states, the District of Columbia, and the U.S. Territories. Though the legal definitions of what constitutes stalking is not uniform in every jurisdiction, the laws consider it a crime to "willfully, maliciously, and repeatedly harass, follow, or cause credible threat to another individual in an attempt to frighten or harm."[62] In addition, other laws may be applicable as well against stalkers, if their behavior warrants it, such as committing physical or sexual assault, breaking and entering, vandalism, and other stalker related victimization.

The first state to outlaw stalking was California. In 1990, it passed legislation to make this a crime following the stalking-murder of actress Rebecca Schaffer.[63] Passage of the Violence Against Women Act (VAWA) as a section of Title IV of the Violent Crime Control and Law Enforcement Act of 1994, made crossing state lines with the intent to injure, harass, or intimidate a spouse or other person involved with intimately a federal crime.[64] The Violence Against Women and Department of Justice Reauthorization Act of 2005 enhanced the Interstate federal stalking law to include cyberstalking.[65]

These laws against stalking notwithstanding, stalking remains a major problem for college students, whose environment and accessibility makes them especially vulnerable. Studies show that only a relatively small number of the approximately 9,653 colleges and universities across the United States have taken adequate steps to assist student victims of stalking on and around their campuses.[66] Moreover, college students who have been stalked have received inadequate justice. The NVAW found that only 13 percent of stalking cases were prosecuted.[67] This low percentage, along with the low reporting rate for stalking victimization, further underlines the difficulties in identifying stalking and treating it as a serious offense.

Nonetheless, colleges have the tools to confront stalking and make campuses safer, including counseling and health services, campus police and security, and a clear association between stalking and sexual victimization of students that is also being addressed.

Chapter 7

HATE CRIME

Hate crime represents another serious concern for college students, campus administrators, and school and local law enforcement. Most students have encountered, witnessed, or heard about acts perpetrated on and around campus that are hate or bias-motivated based on the victim's race, ethnicity, gender, religion, national origin, sexual orientation, or mental or physical disability. There are hate crime statutes federally, in most states, and the District of Columbia. Many states also have civil statutes that allow for seeking restraining orders against those who commit bias-motivated crimes of violence, threats, or property offenses. These statutes tend to vary in defining what constitutes a hate crime. Lack of clarity in definition can lead to confusion in understanding the type of behavior that either is bias-motivated or escalates into such. The occurrence of campus hate crimes often goes unreported, due in part to uncertainty that a crime is being committed or whom to report it to. On the campuses of colleges and universities across the country, diversity is a central aspect of the experience for students from all walks of life. This very environment can also attract those who are less tolerant, resulting in bias driven behavior.

Defining Hate Crime

There have been many definitions applied to hate crime through federal and state statutes, law enforcement, criminologists, educators, and researchers.[1] The fact that these can vary, sometimes dramatically, can make it difficult to get a clear picture of what a hate or bias crime is. This can be especially problematic for hate crime victims being able to differentiate from noncriminal behavior or other types of crimes. More uniformity in definitions is also important for better assessing the scope of hate crime in America and developing effective strategies to confront it.

112

Researchers often view the Federal Bureau of Investigation's (FBI) definition of hate crime as the standard, given it is used as the basis for collection of national data in its Uniform Crime Reporting (UCR) program. According to the FBI:

> A hate crime, also known as a bias crime, is a criminal offense committed against a person, property, or society that is motivated, in whole or in part, by the offender's bias against a race, religion, disability, sexual orientation, or ethnicity/national origin.[2]

A definition of hate crime by The International Association of Chiefs of Police adds gender among the individual traits that causes a person to be targeted, as

> a criminal offense committed against a person, property, or society that is motivated, in whole or in part, by the offender's bias against an individual's or a group's race, religion, ethnic/national origin, gender, age, disability, or sexual orientation.[3]

The National Education Association, that offers education and training for combating hate crimes in schools, defines hate crimes as "offenses motivated by hatred against a victim based on his or her beliefs or mental or physical characteristics, including race, ethnicity, and sexual orientation."[4]

Other definitions of hate crime include one by the nonprofit group LAMBDA GLBT Community Services, which is dedicated to reducing hate crimes, homophobia, discrimination, and equality. They define hate crime as "a criminal act which is motivated, at least in part, because of someone's bias or hatred of a person's or group's perceived race, religion, ethnicity, sexual orientation, or other characteristic."[5]

Hate crime is also often referred to as bias crime. While the terms are generally seen as interchangeable, some researchers differentiate. For instance, according to Frederick Lawrence, "bias crime" focuses more on the role bias plays in motivating one to perpetrate a criminal offense; whereas "hate crime" may include actions that do not involve bias or prejudice.[6]

Washington, DC offers a comprehensive state statute defining bias-related crime as a:

> designated act that demonstrates an accused's prejudice based on the actual or perceived race, color, religion, national origin, sex, age, marital

status, personal appearance, sexual orientation, family responsibility, physical handicap, matriculation, or political affiliation of a victim of the subject designated act.[7]

Hate or bias incidents are further differentiated from hate or ethnic crime. According to the Bureau of Justice Assistance monograph, *Hate Crimes on Campus: The Problem and Efforts to Confront It*, hate or bias incidents "involve behavior that is motivated by bias based on race, religion, ethnicity, national origin, gender, disability, or sexual orientation. These incidents do not involve criminal conduct such as an assault, threats or property damage."[8] Such occurrences as making bias-motivated comments that may be considered degrading would be not seen as a hate crime since the commenter has not accompanied their words with criminal conduct.

In the Department of Justice's *Responding to Hate Crimes and Bias-Motivated Incidences on College/University Campuses*, a hate incident is defined as "an action in which a person is made aware that her/his status is offensive to another, but does not rise to the level of a crime."[9]

For hate crimes, the perpetrator's intent is to harm and humiliate persons perceived to be different based on physical or other characteristics. Hate crime offenders can perpetrate acts of violence, threaten violent behavior verbally, resort to vandalism and other property crime, and use firearms or other weapons in a desire to inspire fear in the individuals targeted. This can leave victims susceptible to further attacks or the threat thereof and experience alienation and helplessness, along with mistrust and apprehension — all of which can have a lasting affect physically and psychologically.[10]

The Dynamics of Hate Crime

How prevalent are hate crimes in our society? Two major sources indicate the widespread nature of hate crime. According to the government reports, the National Crime Victimization Survey (NCVS) and *Uniform Crime Reports* (UCR), between July 2000 and the end of December 2003, there was a yearly average of more than 210,000 hate crime victimizations in the United States (see Table 7.1). Over this span there were nearly 191,000 hate crime incidents in which one or more victims were involved annually. Almost 92,000 of these hate crimes were reported to the police each year.

Table 7.1
Annual Number of Hate Crimes Reported
to the National Victimization Survey

	Incidents	*Victimizations*
Annual number of hate based crimes		
All hate crimes[a]	190,840	210,430
Violent	156,460	176,050
Major violentb	67,290	80,000
Property	34,380	34,380
Annual number reported to police		
All hate crimes[a]	80,760	91,630
Violent	66,650	77,520
Major violent[b]	39,210	47,000
Property	14,110	14,110

[a]Crimes include rape and other sexual assault, robbery, assault, larceny, and burglary. Vandalism is not included.
[b]Major violent crime includes rape and other sexual assault, robbery, and assault either with a weapon or with injury.
SOURCE: U.S. Department of Justice, Bureau of Justice Statistics Special Report, *Hate Crime Reported by Victims and Police* (Washington, DC: Office of Justice Programs, 2005), p. 2.

Amongst hate crime victimizations, the vast majority perpetrated against victims were crimes of violence, of which more than 45 percent were major violent crimes such as rape and other sexual assault, robbery, and assault with a weapon. Nearly six out of ten bias violent crime incidents reported to the police were major violent offenses.

Victim reports indicate that hate crimes are far more likely to be violent than crimes that are not hate associated. As shown in Table 7.2, nearly 84 percent of the hate crimes reported to the NCVS from July 2000 through the end of December 2003 were crimes of violence, compared to around 23 percent of the crimes other than hate. More than three times as many hate crime victimizations were major violent crimes as non hate crime victimizations. For instance, 18.5 percent of hate crime victimizations were aggravated assaults, whereas these constituted 4.5 percent of the victimizations that were other than hate. The percentage of hate crimes that were less serious was nearly four times greater than crimes that were not hate related. The data shows that just over 16 percent of hate crimes were household offenses such as burglary and theft.

Table 7.2
Hate and Other Crime Victimizations, by Type of Crime

Type of Crime	Percent of victimizations by crimes of:	
	Hate	Other than hate[a]
Total	100.0%	100.0%
Violent crime	83.7	22.9
Rape/sexual assault	4.0[b]	1.0
Robbery	5.0	2.5
Aggravated assault	18.5	4.5
With injury	5.0	1.4
Threatened with weapon	13.5	3.1
Simple assault	56.2	15.0
With injury	10.6	3.5
Without injury	17.6	5.5
Verbal threat	28.0	6.0
Personal larceny	0.0b%	0.7%
Household crime	16.3%	76.4%
Burglary	3.7[b]	13.3
Motor vehicle theft	0.3[b]	4.1
Theft	12.3	59.0

[a]*Other than hate crimes* are those described by victims as not having attributes that define hate crimes. Excluded from analysis were those crimes in which the victims did not know or did not answer whether they were targeted as hate victims (5.2% of all victimizations).
[b]Estimate is based on 10 or less sample cases.

SOURCE: U.S. Department of Justice, Bureau of Justice Statistics Special Report, *Hate Crime Reported by Victims and Police* (Washington, DC: Office of Justice Programs, 2005), p. 3.

Most hate crimes are motivated by race. As shown in Table 7.3, more than half the incidents and victimization reported to the NCVS during the period noted were race-motivated hate crimes. Nearly three in ten hate crimes were motivated by ethnicity, while more than three in ten victimizations and incidents were motivated by the victim's association with someone or others objectionable to the hate offender, such as of a different ethnicity. Almost one in five hate crimes were motivated by sexual orientation, roughly one in eight due to religion, and around one in nine as a result of the target's disability. In the overwhelming majority of hate crime incidents and victimizations, the evidence of motivations was seen as making negative comments or using abusive language.

Table 7.3
Motivation and Evidence in Hate Crime[a]

	Percent of hate crime:	
	Incidents	Victimizations
Motivation		
Race	55.4%	56.0%
Association	30.7	30.6
Ethnicity	28.7	27.9
Sexual orientation	18.0	17.9
Perceived characteristic	13.7	13.2
Religion	12.9	12.4
Disability	11.2	10.5
Evidence of Motivation		
Negative comments, hurtful words, abusive language	98.5%	98.5%
Confirmation by police investigation	7.9	8.4
Hate symbols	7.6	7.8

[a]Detail adds to more than 100 percent due to some respondents including more than one motivation or evidence of motivation.

SOURCE: U.S. Department of Justice, Bureau of Justice Statistics Special Report, *Hate Crime Reported by Victims and Police* (Washington, DC: Office of Justice Programs, 2005), p. 3.

The characteristics of hate crime offenders, as reported to the NCVS and the National Incident-Based Reporting System (NIBRS), the latter which is enhanced data from the UCR program, can be seen in Table 7.4. Nearly seven in ten hate crimes were committed by single offenders. More than one in four hate crimes in the NIBRS were perpetrated by two or more offenders. Hate crime offenders are much more likely to be male than female, constituting around three-quarters of the perpetrators. The NCVS data shows a higher percentage of female offenders than the NIBRS.

Almost seven out of ten hate crime perpetrators were white, according to the NIBRS, while the NCVS showed a much closer percentage of white and black offenders. Perpetrators of hate crimes are most likely to be age thirty and older, followed by seventeen and younger, and twenty to twenty-nine. More then half the hate crime offenders in the NCVS were strangers to the victims, compared to less than 40 percent in the

NIBRS. Around seven out of ten hate crimes were committed without the use of a weapon.

Table 7.4
Characteristics of Offenders Reported
by Hate Crime Victims to NCVS and NIBRS

Characteristics of offenders	Percent of hate crime victimizations	
	National Crime Victimization Survey	National Incident-based Reporting System
Number of offenders		
One	67.5%	68.3%
Two or three	16.3	25.7
Four or more	16.2	6.0
Gender		
Male	72.2%	76.4%
Female	21.2	16.5
Both male and female	6.6	7.2
Race		
White	43.9%	68.1%
Black	37.6	20.7
Other	13.2	1.5
More than one racial group	5.4	9.7
Age		
17 or younger	21.0%	24.7%
18–20	6.2	9.7
21–29	21.1	15.9
30 or older	37.8	36.0
More than one age group	14.0	13.6
Victim-offender relationship[a]		
Stranger	51.3%	35.8%
Use of weapons		
Weapon[b]	23.9%	19.4%
Other weapon[c]	—[d]	12.6
No weapon	69.8	64.4
Unknown	6.3	3.6

[a]For the National Incident-Based Reporting System, victim-offender relationship is only collected for crimes against persons.
[b]Includes firearms, knives, and sharp and blunt objects.
[c]Includes motor vehicles, personal weapons (hands, feet, teeth, and others), poison, explosives, incendiary devices, drugs and other items.
[d]Not available.

SOURCE: Adapted from U.S. Department of Justice, Bureau of Justice Statistics Special Report, *Hate Crime Reported by Victims and Police* (Washington, DC: Office of Justice Programs, 2005), p. 11.

Hate crime victim characteristics reported to the NCVS and NIBRS are shown in Table 7.5.

Victims were male and white in around two-thirds of the victimizations in the NIBRS data. It showed that nearly three in ten victims were black, with less than 5 percent other races. The NCVS showed just over 55 percent of the hate crime victims as male and more than 44 percent female; with 85 percent of the victims white and about 9 percent of bias crime victims black.

Around nine in ten victims were non–Hispanic, while more than three out of ten victims were thirty to forty-nine years of age. One-fourth of the NIBRS victims of hate crimes were ages twenty-one to twenty-nine, and around two in ten victims in both data were age seventeen or younger.

Table 7.5
Characteristics of Victims of Hate Crime
Reported to NCVS and NIBRS

	Percent of hate crime victimizations	
	National Crime	*National Incident-based*
Characteristics of offenders	*Victimization Survey*	*Reporting System*
Gender		
Male	55.4%	64.7%
Female	44.6	35.3
Race		
White	85.0%	66.5%
Black	9.2	29.1
Other	5.8	4.4
Ethnicity		
Hispanic	11.4%	8.8%
Non–Hispanic	88.6	91.2
Age		
17 or younger	18.8%	19.1%
18–20	9.3	11.4
21–29	18.1	24.1
30–49	37.3	34.9
50 or older	16.5	10.4

SOURCE: Adapted from U.S. Department of Justice, Bureau of Justice Statistics Special Report, *Hate Crime Reported by Victims and Police* (Washington, DC: Office of Justice Programs, 2005), p. 10.

About 20 percent of all hate crimes occur at school, with nearly four in ten victimizations occurring at a commercial place, on the street, or parking lot. More than one quarter of bias crimes were perpetrated at or close to the victim's residence (see Figure 7.1).

Figure 7.1
Hate Crime by Place of Occurrence

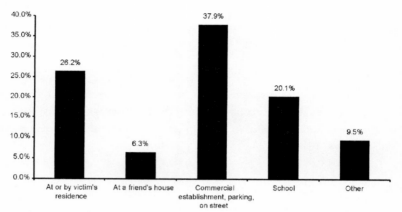

SOURCE: Adapted from U.S. Department of Justice, Bureau of Justice Statistics Special Report, *Hate Crime Reported by Victims and Police* (Washington, DC: Office of Justice Programs, 2005), p. 8.

Most hate crimes are not reported to law enforcement authorities. Approximately 44 percent of hate crimes are reported to the police, with nearly 55 percent unreported. Around one in four such cases are reported by the victim (see Figure 7.2). Comparatively, about half of non-hate violent crime victimizations are reported to the police, with nearly three in ten hate crimes reported by victims.[11]

Other findings on the dynamics of hate crimes in this country include:

- The Human Rights Campaign reported on 651 hate crimes between 1998 and 2002, including 181 murders.[12]
- A report by the Anti-Defamation League found that there were 1,557 anti–Semitic incidents nationwide in 2003.[13]
- The National Coalition of Anti-Violence Programs reported on 2,051 bias-motivated crimes in 2003.[14]
- The National Center for Education Statistics reported that nearly four in ten students between ages twelve to eighteen had seen hate-related graffiti at school in 2003.[15]
- The National Center for Victims of Crime (NCVC) found that there were 602 hate groups and 194 "Patriot" groups active in this country in 2000.[16]

- The Simon Wiesenthal Center has identified more than 8,000 hate and terrorist sites operating on the Internet.[17]
- The Bureau of Justice Statistics reported that an arrest is made in around 20 percent of all bias crime incidents.[18]

Figure 7.2
Reporting Hate Crimes to the Police

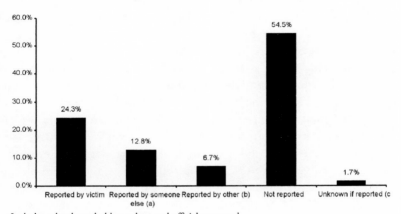

[a]Includes other household members and official personnel.
[b]Includes police on the scene and others.
[c]Estimate is based on 10 or less sample cases.

SOURCE: Adapted from U.S. Department of Justice, Bureau of Justice Statistics Special Report, *Hate Crime Reported by Victims and Police* (Washington, DC: Office of Justice Programs 2005), p. 4.

College Students and Hate Crime

The incidence of hate crime on the campuses of colleges and universities is a subject for debate, as much of the available data is incomplete. However, most experts on bias crime recognize that college students are especially vulnerable to targeting by hate offenders. Recent examples, among many, of hate crimes against college students include[19]:

- An ex-student was convicted of sending an e-mail containing racially derogatory remarks and threats to fifty-nine college students, who were mostly Asian.
- A student pled guilty after being charged with violating the civil

121

rights of three students enrolled at a small college in Massachusetts, including the use of anti–Semitic slurs and threats of force.
- A person was charged with the detonation of two pipe bombs on a predominately African American Florida university campus.
- Two men were sentenced to life in prison after the beating death of a University of Wyoming gay student.

There are currently three principal sources for campus hate crime statistics: (1) UCR program, (2) U.S. Department of Education (ED) Campus Security Statistics, and (3) International Association of College Law Enforcement Administrators (IACLEA). Discrepancies exist in their data due to differing methodologies and interpretations of requirements for reporting hate crime, the limited number of schools supplying information, structural differences in campus law enforcement, and underreporting by victims of bias crime.[20] For instance, while reporting hate and other crimes to either the ED or UCR is mandatory in order for colleges and universities to receive federal funds, only 400 of almost 7,000 institutions of higher education in the United States reported crime data to the UCR in 2002, compared to more than 6,000 schools reporting such data to the ED.[21] These issues notwithstanding, hate crimes have proven to be pervasive on many college campuses.

The UCR found that 13.5 percent of reported hate crimes in 2005 took place at schools or colleges.[22] Of these, 54 percent were motivated by race, 22 percent due to religion, 13 percent based on sexual orientation, and 12 percent related to ethnicity of victim. In a 1998 FBI study of crime on college campuses, in which 450 institutions of higher learning from forty states participated, 49 percent of the schools reported a total of 241 hate crime incidents during the year.[23] Nearly six in ten of these hate crimes were race-motivated, while nearly one in five were motivated by anti–Semitism, and around one out of six as a result of sexual orientation.

In 1998, the IACLEA also surveyed 411 campuses across the United States; with 88 percent reporting at least one incident of hate crime.[24] These colleges experienced 3.8 crimes on average that year, totaling 334 incidents. The hate crimes were motivated by one or more of the following categories: race, ethnicity/national origin, religion, sexual orientation, and disability. Gender was not included among the motives. Over 80 percent of the hate crimes were based upon race or sexual orientation.

A rise in anti–Semitism at institutions of higher education has been of concern to school administrators. The NCVC reported that anti–Semitic incidents on college campuses grew by 15 percent in 2002.[25] This may correlate with a recent increase in the number of anti–Semitic and extremist speakers that student groups have invited on campus.[26]

Bias-motivated crime can have an effect on college student victims in a manner similar to other types of crime victimization. That is, physically, emotionally, financially, and educationally. These can be both short- and long-term. With respect to school, being the target of a hate crime can have an impact on everything from school attendance and performance to socializing and peace of mind on campus. Hate crime victimization can further cause victims to feel rejected and unsupported by the academic community as well as the criminal justice system. One study on bias and hate crime noted that "often professionals who work within the system that serves the victim have the same prejudices and bias as the rest of society and may minimize the impact of the crime on the individual. Hate/bias crime victims feel betrayed and hopeless when they confront institutional prejudice."[27]

Underreporting of Campus Hate Crime

Most indications are that hate crimes are vastly underreported by both schools and victims of bias-motivated offenses, which is similar to other forms of college criminality. Reasons typically attributed to low reporting of campus hate crimes include:

- Reluctance to report victimization due to feelings of isolation.
- Hesitancy to report the hate crime for fear of perpetrator retaliation.
- Victimization was handled in another way.
- Lack of understanding that a crime was committed.
- Difficulty in proving the offense was a hate crime.

- Belief that the college or police would not do anything about it.
- Fears on the part of colleges of stigma associated with labeling a crime on campus as a hate or bias crime.

In their study of obstacles to accurate reporting of hate crimes, Jack McDevitt and associates suggest seven decision points, generally sequential[28]:

- Victim awareness that a crime occurred.
- Victim discernment of hate as the motivating factor for victimization.
- Victim or someone else seeks police intervention.
- Communication by victim or another to the authorities about the perceived crime motivation.
- The constituent of hate is recognized by police.
- The hate element is documented by police and the suspect is charged accordingly with hate or bias crime, or civil rights violations.
- The incident is recorded by police and information is submitted to the UCR, Hate Crime Reporting Unit.

The researchers contend that should a breakdown occur at any of these points of decision, the chances for accurate reporting of hate crime decreases. Other studies have supported this finding.[29]

Shane Windmeyer asserts that hate crimes and incidents that are bias-motivated at colleges and universities will not be dealt with properly until institutions become better informed about the extent and gravity of hate crime.[30] In spite of the relatively low number of colleges and victims reporting or identifying hate crimes, the indication is that "hate crimes on campus are a significant problem. Moreover, there are strong reasons to believe that the problem of hate crimes is more widespread than any statistics are likely to reveal."[31]

What Causes Hate Crime?

Hate crimes are a reflection of various factors, including bigotry, ignorance, economic conditions, poverty, ideology, prevailing attitudes from one generation to another, miscommunication, stereotypes, unemployment, low education, and other types of violent behavior and criminality. These are not mutually exclusive and can also be related to other issues, creating a mindset for hate, and acting on these impulses through criminal behavior.

Criminologists contend that most bias-motivated offenses are committed by "otherwise law-abiding [citizens] who see little wrong with their actions."[32] Though substance abuse often plays a role in hate crime, most experts believe that the primary cause of bias offending is individual prejudice, which "colors people's judgment, blinding the aggressors to the immorality of what they are doing. Such prejudice is most likely rooted in an environment that disdains someone who is 'different' or sees that difference as threatening."[33] The most violent bias crimes, such as those involving particularly brutal homicides or other assaultive behavior, tend to be committed by offenders with a history of serious and violent offending or other acts of aggression.[34]

Some social scientists have associated hate crime to downturns in the economy.[35] Others believe that hate crimes are "sporadic, isolated, uncoordinated, and not tied to economic fluctuation."[36] According to hate crime researchers Donald Green, Jack Glaser, and Andrew Rich: "Rather than economic downturns, neighborhood influxes of ethnically diverse people were most likely to spur bigoted violence. The only time economic hardship relates to hate crime is when established political leaders convince the public that specific groups are to blame."[37] Even without such an indictment, certain circumstances can sway the public against a particular race, ethnic group, or culture to spur hate crimes. An example of this is the spike in violence against Arab-Americans and Muslims following the 9/11 attack perpetrated by al-Qaeda linked Islamist terrorists.[38]

Sociologists have also attributed bias crime to the social norms breaking down, viewing it in a historical perspective in relation to political and economic change. Other researchers have argued that bias-motivated crimes "are not necessarily random, uncontrollable, or inevitable occurrences."[39] On the contrary, most evidence indicates that society and policymakers can create effective strategies for reducing or preventing the occurrence of hate crimes and other types of violence.[40]

Typologies of Hate Offenders

Along with seeking to understand what causes people to become hate offenders, criminologists have also sought to explain hate crime in terms offender typologies. Though perpetrators of bias crimes can fit into more than one typology, their characteristics can generally be associated with a type in particular. Three types of hate offenders have been identified by Jack Levin and Jack McDevitt, as follows[41]:

- *Thrill-seeking offenders* are motivated by the excitement and power derived through hate offending. They tend to commit bias crimes outside their home turf, vandalizing property and attacking persons from groups these offenders see as inferior to them and vulnerable. Thrill seekers are not usually aligned with a hate group. This is the most common kind of hate offender, representing two-thirds of all offender motivations.
- *Reactive offenders* will attack a person or group of individuals on their home turf, whom the perpetrators see as threatening their existence, neighborhood, workplace, or freedom, while validating the aggressive actions as defensive or protection of turf. They are hardly ever associated with organized hate groups, but will seek assistance from such if necessary to deal with threat. One quarter of hate offender motivation falls under this type.
- *Mission offenders* often tend to be psychotic or mentally ill and prone to delusions. They see their mission as eliminating groups perceived as evil or inferior and become deeply paranoid and desperate to fulfill this obligation. These offenders usually commit their hate crimes (mostly violent) alone and often arbitrarily in attacking individuals within the hated group. Mission offenders are the least common perpetrator of hate offenses.

The researchers also depict a fourth type of offender motivation for hate crime, *retaliatory offenders*, in which persons seek retaliation for a perceived affront or attack against someone or everyone within their group.[42]

In a study of ethnoviolence, it was found that more than one in four persons reporting reactive hate episodes were victimized in the work setting.[43] A similar environment exists at colleges and universities, where students from various backgrounds coexist in working toward educational goals. This makes it a likely setting for reactive offenders who may see bias crime as defending their turf against racial and ethnic minorities or other groups.[44]

Impulsive thrill-seeking offenders are also prone to targeting persons in groups they are biased against within the college community, such African Americans and Latinos, and others whom the hate offenders deem inferior. Substance abuse often plays a role in thrill-seeking episodes of hate.[45]

In an examination of offender motivations in self-reported aggression against gays, Karen Franklin described four types of offenders[46]:

- *Self-defense offenders* often assert that their hostile actions were in response to forceful sexual propositions from victims. The bias-motivated offenders seem to base their interpretations and actions on associating homosexuals with being sexual predators.
- *Ideology offenders* tend to attack gays and lesbians due to negative feelings with respect to homosexuality. These offenders choose to take the role of upholding the social norms by attacking moral wrongdoers.
- *Thrill seekers* turn to hate crime due to boredom, for fun and stimulation, and a sense of power.
- *Peer dynamics* perpetrate hate offenses to show how tough they are and reinforce to friends their heterosexuality, while minimizing antagonistic views against homosexuals and the severity of the attack.

With hate crimes and bias incidents becoming more and more common on the campuses of universities and colleges throughout the country, identifying hatemongers is important in developing strategies to better address hate crime, protect students, promote tolerance, and improve the accuracy of campus crime statistics.

Combating Hate Crime on Campus

Since the early 1980s, the issue of hate crime on college and university campuses and elsewhere in the United States has been undertaken by the federal government and most states through legislation aimed at combating bias crimes, apprehending those perpetrating such crimes, and protecting the public and their civil rights from those who spew hate through their words and actions.

A key federal law with respect to campus hate crime is the Crime Awareness and Campus Security Act of 1990.[47] It requires institutions of higher learning that receive federal funding to provide campus crime statistics, including hate crime, in an annual report and reveal procedures for campus safety and knowledge of any crime threats. The Act was amended in 1998 and renamed the Jeanne Clery Disclosure of Campus Security Policy and Campus Crime Statistics Act (or Clery Act).[48] See more on this in Chapter 4. It was further amended in 2003, dictating that schools report crimes by category of bias and notify campus police or local law enforcement of any hate crimes that involve bodily injury.

Also enacted in 1990 was the Hate Crimes Statistics Act (HCSA), which requires the Department of Justice to gather information on crimes that manifest hate or bias on the basis of race, ethnicity, religion, or sexual orientation from law enforcement agencies nationwide and publish the findings annually.[49] Under the Violent Crime Control and Law Enforcement Act of 1994, an amendment to the HCSA required the FBI to also report on hate crimes that were based upon disability.[50]

Other significant federal statutes related to hate crime are as follows:

- Violent Crime Control and Law Enforcement Act of 1994 (called the Crime Bill) requires the United States Sentencing Commission to increase penalties for crimes that are bias-motivated because of race, ethnicity, color, national origin, gender, religion, sexual orientation, disability, or the perception thereof, on any individual.[51]
- Hate Crime Sentencing Enhancement Act is a section of the Violent Crime Control and Law Enforcement Act of 1994, allowing for longer sentences for hate crimes or offenses motivated by a victim's race, ethnicity, national origin, gender, sexual orientation, or disability.[52]
- Church Arson Prevention Act of 1996 requires the collection of

hate crime data as part of the Uniform Crime Reporting program. The Act also created the National Church Arson Task Force to oversee the investigation of arson at churches across the United States and prosecution of arsonists, while also allowing for greater federal jurisdiction for such bias-motivated criminality.[53]

- Violence Against Women Act of 2005 reauthorizes a law first passed in 1994, offering a more comprehensive measure aimed at combating and preventing violence against women, including domestic violence, dating violence, stalking, and college campus crimes of violence. It also allows for civil action on the federal level for gender-motivated violent crime victimization.[54]

An important piece of federal hate-related legislation being considered is:

- Local Law Enforcement Hate Crimes Prevention Act of 2007 (referred to as the Matthew Shepard Act). This Act would expand upon the current federal hate crime statute by adding crimes based on the actual or perceived gender, gender identity, sexual orientation, or disability of a victim.[55]

On the state level, forty-five states and the District of Columbia have enacted hate crime statutes.[56] Allowance for a civil cause of action alongside criminal penalties exists in thirty-one states and the District of Columbia for bias-motivated offenses; while in twenty-seven states and the District of Columbia, there are laws to require the collection of hate crime statistics. Sexual orientation is included in sixteen of the statutes.[57]

Apart from hate crime laws, various organizations exist to combat bias crimes on and off campus. These include the Anti-Defamation League, American-Arab Anti-Discrimination Committee, American Citizens for Justice, Inc., Human Rights Campaign, NAACP, National Asian Pacific American Legal Consortium, and National Gay and Lesbian Task Force.[58] Ultimately, greater attention by campus officials to bias-motivated crimes and improved policies for detection and reporting are still needed to help ensure student safety.

CHAPTER NOTES

Chapter 1

1. National Minimum Drinking Age Act (1984), 23 U.S.C. § 158, P.L. 98–363.

2. Federal-Aid Highway Act (1982), P.L. 97–424; Surface Transportation and Uniform Relocation Assistance Act (1987), P.L. 100–17.

3. "Research Findings on Underage Drinking and the Minimum Legal Drinking Age," http://www.niaaa.nih.gov/AboutNIAAA/NIAAASponsoredPrograms/drinkingage.htm.

4. 23 U.S.C. § 158; Alex Koroknay, "Legislative Analysis for the National Minimum Drinking Age Act," http://www.yria.alcade.net/essays/leg-an.htm.

5. "Research Findings on Underage Drinking"; Robert B. Voas, A. Scott Tippetts, and James C. Fell, "Assessing the Effectiveness of Minimum Legal Drinking Age and Zero Tolerance Laws in the United States," *Accident Analysis and Prevention* 35, 4 (2003): 579–87; James C. Fell, Deborah A. Fisher, Robert B. Voas, Kenneth Blackman, and A. Scott Tippetts, "The Relationship of Underage Drinking Laws to Reductions in Drinking Drivers in Fatal Crashes in the United States," *Accident Analysis and Prevention* 40 (2008): 1430–40; David A. Brent, "Risk Factors for Adolescent Suicide and Suicidal Behavior: Mental and Substance Abuse Disorders, Family Environmental Factors, and Life Stress," *Suicide Life Threat Behavior* 25 (1996): 52–63.

6. "Research Findings on Underage Drinking"; The ESPAD Report 2003: Alcohol and Other Drug Use Among Students in 35 European Countries available online at http://www.monitoringthefuture.org/pubs/espadusa2003.pdf.

7. The Amethyst Initiative, http://www.amethystinitiative.org.

8. U.S. Department of Health and Human Services, Centers for Disease Control and Prevention, "Quick Stats: Underage Drinking," http://www.cdc.gov/Alcohol/quickstats/underage_drinking.htm; U.S. Department of Health and Human Services, National Institute on Alcohol Abuse and Alcoholism, "Statistical Snapshot of Underage Drinking," http://www.niaaa.nih.gov/AboutNIAAA/NIAAASponsoredPrograms/StatisticalSnapshotUnderageDrinking.htm.

9. Jacqueline W. Miller, Timothy S. Naimi, Robert D. Brewer, and Sherry Everett Jones, "Binge Drinking and Associated Health Risk Behaviors Among High School Students," *Pediatrics* 119, 1 (2007): 76–85; R. Barri Flowers, *Kids Who Commit Adult Crimes: A Study of Serious Juvenile Criminality and Delinquency* (Binghamton, NY: Haworth Press, 2002), pp. 43–50.

10. Reported in U.S. Department of Health and Human Services, National Institute on Alcohol Abuse and Alcoholism, *Alcohol Alert* 68 (April 2006), http://pubs.niaaa.nih.gov/publications/aa68/aa68.htm.

11. U.S. Department of Health and Human Services, National Institute on Alcohol Abuse and Alcoholism, "Statistical Snapshot of College Drinking," http://www.niaaa.nih.gov/AboutNIAAA/NIAAASponsoredPrograms/StatisticalSnapshotCollegeDrinking.htm.

12. National Survey on Drug Use and Health, "Underage Alcohol Use Among Full-Time College Students," *NSDUH Report* 31 (2006), http://oas.samhsa.gov/2k6/college/collegeUnderage.htm.

13. *Ibid.*

14. Cited in *Alcohol Alert* 68.

15. Paul E. Greenbaum, Frances K. Del Boca, Jack Darks, and Mark S. Goldman, "Variations in the Drinking Trajectories of Freshmen College Students," *Journal of Consulting and Clinical Psychology* 73 (2005): 229–38.

16. Miller, Naimi, Brewer, and Jones, "Binge Drinking and Associated Health Risk Behaviors"; U.S. Department of Health and Human Services, *The Surgeon General's Call to Action to Prevent and Reduce Underage Drinking* (Rockville, MD: U.S. Department of

Health and Human Services, 2007), http://www.surgeongeneral.gov/topics/underagedrinking; Ralph Hingson, Timothy Heeren, Michael Winter, and Henry Wechsler, "Magnitude of Alcohol-Related Mortality and Morbidity Among U.S. College Students Ages 18–24: Changes from 1998 to 2001," *Annual Review of Public Health* 26 (2005): 259–279.

17. "Underage Alcohol Use Among Full-Time College Students."

18. Quoted in U.S. Department of Health and Human Services, National Institute on Alcohol Abuse and Alcoholism, "College Drinking and its Consequences: New Data," November 2007, p. 2, http://www.collegedrinkingprevention.gov/1College_Bulletin-508_361C4E.pdf.

19. Alcohol Problems and Solutions, "Binge Drinking," http://www2.potsdam.edu/hansondj/BingeDrinking.html.

20. U.S. Department of Justice, Office of Juvenile Justice and Delinquency Prevention, *Drinking in America: Myths, Realities, and Prevention Policy* (Washington, D.C.: U.S. Department of Justice, 2005), http://www.udetc.org/documents/Drinking_in_America.pdf.

21. *Ibid.*

22. Lloyd D. Johnston, Patrick M. O'Malley, Jerald G. Bachman, and John E. Schulenberg, *Monitoring the Future National Survey Results on Drug Use, 1975–2007*, Vol. I: Secondary School Students (Bethesda, MD: National Institute on Drug Abuse, 2008), p. 26.

23. U.S. Department of Health and Human Services, National Institute on Alcohol Abuse and Alcoholism, "Research Findings on College Drinking and the Minimum Legal Drinking Age," http://www.niaaa.nih.gov/AboutNIAAA/NIAAASponsoredPrograms/CollegeDrinkingMLDA.htm; Patricia C. Rutledge, Aesoon Park, and Kenneth J. Sher, "21st Birthday Drinking: Extremely Extreme," *Journal of Consulting and Clinical Psychology* 76, 3 (2008): 511–16.

24. Science Daily, "Binge Drinking Tied to Conditions in the College Environment," July 14, 2008, http://www.sciencedaily.com/releases/2007/08/070831093912.htm.

25. Dennis L. Thombs, R. Scott Olds, and Barbara M. Snyder, "Field Assessment of BAC Data to Study Late-Night College Drinking," *Journal of Studies on Alcohol* 64, 3 (2003): 322–30. *See also* James E. Lange and Robert

B. Voas, "Defining Binge Drinking Quantities Through Resulting Blood Alcohol Concentration," *Psychology of Addictive Behaviors* 84 (2001): 508–18; H. Wesley Perkins, William DeJong, and Jeff Linkenbach, "Estimated Blood Alcohol Levels Reached by 'Binge' and 'Nonbinge' Drinkers: A Survey of Young Adults in Montana," *Psychology of Addictive Behaviors* 15 (2001): 317–20.

26. U.S. Department of Health and Human Services, Substance Abuse and Mental Health Services Administration, *Results from the 2007 National Survey on Drug Use and Health: National Findings* (2008), http://oas.samhsa.gov/NSDUH/2k7NSDUH/2k7results.cfm#2.2.

27. "Statistical Snapshot of College Drinking."

28. U.S. Department of Health and Human Services, National Institute on Alcohol Abuse and Alcoholism, *Alcohol Alert* 58 (October 2002), http://pubs.niaaa.nih.gov/publications/aa58.htm.

29. Cited in Centers for Disease Control and Prevention, "Quick Stats: Underage Drinking."

30. *Ibid. See also* Joseph W. LaBrie, Andrea Rodrigues, Jason Schiffman, and Summer Tawalbeh, "Early Alcohol Initiation Increases Risk Related to Drinking Among College Students," *Journal of Child & Adolescent Substance Abuse* 17, 2 (2007): 125–41.

31. Science Daily, "Underage Drinking Starts Before Adolescence," (September 5, 2007), http://www.sciencedaily.com/releases/2007/08/070831093912.htm.

32. Miranda Hitti, "Underage Drinking Hits Grade School," WebMD Health News, http://children.webmd.com/news/20070831/underage-drinking-hits-grade-school.

33. "Statistical Snapshot of Underage Drinking."

34. Cited in "Quick Stats: Underage Drinking."

35. R. Barri Flowers, *Drugs, Alcohol and Criminality in American Society* (Jefferson, NC: McFarland, 2008), pp. 99–110; Miller, Naimi, Brewer, and Jones, "Binge Drinking and Associated Health Risk Behaviors."

36. Cited in Underage Drinking Research, "8th, 10th, and 12th Grade Drinking," http://www.alcoholstats.com/page.aspx?id=135#4; Institute for Social Research, Survey Research Center, Monitoring the Future: A Continuing

Study of American Youth, http://www.moni toringthefuture.org/; U. S. Department of Health and Human Services, National Institute on Drug Abuse, "NIDA InfoFacts: High School and Youth Trends," http://www.drug abuse.gov/infofacts/HSYouthtrends.htm.

37. International Survey Associates, PRIDE Surveys: 2007–08 National Summary — Grades 6 Thru 12 (September 19, 2008), p. 236, http://www.pridesurveys.com.

38. Cited on Stop Underage Drinking, Portal of Federal Resources, "SAMHSA's 2007 National Survey on Drug Use and Health (NSDUH)," http://www.stopalcoholabuse. gov/Stats.

39. Flowers, *Kids Who Commit Adult Crimes*, pp. 46–49; George W. Dowdall, *College Drinking: Reframing a Social Problem* (New York: Praeger, 2008).

40. Cited in *Alcohol Alert* 58; Hingson, Heeren, Winter, and Wechsler, "Magnitude of Alcohol-Related Mortality and Morbidity."

41. Hingson, Heeren, Winter, and Wechsler, "Magnitude of Alcohol-Related Mortality and Morbidity."

42. *Ibid.*

43. *Ibid.*; Flowers, *Drugs, Alcohol and Criminality in American Society*, pp. 99–105.

44. Hingson, Heeren, Winter, and Wechsler, "Magnitude of Alcohol-Related Mortality and Morbidity."

45. *Ibid.*; Flowers, *Kids Who Commit Adult Crimes*, pp. 43–49.

46. Hingson, Heeren, Winter, and Wechsler, "Magnitude of Alcohol-Related Mortality and Morbidity."

47. Henry Wechsler, Jae Eun Lee, Meichun Kuo, Mark Seibring, Toben F. Nelson, and Hang P. Lee, "Trends in College Binge Drinking During a Period of Increased Prevention Efforts: Findings From Four Harvard School of Public Health Study Surveys, 1993–2001," *Journal of American College Health* 50, 5 (2002): 203–217.

48. Cheryl A. Presley, Jami S. Leichliter, and Phillip W. Meilman, *Alcohol and Drugs on American College Campuses: A Report to Colleges Presidents* (Carbondale, IL: Core Institute, Southern Illinois University, 1998), p. 10.

49. Henry Wechsler, Jae Eun Lee, Toben F. Nelson, and Meichun Kuo, "Underage College Students' Drinking Behavior, Access to Alcohol, and the Influence of Deterrence Policies:

Findings From the Harvard School of Public Health College Alcohol Study," *Journal of American College Health* 50, 5 (2002): 228.

50. See, for example, Henry Wechsler, Jae Eun Lee, Jeana Gledhill-Hoyt, and Toben F. Nelson, "Alcohol Use and Problems at Colleges Banning Alcohol: Results of a National Survey," *Journal of Studies on Alcohol* 62 (2001): 133–41; Henry Wechsler, Jae Eun Lee, Toben F. Nelson, and Hang P. Lee, "Drinking Levels, Alcohol Problems and Secondhand Effects in Substance-Free College Residences: Results of a National Study," *Journal of Studies on Alcohol* 62 (2001): 23–31.

51. Frank J. Chaloupka, Michael Grossman, and Henry Saffer, "The Effects of Price on Alcohol Consumption and Alcohol-Related Problems," *Alcohol Research & Health* 26, 1 (2002): 22–34; Jenny Williams, Frank J. Chaloupka, and Henry Wechsler, "Are There Differential Effects of Price and Policy on College Students' Drinking Intensity?" *Contemporary Economic Policy* 23 (2005): 78–90; Meichun Kuo, Henry Wechsler, Patty Greenberg, and Hang Lee, "The Marketing of Alcohol to College Students: The Role of Low Prices and Special Promotions," *American Journal of Preventive Medicine* 25 (2003): 204–211.

52. Consolidated Appropriations Act of 2004, P.L. 108–199.

53. Stop Underage Drinking, Portal of Federal Resources, "About Us," http://www. stopalcoholabuse.gov/About/; Drug-Free Schools and Communities Act (1986), 20 U.S.C. 3181, P.L. 101–226; U.S. Department of Education, Higher Education Center for Alcohol and Other Drug Abuse and Violence Prevention, "Drug-Free Schools and Communities Act (DFSCA) and Drug and Alcohol Abuse Prevention Regulations," http://www. higheredcenter.org/mandates/dfsca.

54. U.S. Department of Education, "Preventing Underage Drinking: A School-Based Approach," http://www.ed.gov/admins/lead/ safety/training/alcohol/prevent.html.

Chapter 2

1. U.S. Department of Health and Human Services, National Survey on Drug Use and Health, *The NSDUH Report: College Enrollment Status and Past Year Illicit Drug Use*

Among Young Adults: 2002, 2003, and 2004 (Rockville, MD: Office of Applied Studies, 2005), p. 1.

2. "Drug and Alcohol Abuse by College Students: An Issue of Increasing Concern on Campus," http://www.collegedrugabuse.com/; R. Barri Flowers, *Kids Who Commit Adult Crimes: A Study of Serious Juvenile Criminality and Delinquency* (Binghamton, NY: Haworth Press, 2002), pp. 43–50; Cheryl A. Presley, Philip W. Meilman, and Jeffrey R. Cashin, *Alcohol and Drugs on American College Campuses: Use, Consequences, and Perceptions of the Campus Environment, Volume IV: 1992–94* (Carbondale, IL: Core Institute, Southern Illinois University, 1996); Carolyn J. Palmer, "Violence and Other Forms of Victimizations in Residence Halls: Perspectives of Resident Assistants," *Journal of College Student Development* 37, 3 (1996): 268–78.

3. *The NSDUH Report*, p. 1.

4. U.S. Department of Health and Human Services, *Monitoring the Future National Survey Results on Drug Use, 1975–2007: Volume II, College Students and Adults Age 19–45, 2007* (Bethesda, MD: National Institute on Drug Abuse, 2008), p. 258.

5. *Ibid.*

6. *Ibid.*, pp. 258–59.

7. *Ibid.*, pp. 260–62.

8. *Ibid.*, p. 260.

9. Kim Fromme, William R. Corbin, and Marc I. Kruse, "Behavioral Risks During the Transition from High School to College," *Developmental Psychology* 44, 5 (2008): 1497–1504.

10. Kenneth J. Sher and Patricia C. Rutledge, "Heavy Drinking Across the Transition to College: Predicting First-Semester Heavy Drinking from Precollege Variables," *Addictive Behaviors* 32, 4 (2007): 819–35.

11. *Ibid.*, U.S. Department of Health and Human Services, SAMHSA's National Clearinghouse for Alcohol and Drug Information, "Binge Drinking in Adolescents and College Students," http://ncadi.samhsa.gov/govpubs/rpo995/; Alan Reifman and Wendy K. Watson, "Binge Drinking During the First Semester of College: Continuation and Desistance from High School Patterns," *Journal of American College Health* 52, 2 (2003): 73–81; Henry Wechsler, Andrea Davenport, George W. Dowdall, Barbara Moeykens, and Sonia Castillo, "Health and Behavioral Conse-

quences of Binge Drinking in College: A National Survey of Students at 140 Campuses," *Journal of the American Medical Association* 272 (1994): 1672–77.

12. Amelia M. Arria, Vanessa Kuhn, Kimberly M. Caldeira, Kevin E. O'Grady, Kathryn B. Vincent, and Eric D. Wish, "High School Drinking Mediates the Relationship Between Parental Monitoring and College Drinking: A Longitudinal Analysis," *Substance Abuse Treatment, Prevention, and Policy* 3 (2008): 6; John S. Baer, Daniel R. Kivlahan, and G. Alan Marlatt, "High-Risk Drinking Across the Transition from High School to College," *Alcoholism: Clinical and Experimental Research* 19, 1 (2006): 54–58; Frances M. Sessa, "The Influence of Perceived Parenting on Substance Use During the Transition to College: A Comparison of Male Residential and Commuter Students," *Journal of College Student Development* 46 (2005): 62–74.

13. University of Michigan News Service, "Various Stimulant Drugs Show Continuing Gradual Declines Among Teens in 2008, Most Illicit Drugs Hold Steady," December 11, 2008, http://monitoringthefuture.org/data/08data.html#2008data-drugs. *See also* U.S. Department of Health and Human Services, *Monitoring the Future National Survey Results on Adolescent Drug Use: Overview of Key Findings, 2008* (Bethesda, MD: National Institute on Drug Abuse, 2009).

14. *Ibid.*

15. U.S. Department of Health and Human Services, *Monitoring the Future National Survey Results on Drug Use, 1975–2007: Volume I, Secondary School Students, 2007* (Bethesda, MD: National Institute on Drug Abuse, 2008), pp. 94–95, 116–20, 251.

16. *Monitoring the Future National Survey Results on Drug Use, 1975–2007: Volume II*, pp. 240–42.

17. Cited in Narconon Drug Detox Rehab Program in America, "Effects of Heavy Marijuana Use on Learning and Social Behavior," http://www.theroadout.org/drug_information/marijuana/effects_of_heavy_marijuana_use_on_learning_and_social_behavior.html. *See also* Judith S. Brook, Elinor B. Balka, and Martin Whiteman, "Risks for Late Adolescence of Early Adolescent Marijuana Use," *American Journal of Public Health* 89, 10 (1999): 1549–54.

18. Kimberly M. Caldeira, Amelia M. Arria, Kevin E. O'Grady, Kathryn B. Vincent,

and Eric D. Wish, "The Occurrence of Cannabis Use Disorders and Other Cannabis-Related Problems Among First-Year College Students," *Addictive Behaviors* 33, 3 (2008): 397–411.

19. See, for example, Louisa Degenhardt, Wayne Hall, and Michael Lynskey, "Exploring the Association Between Cannabis Use and Depression," *Addiction* 98, 11 (2003): 1493–1504; Robert I. Block and Mohamed M. Ghoneim, "Effects of Chronic Marijuana Use on Human Cognition," *Psychopharmacology* 110 (1993): 219–28; Harrison G. Pope, Jr. and Deborah Yurgelun-Todd, "The Residual Cognitive Effects of Heavy Marijuana Use in College Students," *Journal of the American Medical Association* 275, 7 (1996): 521–27.

20. National Institutes of Health, National Institute on Drug Abuse, Research Report Series — Marijuana Abuse, "How Does Marijuana Use Affect School, Work, and Social Life?" (July 22, 2008), http://www.nida.nih.gov/ResearchReports/Marijuana/Marijuana4.html.

21. Community Epidemiology Work Group, *Epidemiologic Trends in Drug Abuse, Vol. II, Proceedings of the Community Epidemiology Work Group, December 2003* (Bethesda, MD: National Institute on Drug Abuse, 2004). *See also* Denise B. Kandel and Mark Davies, "High School Students Who Use Crack and Other Drugs," *Archives of General Psychiatry* 53, 1 (1996): 71–80.

22. R. Barri Flowers, *Drugs, Alcohol and Criminality in American Society* (Jefferson, NC: McFarland, 2008), pp. 137–45; R. Barri Flowers, *The Adolescent Criminal: An Examination of Today's Juvenile Offender* (Jefferson, NC: McFarland, 2009), pp. 83–97; National Highway Traffic Safety Administration (NHTSA), "Marijuana and Alcohol Combined Severely Impede Driving Performance," *Annals of Emergency Medicine* 35, 4 (2000): 398–99.

23. Office of National Drug Control Policy, "Club Drugs Facts and Figures," http://www.whitehousedrugpolicy.gov/drugfact/club/club_drug_ff.html.

24. CampusHealthandSafety.org, "Date Rape and Club Drugs," http://www.campushealthandsafety.org/drugs/club-drugs/.

25. "Date Rape and Club Drugs"; R. Barri Flowers, *Sex Crimes: Perpetrators, Predators, Prostitutes, and Victims*, 2d ed. (Springfield,

IL: Charles C Thomas, 2006), pp. 54–57; Tennessee Victims of Crime State Coordinating Council, "Date Rape Drugs," http://www.tcadsv.org/Websites/vcscc/daterapedrugs.htm; Laura Hensley Choate, "Sexual Assault Prevention Programs for College Men: An Exploratory Evaluation of the Men Against Violence Model," *Journal of College Counseling* 6 (2003): 166–76.

26. "Date Rape and Club Drugs."

27. "Club Drugs Facts and Figures."

28. Cited in Jeffrey S. Simons, Raluca M. Gaher, Christopher J. Correia, and Jacqueline A. Bush, "Club Drug Use Among College Students," *Addictive Behaviors* 30, 8 (2005): 1620.

29. *Ibid.*

30. *Ibid.*, pp. 1619–24.

31. *Ibid.*

32. National Institutes of Health, National Institute on Drug Abuse, "NIDA InfoFacts: Club Drugs (GHB, Ketamine, and Rohypnol)," http://www.drugabuse.gov/InfoFacts/clubdrugs.html; George S. Yacoubian, Jr., Meghan K. Green, and Ronald J. Peters, "Identifying the Prevalence and Correlates of Ecstasy and Other Club Drug (EOCD) Use Among High School Seniors," *Journal of Ethnicity in Substance Abuse* 2, 2 (2003): 53–66.

33. "Club Drugs Facts and Figures."

34. *Ibid.*; University of Arkansas for Medical Sciences, "'Club Drugs' Are Dangerous, Psychologist Warns Teens," March 21, 2002, http://www.uams.edu/today/2002/032102/club.htm.

35. U.S. Department of Education, Higher Education Center for Alcohol and Other Drug Abuse and Violence Prevention, "Rohypnol," http://www.higheredcenter.org/high-risk/drugs/club-drugs/rohypnol.

36. U.S. Department of Education, Higher Education Center for Alcohol and Other Drug Abuse and Violence Prevention, "GHB," http://www.higheredcenter.org/high-risk/drugs/club-drugs/ghb.

37. "Club Drugs Facts and Figures"; The Partnership for a Drug Free America, "Ketamine," http://www.drugfree.org/Portal/Drug_Guide/Ketamine.

38. Flowers, *Drugs, Alcohol and Criminality in American Society*, pp. 85–95; Addiction Treatment Resources for Parents of Teens and Young Adults, "Club Drugs: Know the Facts," http://www.drugrehabtreatment.com/club-drugs.html; Metropolitan Drug Commission,

"Rave/Club Drugs," http://www.metrodrug.org/drugs/clubdrugs.aspx.

39. U.S. Department of Education, Higher Education Center for Alcohol and Other Drug Abuse and Violence Prevention, "Prescription Abuse Among College Students," http://www.higheredcenter.org/services/assistance/topics/prescription-drug-abuse-among-college-students; Sean Esteban McCabe, Christian J. Teter, Carol J. Boyd, John R. Knight, and Henry Wechsler, "Nonmedical Use of Prescription Opioids Among U.S. College Students," *Addictive Behaviors* 30, 4 (2005): 789–805.

40. Cited in Lori Whitten, "Studies Identify Factors Surrounding Rise in Abuse of Prescription Drugs by College Students," *NIDA Notes* 20, 4 (2006), http://www.drugabuse.gov/NIDA_notes/NNvol20N4/Studies.html.

41. McCabe, Teter, Boyd, Knight, and Wechsler, "Nonmedical Use of Prescription Opioids Among U.S. College Students"; Sean Esteban McCabe, John R. Knight, Christian J. Teter, and Henry Wechsler, "Nonmedical Use of Prescription Stimulants Among U.S. College Students: Prevalence and Correlates From a National Survey," *Addition* 99 (2005): 96–106; Richard Kadison, "Getting an Edge: Use of Stimulants and Antidepressants in College," *New England Journal of Medicine* 353 (2005): 1089–91.

42. Cited in Whitten, "Studies Identify Factors Surrounding Rise in Abuse of Prescription Drugs." *See also* Audrey M. Shillington, Mark B. Reed, James E. Lange, John D. Clapp, and Susan Henry, "College Undergraduate Ritalin Abusers in Southwestern California: Protective and Risk Factors," *Journal of Drug Issues* 36, 4 (2006): 999–1014.

43. Whitten, "Studies Identify Factors Surrounding Rise in Abuse of Prescription Drugs."

44. Sean Esteban McCabe and Christian J. Teter, "Drug Use Related Problems Among Nonmedical Users of Prescription Stimulants: A Web-Based Survey of College Students from a Midwestern University," *Drug Alcohol Depend* 91, 1 (2007): 69–76. *See also* Christian J. Teter, Sean Esteban McCabe, Kristy La-Grange, James A. Cranford, and Carol J. Boyd, "Illicit Use of Specific Prescription Stimulants Among College Students: Prevalence, Motives, and Routes of Administration," *Pharmacology* 26 (2006): 1501–10; Sean P. Bar-

rett, Christine Darredeau, and Robert O. Pihl, "Patterns of Polysubstance Use in Drug Using University Students," *Human Psychopharmacology Clinical Experience* 21 (2006): 225–63.

45. Lynda Erinoff, quoted in Whitten, "Studies Identify Factors Surrounding Rise in Abuse of Prescription Drugs."

46. "Prescription Abuse Among College Students." *See also* Barbara P. White, Kathryn A. Becker-Blease, Kathleen Grace-Bishop, "Stimulant Medication Use, Misuse, and Abuse in an Undergraduate and Graduate Student Sample," *Journal of American College Health* 54 (2006): 261–68.

47. Erinoff, quoted in Whitten, "Studies Identify Factors Surrounding Rise in Abuse of Prescription Drugs."

48. Flowers, *Drugs, Alcohol and Criminality in American Society*, pp. 86–95; Whitten, "Studies Identify Factors Surrounding Rise in Abuse of Prescription Drugs"; Elizabeth Ashton, "Alcohol Abuse Makes Prescription Drug Abuse More Likely," *NIDA Notes* 21, 5 (2008) http://www.nida.nih.gov/NIDA_notes/NNvol21N5/alcohol.html; Sean Esteban McCabe, Brady T. West, and Henry H. Wechsler, "Alcohol-Use Disorders and Nonmedical Use of Prescription Drugs Among U.S. College Students," *Journal of Studies on Alcohol and Drugs* 68, 4 (2007): 543–47.

49. KCTV News Homepage/Health, "Pain Meds Riskier Than Pot, Students Say" (September 3, 2008), http://www.kctv5.com/health/17379322/detail.html.

50. *Ibid.*; Society for Prevention Research, "First Year College Students Think Using Pain Killers and Stimulants Nonmedically is Less Risky Than Cocaine; More Risky Than Marijuana" September 3, 2008, http://www.preventionresearch.org/sprnews.php.

51. *Ibid.*; "Pain Meds Riskier Than Pot, Students Say."

52. "Drug Bust Highlights College Students' Rising Drug Use," *Education Reporter* 270 (July 2008), http://www.eagleforum.org/educate/2008/july08/rising-drug-use.html; Tony Perry, "96 Arrested in San Diego Drug Bust," *Los Angeles Times,* May 7, 2008, http://articles.latimes.com/2008/may/07/local/me-drugbust7.

53. "Drug Bust Highlights College Students' Rising Drug Use."

54. U.S. Department of Justice, Bureau of Justice Statistics Special Report, *Violent Vic-*

timization of College Students, 1995–2002 (Washington, D.C.: Office of Justice Programs, 2005), pp. 1–7; U.S. Department of Justice, Federal Bureau of Investigation, *School Violence, Crime in Schools and Colleges: A Study of Offenders and Arrestees Reported via National Incident-Based Reporting System Data* (October 2007), http://www.fbi.gov/ucr/schoolvio lence/2007/index.html; U.S. Department of Justice, Federal Bureau of Investigation, *Crime in the United States: Preliminary Semiannual Uniform Crime Report, January to June 2008,* January 12, 2009, http://www.fbi.gov/ucr/ 2008prelim/index.html.

55. Flowers, *Drugs, Alcohol and Criminality in American Society,* pp. 146–54; Flowers, *Kids Who Commit Adult Crimes,* pp. 46–50, 60–61; Flowers, *Sex Crimes,* pp. 54–56; Bonnie S. Fisher, Francis T. Cullen, and Michael G. Turner, *The Sexual Victimization of College Women* (Washington, D.C.: National Institute of Justice, Bureau of Justice Statistics, 2000); U.S. Department of Justice, Bureau of Justice Statistics Special Report, *National Crime Victimization Survey: Stalking Victimization in the United States* (Washington, D.C.: Office of Justice Programs, 2009); Patricia Tjaden and Nancy Thoennes, *Stalking in America: Findings From the National Violence Against Women Survey* (Washington, D.C.: National Institute of Justice, 1998).

56. Drug-Free Schools and Communities Act (1986), 20 U.S.C. 3181, P.L. 101–226; U.S. Department of Education, Higher Education Center for Alcohol and Other Drug Abuse and Violence Prevention, "Drug-Free Schools and Communities Act (DFSCA) and Drug and Alcohol Abuse Prevention Regulations," http://www.higheredcenter.org/mandates/dfs ca.

57. Student Right-to-Know and Campus Security Act (1990), P.L. 101–452.

58. Crime Awareness and Campus Security Act (1990), Title II of P.L. 101–542.

Chapter 3

1. U.S. Department of Justice, Bureau of Justice Statistics Special Report, *Violent Victimization of College Students, 1995–2002* (Washington, D.C.: Office of Justice Programs, 2005), p. 3.

2. *Ibid.,* pp. 1–7; Jamie Alexander, "A Look at College Student Victimization," *Front Sight Newsletter* (April 2004), http://www. frontsight.com/promotion/16/college.htm.

3. *Violent Victimization of College Students,* p. 5.

4. *Ibid.,* pp. 1–7.

5. U.S. Department of Justice, Federal Bureau of Investigation, School Violence, *Crime in Schools and Colleges: A Study of Offenders and Arrestees Reported via National Incident-Based Reporting System Data,* http:// www.fbi.gov/ucr/schoolviolence/2007/intro duction.htm.

6. U.S. Department of Justice, Federal Bureau of Investigation, *Crime in the United States 2007* (Washington, D.C.: Criminal Justice Information Services Division, 2008), http://www.fbi.gov/ucr/cius2007/offenses/ex panded_information/data/shrtable_02.html.

7. *Crime in Schools and Colleges.*

8. School Violence Resource Center, SVRC Fact Sheet, "Murders Involving the College Population," www.svrc.net/Files/Mur ders.pdf.

9. *Ibid.*; Mark Clayton, "Latest Murders Highlight Rise in Campus Crime," *Christian Science Monitor* (January 22, 2002), http:// www.csmonitor.com/2002/0122/p03s01-ussc.html.

10. My Student Health Zone, "Personal Safety," http://kidshealth.org/PageManager. jsp?dn=studenthealthzone&article_set=39373 &lic=180&cat_id=20305.

11. U.S. Department of Education, National Center for Education Statistics, *Indicators of School Crime and Safety: 2007* (Washington, D.C.: Institute of Education Sciences, 2007), p. 6.

12. *Ibid.*

13. R. Barri Flowers, *Murder, At the End of the Day and Night: A Study of Criminal Homicide Offenders, Victims, and Circumstances* (Springfield, IL: Charles C. Thomas, 2002), pp. 142–55; R. Barri Flowers, *Kids Who Commit Adult Crimes: A Study of Serious Juvenile Criminality and Delinquency* (Binghamton, NY: Haworth Press, 2002), pp 51–61.

14. Flowers, *Murder, At the End of the Day and Night,* pp. 142–43; Flowers, *Kids Who Commit Adult Crimes,* pp. 52–53; Wikipedia, the Free Encyclopedia, "School Shooting," http://en.wikipedia.org/wiki/School_mas sacre.

15. R. Barri Flowers and H. Loraine Flowers, *Murders in the United States: Crimes, Killers and Victims of the Twentieth Century* (Jefferson, NC: McFarland, 2004), pp. 37–38, 187.

16. *Ibid.*; Flowers, *Murder, At the End of the Day and Night*; Flowers, *Kids Who Commit Adult Crimes*; "School Shooting."

17. Wikipedia, the Free Encyclopedia, "List of School-Related Attacks," http://en.wikipedia.org/wiki/List_of_school-related_attacks.

18. "School Shooting."

19. R. Barri Flowers, *Male Crime and Deviance: Exploring Its Causes, Dynamics and Nature* (Springfield, IL: Charles C Thomas, 2003); Henry Wechsler, Matthew Miller, and David Hemenway, "College Alcohol Study: Guns at College," Harvard School of Public Health (2005), http://www.hsph.harvard.edu/cas/Documents/guns.

20. Flowers, *Murder, At the End of the Day and Night*; Flowers, *Kids Who Commit Adult Crimes*; Andrea Aldridge, "Killing Kids: Experts Offer Explanations for School Violence," *Unionite Online: The Union University Magazine* 51, 2 (2000), http://www.uu.edu/Unionite/winter00/killingkids.htm; Peter Langman, *Why Kids Kill: Inside the Minds of School Shooters* (New York: Palgrave Macmillan, 2009).

21. Douglas Lederman, "Weapons on Campus? Officials Warn That Colleges Are Not Immune From the Scourge of Handguns," *Chronicle of Higher Education* (March 9, 1994): A33–A34.

22. Wechsler, Miller, and Hemenway, "College Alcohol Study"; W. David Nichols, "Violence on Campus: The Intruded Sanctuary," *FBI Law Enforcement Bulletin* 64, 6 (1995): 1–5; Cheryl A. Presley, Philip W. Meilman, and Jeffrey R. Cashin, "Weapon Carrying and Substance Abuse Among College Students," *Journal of American College Health* 46, 1 (1997): 3–8.

23. Wechsler, Miller, and Hemenway, "College Alcohol Study"; Cheryl A. Presley, Philip W. Meilman, and Rob Lyerla, *Alcohol and Drugs on College Campuses: Use, Consequence, and Perceptions of the Campus Environment* (Carbondale, IL: Core Institute, 1993).

24. Cited in Wechsler, Miller, and Hemenway, "College Alcohol Study."

25. *Ibid.*

26. *Ibid.*

27. *Ibid.*

28. Flowers, *Murder, At the End of the Day and Night*, pp. 20–32; Flowers, *Male Crime and Deviance*; R. Barri Flowers, *Domestic Crimes, Family Violence and Child Abuse: A Study of Contemporary American Society* (Jefferson, NC: McFarland, 2000), pp. 62–70; Lowell W. Gerson, "Alcohol-Related Acts of Violence: Who Was Drinking and Where the Acts Occurred," *Journal of Studies on Alcohol and Drugs* 39, 7 (1978): 1294–96.

29. *Crime in Schools and Colleges*; Flowers and Flowers, *Murders in the United States*; Flowers, *Murder, At the End of the Day and Night*.

30. "School Shooting"; Wechsler, Miller, and Hemenway, "College Alcohol Study"; Lederman, "Weapons on Campus?"; Donna Leinwand, "4 States, Among Last Holdouts, Eye Open-Carry Gun Laws," *USA Today* (February 11, 2009), http://www.usatoday.com/news/nation/2009-02-11-guns_N.htm.

31. Chelsey Delaney, "Concealed Gun Bill Sparks Debate: Will Allowing College Students to Pack Heat Make Texas Campuses Safer?" ABC News (February 6, 2009), http://abcnews.go.com/OnCampus/Story?id=68056 80&page=1; Brady Campaign to Prevent Gun Violence, Brady Blog (June 18, 2008), http://www.bradycampaign.org/blog/?s=louisiana+campus.

32. Katie Thisdell, "JMU May Join Va. Tech in New Gun Policies," *The Breeze* (September 4, 2008), http://www.thebreeze.org/2008/09-04/news2.html.

33. Delaney, "Concealed Gun Bill Sparks Debate."

34. Flowers, *Kids Who Commit Adult Crimes*; Flowers, *Murder, At the End of the Day and Night*; Aldridge, "Killing Kids."

35. Quoted in Aldridge, "Killing Kids."

36. *Ibid.*

37. Flowers, *Domestic Crimes*; Flowers, *Murder, At the End of the Day and Night*; Langman, *Why Kids Kill*; Katherine S. Newman, Cybelle Fox, Wendy Roth, Jal Mehta, and David Harding, *Rampage: The Social Roots of School Shootings* (New York: Basic Books, 2005).

38. Langman, *Why Kids Kill*; Newman, Fox, Roth, Mehta, and Harding, *Rampage: The Social Roots of School Shootings*; Flowers, *Murder, At the End of the Day and Night*.

39. David Lester, *Serial Killers: The Insatiable Passion* (Philadelphia, PA: Charles Press, 1995), p. 65.

40. Donald T. Lunde, *Murder and Madness* (New York: Norton, 1979).

41. Quoted in Brenda Harkness, "Portraying a Mass Killer," http://www.mnash.edu.au/pubs/montage/Montage_97_02/killer.html

42. Flowers, *Murder, At the End of the Day and Night*; Flowers, *Kids Who Commit Adult Crimes*, pp. 52–54, 89–91; R. Barri Flowers, *The Adolescent Criminal: An Examination of Today's Juvenile Offender* (Jefferson, NC: McFarland, 2009), pp. 22–31.

43. Aldridge, "Killing Kids"; Flowers, *Murder, At the End of the Day and Night*.

44. Student Right-to-Know and Campus Security Act (1990), P.L. 101–452.

45. Crime Awareness and Campus Security Act (1990), Title II of P.L. 101–542.

46. Jeanne Clery Disclosure of Campus Security Policy and Campus Crime Statistics Act (1998), 20 U.S.C. § 1092(f).

47. Higher Education Opportunity Act (2008), P.L. 110–315.

48. *Ibid.*

49. *Ibid.*; *Crime in Schools and Colleges.*

50. U.S. Department of Justice, National Institute of Justice, "Laws to Make Campuses Safer" (October 1, 2008), http://www.ojp.usdoj.gov/nij/topics/crime/rape-sexual-violence/campus/laws.htm.

51. *Ibid.*

52. *Ibid.*

53. Security on Campus, Inc., "2008 Clery Act Amendments: Included in Higher Education Opportunity Act (P.L. 110–315) Enacted into Law August 14, 2008; Effective Immediately," http://www.securityoncampus.org/index.php?option=com_content&view=article&id=345%3A2008cleryactamendments&catid=64%3Acleryact&Itemid=60.

54. U.S. Department of Justice, Bureau of Justice Statistics Special Report, *Campus Law Enforcement, 2004–05* (Washington, D.C.: Office of Justice Programs, 2008), p. 1.

55. *Ibid.*

56. U.S. Secret Service, National Threat Assessment Center, "Preventing School Shootings: A Summary of a U.S. Secret Service Safe School Initiative Report," *National Institute of Justice Journal* 248 (2002): 10–15, http://www.ncjrs.gov/rr/vol4_2/38.html; Sam Houston University, "Right to Know and Campus Security Act of 1990," http://www.shsu.edu/students/righttoknow.html.

Chapter 4

1. U.S. Department of Justice, Bureau of Justice Statistics, Crime Victimization in the United States — Statistical Tables Index, http://www.ojp.usdoj.gov/bjs/abstract/cvus/definitions.htm#rape_sexual_assault.

2. R. Barri Flowers, *Sex Crimes: Perpetrators, Predators, Prostitutes, and Victims*, 2d ed. (Springfield, IL: Charles C Thomas, 2006), pp. 22–25; Joel Epstein and Stacia Langenbahn, *The Criminal Justice and Community Response to Rape* (Washington, D.C.: National Institute of Justice, 1994), p. 7.

3. R. Barri Flowers, *The Victimization and Exploitation of Women and Children: A Study of Physical, Mental and Sexual Maltreatment in the United States* (Jefferson, NC: McFarland, 1994), p. 144.

4. Flowers, *Sex Crimes.*

5. R. Barri Flowers, *Women and Criminality: The Woman as Victim, Offender, and Practitioner* (Westport, CT: Greenwood Press, 1987), p. 28.

6. Kaare Svalastoga, "Rape and Social Structure," *Pacific Sociological Review* 5 (1962): 48–53.

7. Dean Kilpatrick, "Sexual Assault," in Grace Coleman, Mario Gaboury, Morna Murray, and Anne Seymour, eds., *National Victim Assistance Academy* (Washington, D.C.: U.S. Office for Victims of Crime, 1999), http://www.ojp.usdoj.gov/ovc/assist/nvaa99/welcome.html; Laura Rymel, *What is the Difference Between Rape and Sexual Assault?* (Little Rock, AR: School Violence Resource Center, 2004), pp. 1–2.

8. Heather M. Karjane, Bonnie S. Fisher, and Francis T. Cullen, *Campus Sexual Assault: How America's Institutions of Higher Education Respond* (Newton, MA: Educational Development Center, Inc., 2002), pp. 32–34; Patricia Searles and Ronald J. Berger, "The Current Status of Rape Reform Legislation: An Examination of State Statutes," *Women's Rights Law Reporter* 10 (1987): 25–43.

9. The Illinois Criminal Sexual Assault Act (1983), 720 ILCS 5/12–13.

10. Vice President For Campus Life and

Dean of Students in the University, "Sexual Assault and Sexual Abuse," http://sexualviolence.uchicago.edu/assault.shtml.

11. Kilpatrick, "Sexual Assault"; Cornell Law School, Legal Information Institute, U.S. Code Collection, Title 18, Part 1, Chapter 109A, http://www4.law.cornell.edu/uscode/html/uscode18/usc_sup_01_18_10_I_20_109A.html.

12. Title 18, Part 1, Chapter 109A (1986), § 2242, Sexual Abuse.

13. Title 18, Part 1, Chapter 109A (1986), § 2241, Aggravated Sexual Abuse.

14. Jeanne Clery Disclosure of Campus Security Policy and Campus Crime Statistics Act, (1998), 20 U.S.C. § 1092(f). *See also* Bonnie S. Fisher, "Campus Crime and Fear of Victimization: Judicial, Legislative and Administrative Responses," *The Annals of the American Academy of Political and Social Science* 539 (1995): 85–101.

15. Karjane, Fisher, and Cullen, *Campus Sexual Assault*, pp. 32–33; U.S. Department of Justice, Federal Bureau of Investigation, *Uniform Crime Reports*, http://www.fbi.gov/ucr/ucr.htm.

16. U.S. Department of Justice, Bureau of Justice Statistics Special Report, *Violent Victimization of College Students, 1995–2002* (Washington, D.C.: Office of Justice Programs, 2005), p. 2; Rape, Abuse and Incest National Network, "How Often Does Sexual Assault Occur?" http://www.rainn.org/get-information/statistics/frequency-of-sexual-assault.

17. Cited in Rape, Abuse and Incest National Network, "Who Are the Victims?" http://www.rainn.org/get-information/statistics/sexual-assault-victims.

18. Cited in *ibid.*; "Statistics," http://www.rainn.org/statistics; Walter S. DeKeseredy and Katharine Kelly, "The Incidence and Prevalence of Women Abuse in Canadian University and College Dating Relationships," *Canadian Journal of Sociology* 18 (1993): 137–59.

19. Bonnie S. Fisher, Francis T. Cullen, and Michael G. Turner, *The Sexual Victimization of College Women* (Washington, D.C.: National Institute of Justice, Bureau of Justice Statistics, 2000); Mary P. Koss, Christine A Gidycz, and Nadine Wisniewski, "The Scope of Rape: Incidence and Prevalence of Sexual Aggression and Victimization in a National Sample of Higher Education Students," *Jour-*

nal of Consulting and Clinical Psychology 55, 2 (1987): 162–70.

20. Fisher, Cullen, and Turner, *The Sexual Victimization of College Women*; Koss, Gidycz, and Wisniewski, "The Scope of Rape."

21. Koss, Gidycz, and Wisniewski, "The Scope of Rape"; Fisher, Cullen, and Turner, *The Sexual Victimization of College Women*, p. 17; Arnie S. Kahn and V. Andreoli Mathie, "Understanding the Unacknowledged Rape Victim," in C. B. Travis and J. W. White, eds., *Sexuality, Society, and Feminism: Psychological Perspectives on Women* (Washington, D.C.: American Psychological Association, 2000), pp. 377–403.

22. Fisher, Cullen, and Turner, *The Sexual Victimization of College Women*; Karjane, Fisher, and Cullen, *Campus Sexual Assault*, pp. 4–5.

23. Flowers, *Sex Crimes*, pp. 51–58; Karjane, Fisher, and Cullen, *Campus Sexual Assault*, p. 4; Michele A. Paludi, *Sexual Harassment on College Campuses: Abusing the Ivory Power*, 2d ed. (Albany, NY: State University of New York Press, 1996).

24. Fisher, Cullen, and Turner, *The Sexual Victimization of College Women*, p. 9.

25. *Ibid.*

26. Koss, Gidycz, and Wisniewski, "The Scope of Rape."

27. Christopher P. Krebs, Christine H. Lindquist, Tara D. Warner, Bonnie S. Fisher, and Sandra L. Martin, *The Campus Sexual Assault (CSA) Study* (Rockville, MD: National Institute of Justice, 2007), pp. vii–xii.

28. Charlene L. Muehlenhard and Melaney A. Linton, "Date Rape and Sexual Aggression in Dating Situations: Incidence and Risk Factors," *Journal of Counseling Psychology* 34, 2 (1987): 186–96.

29. Kathy Douglas, Janet L. Collins, Charles Warren, Laura Kann, Robert Gold, Sonia Clayton, James G. Ross, and Lloyd J. Kolbe, "Results From the 1995 National College Health Risk Behavior Survey," *Journal of the American College Health Association* 46, 2 (1997): 55–66.

30. Fisher, Cullen, and Turner, *The Sexual Victimization of College Women*, pp. 15–20, 23–30; Bonnie S. Fisher, Leah E. Daigle, Francis T. Cullen, and Michael G. Turner, "Reporting Sexual Victimization To The Police And Others: Results From a National-Level Study of College Women," *Criminal Justice and Behavior* 30, 1 (2003): 6–38.

31. Karjane, Fisher, and Cullen, *Campus Sexual Assault*, p. xiii.

32. Krebs, Lindquist, Warner, Fisher, and Martin, *The Campus Sexual Assault (CSA) Study*, p. viii; National Center for Victims of Crime and Crime Victims Research and Treatment Center, *Rape in America: A Report to the Nation* (Arlington, VA: National Center for Victims of Crime, 1992); Melissa Holmes, Heidi S. Resnick, Dean G. Kilpatrick, and Connie L. Best, "Rape-Related Pregnancy: Estimates and Descriptive Characteristics from a National Sample of Women," *American Journal of Obstetrics and Gynecology* 175, 2 (1996): 320–24; Ted Miller, Mark A. Cohen, and Brian Wiersema, *Victim Costs and Consequences: A New Look* (Washington, D.C.: National Institute of Justice, 1996).

33. Cited in Rymel, *What is the Difference Between Rape and Sexual Assault?*, p. 6.

34. Fisher, Cullen, and Turner, *The Sexual Victimization of College Women*, p. 23.

35. Vernon R. Wiehe and Ann Richards, *Intimate Betrayal: Understanding and Responding to the Trauma of Acquaintance Rape* (Thousand Oaks, CA: Sage, 1995).

36. Mary P. Koss, Thomas E. Dinero, Cynthia A. Seibel, and Susan L. Cox, "Stranger and Acquaintance Rape: Are There Differences in the Victim's Experience?" *Psychology of Women Quarterly* 12, 1 (2006): 1–24.

37. Karjane, Fisher, and Cullen, *Campus Sexual Assault*, pp. vii, 9; Bernice Lott, Mary E. Reilly, and Dale Howard, "Sexual Assault and Harassment: A Campus Community Study," *Signs: Journal of Women in Culture and Society* 8, 2 (1982): 297–319.

38. Karjane, Fisher, and Cullen, *Campus Sexual Assault*, p. 5; Barrie Bondurant, "University Women's Acknowledgment of Rape: Individual, Situational, and Social Factors," *Violence Against Women: An International and Interdisciplinary Journal* 7, 3 (2001): 294–314; Martin D. Schwartz and Molly S. Leggett, "Bad Dates or Emotional Trauma? The Aftermath of Campus Sexual Assault," *Violence Against Women: An International and Interdisciplinary Journal* 5, 3 (1999): 251–71.

39. Fisher, Cullen, and Turner, *The Sexual Victimization of College Women*, p. 15.

40. Koss, Dinero, Seibel, and Cox, "Stranger and Acquaintance Rape."

41. Bondurant, "University Women's Acknowledgment of Rape"; Fisher, Daigle, Cullen, and Turner, "Reporting Sexual Victimization To The Police And Others"; Carol Bohmer and Andrea Parrot, *Sexual Assault on Campus: The Problem and the Solution* (New York: Lexington, 1993).

42. Krebs, Lindquist, Warner, Fisher, and Martin, *The Campus Sexual Assault (CSA) Study*, pp. 2–10; Fisher, Daigle, Cullen, and Turner, "Reporting Sexual Victimization To The Police And Others."

43. Karjane, Fisher, and Cullen, *Campus Sexual Assault*, pp. 9–11; Bohmer and Parrot, *Sexual Assault on Campus*.

44. Bohmer and Parrot, *Sexual Assault on Campus*; Robert Potter, Jeanne Krider, and Pamela McMahon, "Examining Elements of Campus Sexual Violence Policies: Is Deterrence or Health Promotion Favored?" *Violence Against Women* 6 (2000): 1345–62; Helen A. Neville and Aalece O. Pugh, "General and Cultural Specific Factors Influencing African American Women's Reporting Patterns and Perceived Social Support Following Sexual Assault," *Violence Against Women* 3, 4 (1997): 361–81.

45. Rape, Abuse and Incest National Network, "Statistics."

46. Flowers, *Sex Crimes*; Fisher, Cullen, and Turner, *The Sexual Victimization of College Women*; Bondurant, "University Women's Acknowledgment of Rape"; Margaret J. McGregor, Ellen Wiebe, Stephen A. Marion, and Cathy Livingstone, "Why Don't More Women Report Sexual Assault to the Police?" *Canadian Medical Association Journal* 165, 2 (2000): 659–60.

47. Mary P. Koss, "Hidden Rape: Sexual Aggression and Victimization in a National Sample of Students in Higher Education," in Ann W. Burgess, ed., *Rape and Sexual Assault II* (New York: Garland, 1988), pp. 3–25.

48. Fisher, Daigle, Cullen, and Turner, "Reporting Sexual Victimization To The Police And Others"; Fisher, Cullen, and Turner, *The Sexual Victimization of College Women*.

49. Mary P. Frintner and Laura Rubinson, "Acquaintance Rape: The Influence of Alcohol, Fraternity Membership, and Sports Team Membership," *Journal of Sex Education and Therapy* 12 (1993): 272–84.

50. Commission on Substance Abuse at Colleges and Universities, *Rethinking Rites of Passage: Substance Abuse on America's Campuses*

(New York: Columbia University, Center on Addiction and Substance Abuse, 1994).

51. Dennis M. Greene and Rachel L. Navarro, "Situation-Specific Assertiveness in the Epidemiology of Sexual Victimization Among University Women: A Prospective Path Analysis," *Psychology of Women Quarterly* 22 (1998): 589–604; Meichun Mohler-Kuo, George W. Dowdall, Mary P. Koss, and Henry Wechsler, "Correlates of Rape While Intoxicated in a National Sample of College Women," *Journal of Studies on Alcohol* 65, 1 (2004): 37–45.

52. Mohler-Kuo, Dowdall, Koss, and Wechsler, "Correlates of Rape While Intoxicated."

53. Your Total Health, "Drug Use a Factor in Two-Thirds of Sexual Assaults," *Health Day News* (June 1, 2006), http://yourtotalhealth. ivillage.com/drug-use-factor-in-twothirds-sexual-assaults.html.

54. R. Barri Flowers, *Drugs, Alcohol and Criminality in American Society* (Jefferson, NC: McFarland, 2008), pp. 103–111; U.S. Department of Education, Higher Education Center for Alcohol and Other Drug Abuse and Violence Prevention, "Other Drugs," http://www.higheredcenter.org/high-risk/drugs/.

55. Stacey Copenhaver and Elizabeth Grauerholz, "Sexual Victimization Among Sorority Women: Exploring the Link Between Sexual Violence and Institutional Practices," *Sex Roles: A Journal of Research* 24 (1991): 31–41.

56. Krebs, Lindquist, Warner, Fisher, and Martin, *The Campus Sexual Assault (CSA) Study*, p. xvi.

57. Leandra Lackie and Anton F. de Man, "Correlates of Sexual Aggression Among Male University Students," *Sex Roles: A Journal of Research* 37 (1997): 451–57.

58. Frintner and Rubinson, "Acquaintance Rape."

59. Theresa J. Brown, Kenneth E. Sumner, and Romy Nocera, "Understanding Sexual Aggression Against Women: An Examination of the Role of Men's Athletic Participation and Related Variables," *Journal of Interpersonal Violence* 17, 9 (2002): 937–52.

60. Scot B. Boeringer, "Associations of Rape-Supportive Attitudes with Fraternal and Athletic Participation," *Violence Against Women* 5, 1 (1999): 81–90. *See also* Joy Garrett-Gooding and Richard Senter, Jr., "Attitudes and Acts of Sexual Aggression on a University Campus," *Sociological Inquiry* 57, 4 (2007): 348–71.

61. Bohmer and Parrot, *Sexual Assault on Campus*; Patricia Y. Martin and Robert A. Hummer, "Fraternities and Rape on Campus," *Gender and Society* 3, 4 (1989): 457–73; Rana Sampson, *Acquaintance Rape of College Students* (Washington, D.C.: Office of Community Oriented Policing Services, 2002), p. 14.

62. Chris O'Sullivan, "Acquaintance Gang Rape on Campus," in Andrea Parrot and Laurie Bechhofer, eds., *Acquaintance Rape: The Hidden Crime* (New York: John Wiley, 1991), pp. 140–56.

63. Fisher, Cullen, and Turner, *The Sexual Victimization of College Women*, pp. 17–18.

64. Krebs, Lindquist, Warner, Fisher, and Martin, *The Campus Sexual Assault (CSA) Study*, p. xii.

65. Paige Hall Smith, Jacquelyn W. White, and Lindsay J. Holland, "A Longitudinal Perspective on Dating Violence Among Adolescent and College-Age Women," *American Journal of Public Health* 93, 7 (2003): 1104–09; Anne G. Walch and W. Eugene Broadhead, "Prevalence of Lifetime Sexual Victimization Among Women Patients," *Journal of Family Practice* 35 (1992): 511–16; Diana E. H. Russell, *The Secret Trauma: Incest in the Lives of Girls and Women* (New York: Basic Books, 1986).

66. Kimberly A. Hanson and Christine A. Gidcyz, "Evaluation of a Sexual Assault Program," *Journal of Consulting and Clinical Psychology* 61, 6 (1993): 1046–52.

67. Cited in Rymel, *What is the Difference Between Rape and Sexual Assault?*, p. 4.

68. Melissa J. Himelein, "Risk Factors for Sexual Victimization in Dating: A Longitudinal Study of College Women," *Psychology of Women Quarterly* 19, 1 (2006): 31–48.

69. Christine A. Gidcyz, Kimberly Hanson, and Melissa J. Layman, "A Prospective Analysis of the Relationships Among Sexual Assault Experiences: An Extension of Previous Findings," *Psychology of Women Quarterly* 19, 1 (1995): 5–29.

70. Nicole T. Harrington and Harold Leitenberg, "Relationship Between Alcohol Consumption and Victim Behaviors Immediately Preceding Sexual Aggression by an Acquain-

tance," *Violence and Victims* 9, 4 (1994): 315–24.

71. Education: Red Orbit, "A Dangerous Transition: High School to the First Year of College" (February 11, 2008), http://www.red orbit.com/news/education/1250094/a_dan gerous_transition_high_school_to_the_first_y ear_of/.

72. Maria Testa, Jennifer A. Livingston, and Kenneth E. Leonard, "Women's Substance Use and Experiences of Intimate Partner Violence: A Longitudinal Investigation Among A Community Sample," *Addictive Behaviors* 28, 9 (2003): 1649–64; Kimberly A. Tyler, Dan R. Hoyt, and Les B. Whitbeck, "Coercive Sexual Strategies," *Violence and Victims* 13, 1 (1998): 47–61.

73. Krebs, Lindquist, Warner, Fisher, and Martin, *The Campus Sexual Assault (CSA) Study*, pp. 2–6; R. Barri Flowers, *Kids Who Commit Adult Crimes: A Study of Serious Juvenile Criminality and Delinquency* (Binghamton, NY: Haworth Press, 2002), pp. 75–83; W. David Watts and Anne Marie Ellis, "Sexual Abuse, Drinking and Drug Use: Implications for Prevention," *Journal of Drug Education* 23 (1993): 183–200; Carla E. Grayson and Susan Nolen-Hoeksema, "Motives to Drink as Mediators Between Childhood Sexual Assault and Alcohol Problems in Adult Women," *Journal of Traumatic Stress* 18, 2 (2005): 137–45.

74. Rymel, *What is the Difference Between Rape and Sexual Assault?*, p. 8; Alan Berkowitz, "College Men as Perpetrators of Acquaintance Rape and Sexual Assault: A Review of Recent Research," *Journal of American College Health* 40 (1992): 175–81.

75. Rymel, *What is the Difference Between Rape and Sexual Assault?*, p. 8; Mary E. Reilly, Bernice Lott, Donna Caldwell, and Luisa DeLuca, "Tolerance for Sexual Harassment Related to Self-Reported Sexual Victimization," *Gender and Society* 6, 1 (1992): 122–38; Muehlenhard and Linton, "Date Rape and Sexual Aggression in Dating Situations."

76. Martha R. Burt, "Cultural Myths and Support for Rape," *Journal of Personality and Social Psychology* 38 (1980): 217–30.

77. R. Barri Flowers, *The Adolescent Criminal: An Examination of Today's Juvenile Offender* (Jefferson, NC: McFarland, 2009), pp. 133–39.

78. Jeanne Cyriaque, "The Chronic Serious Offender: How Illinois Juveniles 'Match Up,'" *Illinois* (February 1982), pp. 4–5.

79. Bohmer and Parrot, *Sexual Assault on Campus*; Peggy Sanday, *Fraternity Gang Rape: Sex, Brotherhood, and Privilege on Campus* (New York: New York University Press, 1990).

80. Fisher, Cullen, and Turner, *The Sexual Victimization of College Women*, p. 19.

81. *Ibid.*, p. 17.

82. Koss, Gidycz, and Wisniewski, "The Scope of Rape."

83. Eugene. J. Kanin and Stanley R. Parcell, "Sexual Aggression: A Second Look at the Offended Female," *Archives of Sexual Behavior* 6 (1977): 67–76.

84. John Briere and Neil M. Malamuth, "Predicting Self-Reported Likelihood of Sexually Abusive Behavior: Attitudinal Versus Sexual Explanations," *Journal of Research in Personality* 17 (1983): 315–23.

85. Flowers, *Kids Who Commit Adult Crimes*; Krebs, Lindquist, Warner, Fisher, and Martin, *The Campus Sexual Assault (CSA) Study*, pp. 6–10.

86. Krebs, Lindquist, Warner, Fisher, and Martin, *The Campus Sexual Assault (CSA) Study*, p. vii.

87. Flowers, *Sex Crimes*; Stanley L. Brodsky and Susan C. Hobart, "Blame Models and Assailant Research," *Criminal Justice and Behavior* 5 (1978): 379–88.

88. Paul H. Gebhard, John H. Gagnon, Wardell B. Pomeroy, and Cornelia V. Christenson, *Sex Offenders: An Analysis of Types* (New York: Harper & Row, 1965), pp. 198–204.

89. Flowers, *Women and Criminality*, p. 38; A. Nicholas Groth, Ann W. Burgess, and Lynda L. Holmstrom, "Rape: Power, Anger, and Sexuality," *American Journal of Psychiatry* 34 (1977): 1239–43.

90. Robert E. Freeman-Longo and Geral T. Blanchard, *Sexual Abuse in America; Epidemic of the 21st Century* (Brandon, VT: Safer Society Press, 1998), pp. 48–49; A Nicholas Groth and H. Jean Birnbaum, *Men Who Rape: The Psychology of the Offender* (New York: Plenum, 1979).

91. Diana Scully and Joseph Marolla, "Incarcerated Rapists: Exploring a Sociological Mode," *Final Report for Department of Health and Human Services* (Washington, D.C.: Government Printing Office, 1983), p. 63.

92. Student Right-to-Know and Campus Security Act (1990), 20 U.S.C. § 1092.

93. Wikipedia, the Free Encyclopedia, "Clery Act," http://en.wikipedia.org/wiki/Clery_Act.

94. Campus Sexual Assault Victims' Bill of Rights (1992), P.L. 102–325.

95. Security on Campus, Inc., "Security on Campus, Inc. Major Legislative Accomplishments," http://www.securityoncampus.org/index.php?option=com_content&view=article&id=295:majoraccomplishments&catid=58:federallegislation&Itemid=92.

96. *Ibid.*

97. Karjane, Fisher, and Cullen, *Campus Sexual Assault*, p. viii.

Chapter 5

1. R. Barri Flowers, *Kids Who Commit Adult Crimes: A Study of Serious Juvenile Criminality and Delinquency* (Binghamton, NY: Haworth Press, 2002), pp. 75–78.

2. Dating Violence Resource Center, "Campus Dating Violence Fact Sheet," http://www.ncvc.org/ncvc/main.aspx?dbID=DB_DatingViolenceResourceCenter101.

3. Women's Resource Center, "Stop Dating Violence," http://www.uh.edu/wrc/DatingViolence.html.

4. The Equity Office, "Statistics on Dating Violence," January 11, 2007, http://www.acadiau.ca/president/equity/harassment_sexual_dating.htm.

5. See, for example, Robert E. Billingham and Alan R. Sack, "Conflict Resolution Tactics and the Level of Emotional Commitment Among Unmarrieds," *Human Relations* 40 (1987): 59–74; Katherine E. Lane and Patricia A. Gwartney-Gibbs, "Violence in the Context of Dating and Sex," *Journal of Family Issues* 6, 1 (1985): 45–49.

6. David B. Sugarman and Gerald T. Hotaling, "Dating Violence: A Review of Contextual and Risk Factors, in Barrie Levy, ed., *Dating Violence: Young Women in Danger* (Seattle: Seal Press, 1998).

7. *Ibid.*; Flowers, *Kids Who Commit Adult Crimes*, pp. 75–83.

8. *Ibid.*; Sugarman and Hotaling, "Dating Violence."

9. National Center for Victims for Crime's report, Dating Violence on Campus, http://www.ncvc.org/ncvc/AGP.Net/Compo

nents/documentViewer/Download.aspxnz?DocumentID=37929.

10. "Campus Dating Violence Fact Sheet."

11. Cited in "Stop Dating Violence."

12. Cited in United Way of King County, "Teen Dating Violence," http://www.uwkc.org/kcca/impact/DVSA/teen.asp; Christine Wekerle and David A. Wolfe, "Dating Violence in Mid-Adolescence: Theory, Significance, and Emerging Prevention Initiatives," *Clinical Psychology Review* 19 (1999): 435–56.

13. Christine M. Forke, Rachel K. Myers, Marina Catallozzi, and Donald F. Schwarz, "Relationship Violence Among Female and Male College Undergraduate Students," *Archives Of Pediatrics & Adolescent Medicine* 162, 7 (2008): 634–41.

14. Cited in Asian & Pacific Islander Women and Family Safety Center, "Informational: Dating Violence Statistics," http://www.apiwfsc.org/apiwfsc/statistics_dating_violence.html.

15. *Ibid.*

16. Mary P. Koss, "Hidden Rape: Sexual Aggression and Victimization in a National Sample of Students in Higher Education," in Ann W. Burgess, ed., *Rape and Sexual Assault II* (New York: Garland, 1988).

17. Eugene J. Kanin and Stanley R. Parcell, "Sexual Aggression: A Second Look at the Offended Female," *Archives of Sexual Behavior* 6 (1977): 67–76.

18. Cited in "Campus Dating Violence Fact Sheet."

19. *Ibid.*

20. *Ibid.*

21. Patricia Tjaden and Nancy Thoennes, *Full Report of the Prevalence, Incidence, and Consequences of Violence Against Women: Findings From the National Violence Against Women Survey* (Washington, D.C.: National Institute of Justice; 2000).

22. Cited in "Dating and Domestic Violence on Campus," http://www.thesafespace.org/pdf/handout_dv_on_campus.pdf.

23. *Ibid.*

24. Cited in "Campus Dating Violence Fact Sheet."

25. *Ibid.*

26. Forke, Myers, Catallozzi, and Schwarz, "Relationship Violence Among Female and Male College Undergraduate Students."

27. Cited in "Campus Dating Violence Fact Sheet."

28. U.S. Department of Justice, Bureau of Justice Statistics, "Intimate Partner Violence in the United States," http://www.ojp.usdoj.gov/bjs/intimate/ipv.htm.

29. Cited in "Informational: Dating Violence Statistics."

30. Cited in Christine Sellers and Max Bromley, "Violent Behavior in College Student Dating Relationships: Implications for Campus Providers," *Journal of Contemporary Justice* 12, 1 (1996): 1–27.

31. "Campus Dating Violence Fact Sheet"; U.S. Department of Justice, Office of Justice Programs, "Laws to Make Campuses Safer," http://www.ojp.usdoj.gov/nij/topics/crime/rape-sexual-violence/campus/laws.htm.

32. M. S. Plass and J. C. Gessner, "Violence in Courtship Relations: A Southern Example," *Free Inquiry in Creative Sociology* 11 (1983): 198–202; Bruce Roscoe and Tammy Kelsey, "Dating Violence Among High School Students," *Psychology* 23, 1 (1986): 53–59.

33. Mary R. Laner, "Competition and Combativeness in Courtship: Reports From Men," *Journal of Family Violence* 4, 1 (1989): 47–62.

34. Ileana Arias, Mary Samios, and K. Daniel O'Leary, "Prevalence and Correlates of Physical Aggression During Courtship," *Journal of Interpersonal Violence* 2, 1 (1987): 82–90; Linda L. Marshall and Patricia Rose, "Gender, Stress, and Violence in Adult Relationships of a Sample of College Students," *Journal of Social and Personal Relationships* 4 (1987): 299–316.

35. J. D. Goodchilds and G. L. Zellman, "Sexual Signaling and Sexual Aggression in Adolescent Relationships," in Neil Malamuth and E. Donnerstein, eds., *Pornography and Sexual Aggression* (Orlando, FL: Academic Press, 1984); Neil M. Malamuth, "Rape Proclivity Among Males," *Journal of Social Issues* 37, 4 (1981): 138–57.

36. Flowers, *Kids Who Commit Adult Crimes*, pp. 75–83; R. Barri Flowers, *Domestic Crimes, Family Violence and Child Abuse: A Study of Contemporary American Society* (Jefferson, NC: McFarland, 2000), pp. 167–74.

37. Cressida Wasserman, "Dating Violence on Campus: A Fact of Life," U.S. Department of Education's Higher Education Center for Alcohol and Other Drug Abuse and Violence Prevention, pp. 17–21, http://www.highered

center.org/resources/dating-violence-campus-fact-life.

38. *Ibid.*

39. Bonnie S. Fisher, Francis T. Cullen, and Michael G. Turner, *The Sexual Victimization of College Women* (Washington, D.C.: National Institute of Justice, Bureau of Justice Statistics, 2000). *See also* Carolyn Palmer, *Violent Crimes and Other Forms of Victimization in Residence Halls* (Asheville, NC: College Administration Publications, 1993).

40. Timothy C. Hart, *Violent Victimization of College Students* (Washington, D.C.: U.S. Department of Justice, Bureau of Justice Statistics, 2003).

41. Bonnie S. Fisher, Francis T. Cullen, and Michael G. Turner, "Being Pursued: Stalking Victimization in a National Study of College Women," *Criminology and Public Policy* 1, 2 (2002): 257–308.

42. Cited in Wasserman, "Dating Violence on Campus," p. 19.

43. *Ibid.*; Carolyn J. Palmer, "Violence and Other Forms of Victimization in Residence Halls: Perspectives of Resident Assistants," *Journal of College Student Development* 37, 3 (1996): 268–78.

44. Forke, Myers, Catallozzi, and Schwarz, "Relationship Violence Among Female and Male College Undergraduate Students"; Paige Hall Smith, Jacquelyn W. White, and Lindsay J. Holland, "A Longitudinal Perspective on Dating Violence Among Adolescent and College-Age Women," *American Journal of Public Health* 93, 7 (2003):1104–09; Flowers, *Domestic Crimes, Family Violence and Child Abuse*; Kenneth A. Chase, Dominique Treboux, and K. Daniel O'Leary, "Characteristics of High-risk Adolescents' Dating Violence," *Journal of Interpersonal Violence* 17, 1 (2002): 33–49.

45. Smith, White, and Holland, "A Longitudinal Perspective on Dating Violence."

46. Forke, Myers, Catallozzi, and Schwarz, "Relationship Violence Among Female and Male College Undergraduate Students."

47. Flowers, *Kids Who Commit Adult Crimes*, pp. 75–82; Smith, White, and Holland, "A Longitudinal Perspective on Dating Violence"; Barrie Levy, "Abusive Teen Dating Relationship: An Emerging Issue for the 90s," *Response to the Victimization of Women and Children* 13, 1 (1990): 59; Maura O'Keefe and Leah Aldridge, "Teen Dating Violence: A Re-

view of Risk Factors and Prevention Efforts," National Online Resource Center on Violence Against Women, http://new.vawnet.org/category/Main_Doc.php?docid=409.

48. Cited in "Informational: Dating Violence Statistics."

49. Cited in "Teen Dating Violence."

50. Cited in Carrie Mulford and Peggy C. Giordano, *Teen Dating Violence: A Closer Look at Adolescent Romantic Relationships* (Washington, D.C.: National Institute of Justice, 2008), http://www.ojp.usdoj.gov/nij/journals/261/teen-dating-violence.htm.

51. *Ibid.*

52. Cited in R. Barri Flowers, *Sex Crimes: Perpetrators, Predators, Prostitutes, and Victims*, 2d ed. (Springfield, IL: Charles C Thomas, 2006), pp. 51–60.

53. Sheila Kuehl, "Legal Remedies for Teen Dating Violence," in Barrie Levy, ed., *Dating Violence: Young Women in Danger* (Seattle: Seal Press, 1998), p. 209; Centers for Disease Control and Prevention, National Center for Injury Prevention and Control, "Dating Abuse fact Sheet," http://www.cdc.gov/ncipc/dvp/DatingViolence.htm; Alabama Coalition Against Domestic Violence, "Dating Violence," http://www.acadv.org/dating.html; Sarah Avery-Leaf, Michele Cascardi, K. Daniel O'Leary, and Annmarie Cano, "Efficacy of a Dating Violence Prevention Program on Attitudes Justifying Aggression," *Journal of Adolescent Health* 21 (1997): 11–7.

54. National Center for Victims of Crime, "Teen Dating Violence Fact Sheet"; Carolyn T. Halpern, Mary L. Young, Martha W. Waller, Sandra L. Martin, and Lawrence L. Kupper, "Prevalence of Partner Violence in Same-Sex Romantic Relationships in a National Sample of Adolescents," *Journal of Adolescent Health* 35 (2004): 124–131.

55. Cited in "Informational: Dating Violence Statistics"; Flowers, *Kids Who Commit Adult Crimes*; Bert H. Hoff, "Battered Men: The Hidden Side of Domestic Violence," MenWeb, http://www.menweb.org/battered/fiebertdate.htm#10.

56. Billingham and Sack, "Conflict Resolution Tactics and the Level of Emotional Commitment Among Unmarrieds"; M. O'-Keefe, K. Brockopp, and E. Chew, "Teen Dating Violence," *Social Work* 31 (1986): 465–68; Alice Lo Waiping and Michael J. Sporakowski, "The Continuation of Violent Dating Rela-

tionships Among College Students," *Journal of College Student Development* 30 (1989): 432–39.

57. Flowers, *Sex Crimes*, pp. 51–60; Centers for Disease Control and Prevention, "Physical Dating Violence Among High School Students–United States, 2003," *Morbidity and Mortality Weekly Report* 55, 19 (2006): 532–535; Vangie A. Foshee, "Gender Differences in Adolescent Dating Abuse Prevalence, Types, and Injuries," *Health Education Research* 11, 3 (1996): 275–286.

58. Forke, Myers, Catallozzi, and Schwarz, "Relationship Violence Among Female and Male College Undergraduate Students."

59. Rohini Luthra and Christine A. Gidycz, "Dating Violence Among College Men and Women," *Journal of Interpersonal Violence* 21, 6 (2006): 717–31.

60. Cited in Hoff, "Battered Men"; Flowers, *Domestic Crimes, Family Violence and Child Abuse*, pp. 92–96.

61. Martin S. Fiebert and Denise M. Gonzalez, "College Women Who Initiate Assaults on their Male Partners and the Reasons Offered for Such Behavior," *Psychological Reports* 80 (1997): 583–590.

62. K. Daniel O'Leary, A. M. Smith Slep, Sarah Avery-Leaf, and Michele Cascardi, "Gender Differences in Dating Aggression Among Multiethnic High School Students," *Journal of Adolescent Health* 42 (2008): 473–479.

63. Timothy A. Roberts and Jonathan D. Klein, "Intimate Partner Abuse and High-Risk Behavior in Adolescents," *Archives of Pediatrics and Adolescent Medicine* 157 (2003): 375–80.

64. Carolyn T. Halpern, Selene G. Oslak, Mary L. Young, Sandra L. Martin, and Lawrence L. Kupper, "Partner Violence Among Adolescents in Opposite-Sex Romantic Relationships: Findings From the National Longitudinal Study of Adolescent Health," *American Journal of Public Health* 91, 10 (2001): 1679–85.

65. Cited in Advocates for Youth, "The facts: Dating Violence Among Adolescents," http://www.advocatesforyouth.org/publications/factsheet/fsdating.htm; "Informational: Dating Violence Statistics." *See also* Denise Gamache, "Domination and Control; The Social Context of Dating Violence," in Barrie Levy, ed., *Dating Violence: Young Women in Danger* (Seattle: Seal Press, 1998).

66. Halpern, Young, Waller, Martin, and Kupper, "Prevalence of Partner Violence in Same-Sex Romantic and Sexual Relationships in a National Sample of Adolescents."

67. Naomi Freedner, Lorraine H. Freed, Y. Wendy Yang, and S. Bryn Austin, "Dating Violence Among Gay, Lesbian, and Bisexual Adolescents: Results From a Community Survey," *Journal of Adolescent Health* 31 (2002): 469–74.

68. Cited in Flowers, *Kids Who Commit Adult Crimes*, pp. 75–84; Cheryl A. Presley, Jami S. Leichliter, and Philip W. Meilman, *Alcohol and Drugs on American College Campuses: A Report to College Presidents* (Carbondale, IL: Southern Illinois University, 1999); Antonia Abbey, "Acquaintance Rape and Alcohol Consumption on College Campuses: How Are They Linked?" *Journal of American College Health* 39 (1991): 165–169.

69. Cited in Presley, Leichliter, and Meilman, *Alcohol and Drugs on American College Campuses.*

70. Cited in Anne Seymour, Morna Murray, Jane Sigmon, Melissa Hook, Christine Edmunds, Mario Gaboury, and Grace Coleman, *2000 National Victim Assistance Academy* (Washington, D.C.: U.S. Department of Justice, Office for Victims of Crime, 2008).

71. See, for example, S. Brodbelt, "College Dating and Violence," *College Student Journal* 17 (1983): 273–77; Angela R. Gover, "Risky Lifestyles and Dating Violence: A Theoretical Test of Violent Victimization," *Journal of Criminal Justice* 32, 1 (2004): 171–80; Jay G. Silverman, Anita Raj, Lorelei A. Mucci, and Jeanne E. Hathaway, "Dating Violence Against Adolescent Girls and Associated Substance Use, Unhealthy Weight Control, Sexual Risk Behavior, Pregnancy, and Suicidality," *Journal of the American Medical Association* 286, 5 (2001): 572–79.

72. Flowers, *Sex Crimes*, pp. 51–60; Flowers, *Kids Who Commit Adult Crimes*, pp. 75–83; University of Chicago, Vice President for Campus Life and Dean of Students, "Sexual Violence: Acquaintance/Date Rape," http://sexualviolence.uchicago.edu/daterape.shtml.

73. Flowers, *Kids Who Commit Adult Crimes*, pp. 77–82; Flowers, *Sex Crimes*, pp. 53–59; Flowers, *Domestic Crimes, Family Violence and Child Abuse*, pp. 168–72; David A. Wolfe, Christine Wekerle, Katreena Scott, Anna-Lee Straatman, and Carolyn Grasley,

"Predicting Abuse in Adolescent Dating Relationships Over 1 Year: The Role of Child Maltreatment and Trauma," *Journal of Abnormal Psychology* 113, 3 (2004): 406–15.

74. Sugarman and Hotaling, "Dating Violence"; Carol K. Sigelman, Carol J. Berry, and Katharine A. Wiles, "Violence in College Students' Dating Relationships," *Journal of Applied Social Psychology* 14, 6 (1984): 530–48.

75. Mulford and Giordano, *Teen Dating Violence*; Rebecca E. Dobash and Russell P. Dobash, *Violence Against Wives: A Case Against the Patriarchy* (London: Open Books, 1980); Michael S. Kimmel, "Gender Symmetry in Domestic Violence: A Substantive and Methodological Research Review," *Violence Against Women* 8 (2002): 1332–63.

76. National Center for Victims of Crime, "Minor's Access to Protective Orders," http://www.ncvc.org/ncvc/main.aspx?dbName=DocumentViewer&DocumentID=++32674.

77. Student Right-to-Know and Campus Security Act (1990), 20 U.S.C. § 1092.

78. Campus Sexual Assault Victims' Bill of Rights (1992), P.L. 102–325.

79. Higher Education Amendments (1998), P.L. 105–244.

80. Cited in Wasserman, "Dating Violence on Campus," pp. 20–21; Heather M. Karjane, Bonnie S. Fisher, and Francis T. Cullen, *Campus Sexual Assault: How America's Institutions of Higher Education Respond* (Newton, MA: Education Development Center, Inc., 2002).

Chapter 6

1. Lorraine Sheridan and Graham M. Davies, "Stalking: The Elusive Crime," *Legal and Criminological Psychology* 6, 2 (2001): 133–47; Lorraine Phillips, Ryan Quirk, Barry Rosenfeld, and Maureen O'Connor, "Is It Stalking? Perceptions of Stalking Among College Undergraduates," *Criminal Justice and Behavior* 31, 1 (2004): 73–96.

2. U.S. Department of Justice, Bureau of Justice Statistics Special Report, *National Crime Victimization Survey: Stalking Victimization in the United States* (Washington, D.C.: Office of Justice Programs, 2009), p. 3.

3. National Center for Victims of Crime, Stalking Resource Center, "Criminal Stalking

Laws by State/Oregon," http://www.ncvc.org/src/main.aspx?dbID=DB_Oregon179.

4. North Dakota Council on Abused Women's Services, Coalition Against Sexual Assault in North Dakota, "What is Stalking? Definitions," http://www.ndcaws.org/harassment/stalkinglaws.asp.

5. *Stalking Victimization in the United States*, p. 1.

6. *Ibid.*

7. Cited in U.S. Department of Justice, Office of Justice Programs, "Stalking," http://www.ojp.usdoj.gov/nij/topics/crime/stalking/welcome.htm#tja. See also Patricia Tjaden and Nancy Thoennes, *Stalking in America: Findings From the National Violence Against Women Survey* (Washington, D.C.: National Institute of Justice, 1998).

8. Tjaden and Thoennes, *Stalking in America*, p. 2.

9. Idaho State University, Department of Public Safety, "Stalking on Campus," http://www.isu.edu/pubsafe/crime_prevention/Stalking_On_Campus.shtml.

10. Lambèr Royakkers, "The Dutch Approach to Stalking Laws," *California Criminal Law Review* 3 (2000): 7.

11. 2002 National Victim Assistance Academy, Chapter 22: Special Topics, "Section 2: Stalking," http://www.ojp.usdoj.gov/ovc/assist/nvaa2002/chapter22_2.html.

12. *Stalking Victimization in the United States*, p. 1.

13. *Ibid.*, pp. 1–9.

14. Tjaden and Thoennes, *Stalking in America*, pp. 2–3.

15. *Ibid.*, p. 4.

16. Kathleen C. Basile, Monica H. Swahn, Jieru Chen, and Linda E. Saltzman, "Stalking in the United States: Recent National Prevalence Estimates," *American Journal of Preventive Medicine* 31 (2006): 172–75.

17. Brian H. Spitzberg and William R. Cupach, "State of the Art of Stalking: Taking Stock of the Emerging Literature," *Aggression and Violent Behavior* 12, 1 (2007): 64–86.

18. Tjaden and Thoennes, *Stalking in America*, pp. 2–8; Kris Mohandie, J. Reid Meloy, Mila Green McGowan, and Jenn Williams, "The RECON Typology of Stalking: Reliability and Validity Based upon a Large Sample of North American Stalkers," *Journal of Forensic Sciences* 51, 1 (2006): 147–55.

19. Jacquelyn C. Campbell, Daniel Webster, Jane Koziol-McLain, Carolyn Block, Doris Campbell, Mary Ann Curry, Faye Gary, Nancy Glass, Judith McFarlane, Carolyn Sachs, Phyllis Sharps, Yvonne Ulrich, Susan A. Wilt, Jennifer Manganello, Xiao Xu, Janet Schollenberger, Victoria Frye, and Kathryn Laughon, "Risk Factors for Femicide in Abusive Relationships: Results from a Multisite Case Control Study," *American Journal of Public Health* 93, 7 (2003): 1089–97; R. Barri Flowers, *Murder, At the End of the Day and Night: A Study of Criminal Homicide Offenders, Victims, and Circumstances* (Springfield, IL: Charles C Thomas, 2002), pp. 51–60.

20. Barry Rosenfeld, "Violence Risk Factors in Stalking and Obsessional Harassment," *Criminal Justice and Behavior* 31 (2004): 1.

21. Robert A. Wood and Nona L. Wood, "Stalking the Stalker: A Profile of Offenders," *FBI Law Enforcement Bulletin* 71, 12 (2002): 1–7.

22. Karl A. Roberts, "Women's Experience of Violence During Stalking by Former Romantic Partners," *Violence Against Women* 11 (2005): 89–114.

23. Eric Blaauw, Frans W. Winkel, Ella Arensman, Lorraine Sheridan, and Adriënne Freeve, "The Toll of Stalking: The Relationship Between Features of Stalking and Psychopathology of Victims," *Journal of Interpersonal Violence* 17, 1 (2002): 50–63.

24. *Stalking Victimization in the United States*, p. 4; Tjaden and Thoennes, *Stalking in America*, p. 2; Lorraine P. Sheridan, Eric Blaauw, and Graham M. Davies, "Stalking: Knowns and Unknowns," *Trauma, Violence, and Abuse* 4, 2 (2003): 148–62.

25. Bonnie S. Fisher, Francis T. Cullen, and Michael G. Turner, *The Sexual Victimization of College Women* (Washington, D.C.: National Institute of Justice, Bureau of Justice Statistics, 2000), p. 28; R. Barri Flowers, *Male Crime and Deviance: Exploring Its Causes, Dynamics and Nature* (Springfield, IL: Charles C Thomas, 2003).

26. The California Coalition Against Sexual Assault, *Campus Stalking* (Washington, D.C.: U.S. Department of Justice, 2002), p. 2. *See also* Emily Spence-Diehl, *Stalking: A Handbook for Victims* (Holmes Beach, FL: Learning Publications, 1999).

27. Fisher, Cullen, and Turner, *The Sexual Victimization of College Women*, pp. 27–30.

28. Elizabeth E. Mustaine and Richard Tewksbury, "A Routine Activity Theory Explanation of Women's Stalking Victimizations," *Violence Against Women* 5, 1 (1999): 43–62.

29. Tjaden and Thoennes, *Stalking in America*, p. 4.

30. Beth Bjerregaard, "An Empirical Study of Stalking Victimization," *Violence and Victims* 15, 4 (2000): 389–406. *See also* Karen L. Yanowitz, "Influence of Gender and Experience on College Students' Stalking Schemas," *Violence and Victims* 21, 1 (2006): 91–100.

31. Cited in Miranda Hitti, "Stalkers a Problem For Students," Web MD Health News (September 28, 2004), http://www.web md.com/parenting/news/20040928/stalkers-problem-for-students.

32. Fisher, Cullen, and Turner, *The Sexual Victimization of College Women*, p. 28.

33. Dating Violence Resource Center, "Campus Dating Violence Fact Sheet," http://www.ncvc.org/ncvc/main.aspx?dbID=DB_D atingViolenceResourceCenter101; Cressida Wasserman, "Dating Violence on Campus: A Fact of Life," U.S. Department of Education's Higher Education Center for Alcohol and Other Drug Abuse and Violence Prevention, pp. 16–17, http://www.higheredcenter.org/ resources/dating-violence-campus-fact-life; Keith E. Davis and Irene H. Frieze, "Research on Stalking: What Do We Know and Where Do We Go?" *Violence and Victims* 15, 4 (2000): 473–87.

34. Rosenfeld, "Violence Risk Factors in Stalking and Obsessional Harassment"; Troy McEwan, Paul E. Mullen, and Rosemary Purcell, "Identifying Risk Factors in Stalking: A Review of Current Research," *International Journal of Law and Psychiatry* 30, 1 (2007): 1–9.

35. Cited in Andrew Brownstein, "In the Campus Shadows, Women Are Stalkers as Well as the Stalked," The Chronicle of Higher Education (December 8, 2000), http://chron icle.com/free/v47/i15/15a04001.htm; Paul E. Mullen, Michele Pathé, and Rosemary Purcell, *Stalkers and Their Victims*, 2d ed. (Cambridge: Cambridge University Press, 2000).

36. Yanowitz, "Influence of Gender and Experience on College Students' Stalking Schemas"; Phillips, Quirk, Rosenfeld, and O'Connor, "Is It Stalking? Perceptions of Stalking Among College Undergraduates";

Eileen M. Alexy, Ann W. Burgess, Timothy Baker, and Shirley A. Smoyak, "Perceptions of Cyberstalking Among College Students," *Brief Treatment and Crisis Intervention* 5, 3 (2005): 279–289.

37. Cited in Andrew Brownstein, "In the Campus Shadows, Women Are Stalkers as Well as the Stalked"; J. Reid Meloy and Cynthia Boyd, "Female Stalkers and Their Victims," *Journal of the American Academy of Psychiatry and the Law* 31 (2003): 211–19.

38. Hitti, "Stalkers a Problem For Students"; Fisher, Cullen, and Turner, *The Sexual Victimization of College Women*, pp. 28–29.

39. American Association of University Women, *Drawing the Line: Sexual Harassment on Campus* (Washington, D.C.: AAUW Educational Foundation, 2005), pp. 2–3; Susan Kinzie, "Many Cases Unreported, Survey Finds," *Washington Post* (January 25, 2006), p. A2.

40. Judith M. McFarlane, Jacquelyn C. Campbell, Susan Wilt, Carolyn J. Sachs, Yvonne Ulrich, and Xiao Xu, "Stalking and Intimate Partner Femicide," *Homicide Studies* 3, 4 (1999): 300–16.

41. Fisher, Cullen, and Turner, *The Sexual Victimization of College Women*, pp. 29–30.

42. Karen Osterholm, Deborah E. Horn, and William A. Kritsonis, "College Professors as Potential Victims of Stalking: Awareness and Prevention: National Implications," *Focus on Colleges, Universities and Schools* 1, 1 (2007): 2–4; Piper Fogg and Sharon Walsh, "The Question of Sex Between Professors and Students," *Chronicle of Higher Education* 48, 30 (2002): A8–A9.

43. Osterholm, Horn, and Kritsonis, "College Professors as Potential Victims of Stalking: Awareness and Prevention," p. 3; Spitzberg and Cupach, "State of the Art of Stalking," pp. 64–68.

44. *Campus Stalking*, p.4.

45. "Stalking," Wikipedia, the Free Encyclopedia, http://en.wikipedia.org/wiki/Stalk ing; Kristine K. Kienlen, D. L. Birmingham, Kenneth B. Solberg, J. T. O'Regan, and J. Reid Meloy, "A Comparative Study of Psychotic and Nonpsychotic Stalking," *Journal of the American Academy of Psychiatry and the Law* 25, 3 (1997): 317–34.

46. Mullen, Pathé, and Purcell, *Stalkers and Their Victims*; Kienlen, Birmingham, Sol-

berg, O'Regan, and Meloy, "A Comparative Study of Psychotic and Nonpsychotic Stalking."

47. Ronnie B. Harmon, Richard Rosner, and Howard Owens, "Obsessional Harassment and Erotomania in a Criminal Court Population," *Journal of Forensic Sciences* 40, 2 (1995): 188–96.

48. Michael A. Zona, Kaushal K. Sharma, and John Lane, "A Comparative Study of Erotomanic and Obsessional Subjects in a Forensic Sample," *Journal of Forensic Sciences* 38, 4 (1993): 894–903.

49. Paul E. Mullen, Michele Pathé, Rosemary Purcell, and Geoffrey W. Stuart, "Study of Stalkers," *American Journal of Psychiatry* 156 (1999): 1244–49.

50. U.S. Department of Justice, *1999 Report on Cyberstalking: a New Challenge for Law Enforcement Industry*, A Report from the Attorney General to the Vice President, August 1999, http://www.usdoj.gov/criminal/cybercrime/cyberstalking.htm.

51. Paul Bocij, "Corporate Cyber stalking: An Invitation to Build Theory," *First Monday* 7, 11 (2002), http://firstmonday.org/issues/issue7_11/bocij/index.html; P. Bocij and Leroy McFarlane, "Online harassment: Towards a Definition of Cyber Stalking," *Prison Service Journal* 139 (2002): 31–38.

52. Quoted in "Cyberstalking," Wikipedia, the Free Encyclopedia, http://en.wiki pedia.org/wiki/Cyberstalking. *See also* Paul Bocij, *Cyberstalking: Harassment in the Internet Age and How to Protect Your Family* (New York: Praeger, 2004), pp. 9–10.

53. Bocij, *Cyberstalking: Harassment in the Internet Age*; Karuppannan Jaishankar and Velmurugan Uma Sankary, "Cyber Stalking: A Global Menace in the Information Super Highway," http://www.erces.com/journal/articles/archives/volume2/v03/v02.htm.

54. *Campus Stalking*, p. 2.

55. *1999 Report on Cyberstalking*.

56. *Ibid.*; Robert D'Ovidio and James Doyle, "A Study on Cyberstalking: Understanding Investigative Hurdles," *FBI Law Enforcement Bulletin* 72, 3 (2003): 10–17.

57. *Ibid. See also* Bonnie S. Fisher, Francis T. Cullen, and Michael G. Turner, "Being Pursued: Stalking Victimization in a National Study of College Women," *Criminology and Public Policy* 1, 2 (2002): 257–308.

58. Alexy, Burgess, Baker, and Smoyak,

"Perceptions of Cyberstalking Among College Students."

59. B. H. Spitzberg and G. Hoobler, "Cyberstalking and the Technologies of Interpersonal Terrorism," *New Media and Society* 4 (2002): 71–92.

60. Rebecca K. Lee, "Romantic and Electronic Stalking in a College Context," *William & Mary Journal of Women and the Law* 4 (1998): 373–466.

61. Bully Online, "Issues Related to Bullying," http://www.bullyonline.org/related/stalking.htm; Matthew Chapman, "My Wife Left Me for a Cyber love-Rat," *BBC News* (August 17, 2002), http://news.bbc.co.uk/1/hi/uk/2197441.stm.

62. "Section 2: Stalking."

63. Tami Port, "Stalking Crime Antistalking Laws," August 28, 2007, http://personali tydisorders.suite101.com/article.cfm/stalk ing_law.

64. *Ibid.*; Violent Crime Control and Law Enforcement Act (1994), P.L. 103–322.

65. Violence Against Women and Department of Justice Reauthorization Act (2005), H.R. 3042; 18 U.S.C. § 2261A Interstate Stalking, § 2261A(1), § 2261A(2) (1996).

66. Patricia Q. Brown, *Institution in the United States: 1993–94, 1998–99* (Washington, D.C.: National Center for Education, 2001).

67. Tjaden and Thoennes, *Stalking in America*.

Chapter 7

1. Michael Shively, *Study of Literature and Legislation on Hate Crime in America* (Cambridge, MA: Abt Associates Inc., 2005), pp. 12–21; James J. Nolan III, Jack McDevitt, Shea Cronin, and Amy Farrell, "Learning to See Hate Crimes: A Framework for Understanding and Clarifying Ambiguities in Bias Crime Classification," *The Justice Professional* 17, 1 (2004): 91–105; Kellina M. Craig and Craig R. Waldo, "'So, What's a Hate Crime Anyway?' Young Adults' Perceptions of Hate Crimes, Victims, and Perpetrators," *Law and Human Behavior* 20, 2 (1996): 113–129.

2. U.S. Department of Justice, Federal Bureau of Investigation, Crime in the United States 2004, "Hate Crime," http://www.fbi.

gov/ucr/cius_04/offenses_reported/hate_crim
e/index.html.

3. Quoted in Department of Criminal
Justice Services, "Law Enforcement Services
Section Sample Directives: Policies in Action,"
July 2000, http://www.dcjs.virginia.gov/cple/
SampleDirectives/inAction/policy.cfm?&id=2

4. Quoted in Shively, *Study of Literature
and Legislation on Hate Crime in America*, p.
51.

5. LAMBDA GLBT Community Services, http://www.lambda.org/.

6. Frederick M. Lawrence, *Punishing
Hate: Bias Crimes Under American Law* (Cambridge, MA: Harvard University Press, 2002).

7. Quoted in Shively, *Study of Literature
and Legislation on Hate Crime in America*, p.
19.

8. U.S. Department of Justice, *Hate
Crimes on Campus: The Problem and Efforts to
Confront It* (Washington, D.C.: Bureau of Jus-
tice Assistance, 2001), p. 17.

9. U.S. Department of Justice, *Responding
to Hate Crimes and Bias-Motivated Incidences
on College/University Campuses* (Washington,
D.C.: Community Relations Service, 2000),
p. 2.

10. *Ibid.*, pp. 2–3.

11. U.S. Department of Justice, Bureau of
Justice Statistics Special Report, *Hate Crime
Reported by Victims and Police* (Washington,
D.C.: Office of Justice Programs, 2005), p. 4.

12. Cited in Shively, *Study of Literature and
Legislation on Hate Crime in America*, p. 69.
See also Human Rights Campaign, http://
www.hrc.org/.

13. Cited in Shively, *Study of Literature and
Legislation on Hate Crime in America*, p. 68.
See also ADL: Fighting Anti-Semitism, Big-
otry, and Extremism, http://www.adl.org/.

14. Cited in Shively, *Study of Literature and
Legislation on Hate Crime in America*, p. 69.
See also National Coalition of Anti-Violence
Programs, http://www.ncavp.org/.

15. U.S. Department of Education, National Center for Education Statistics, *Indicators of School Crime and Safety: 2005* (Washington, D.C.: Institute of Education Sciences,
2005), p. vi.

16. Cited in Anne Seymour, Melissa
Hook, and Carl Grimes, "Hate and Bias
Crime," in Anne Seymour, Morna Murray,
Jane Sigmon, Melissa Hook, Christine Ed-
munds, Mario Gaboury, and Grace Coleman,

eds., *National Victim Assistance Academy Textbook* (Washington, D.C.: U.S. Department of
Justice, Office for Victims of Crime, 2002).

17. "Report From Friends of Simon
Wiesenthal Center Reveals Internet Hate Sites
on the Rise; Center Honours Local Police,"
Reuters (October 20, 2008), http://www.
reuters.com/article/pressRelease/idUS135228
+20-Oct-2008+MW20081020.

18. Cited in Seymour, Hook, and Grimes,
"Hate and Bias Crime."

19. *Hate Crimes on Campus*, pp. 3–4; R.
Barri Flowers, *Murder, At the End of the Day
and Night: A Study of Criminal Homicide Offenders, Victims, and Circumstances* (Springfield, IL: Charles C Thomas, 2001), pp. 142–
44.

20. *Hate Crimes on Campus*, pp. 4–5; Shively, *Study of Literature and Legislation on Hate
Crime in America*, pp. iii–iv, 59–66.

21. Cited in Shively, *Study of Literature and
Legislation on Hate Crime in America*, p. iv.

22. Cited in Gayla Martindale, "Hate
Crimes on Campus," StateUniversity.com
Blog, http://www.stateuniversity.com/blog/
permalink/College-Hate-Crimes.html. *See
also* Nadine Recker Rayburn, Mitchell Earleywine, and Gerald C. Davison, "Base Rates of
Hate Crime Victimization Among College
Students," *Journal of Interpersonal Violence* 18,
10 (2003): 1209–21.

23. Cited in *Hate Crimes on Campus*, p. 5.

24. *Ibid.*

25. Cited in Seymour, Hook, and Grimes,
"Hate and Bias Crime."

26. Anti-Defamation League, "Focus on
the College Campus," http://www.cbssports.
com/nba/scoreboard.

27. Seymour, Hook, and Grimes, "Hate
and Bias Crime."

28. Jack McDevitt, Jennifer M. Balboni,
and Susan Bennett, *Improving the Quality and
Accuracy of Bias Crime Statistics Nationally: An
Assessment of the First Ten Years of Bias Crime
Data Collection* (Washington, D.C.: Bureau
of Justice Statistics, 2000).

29. See for example James J. Nolan III,
Yoshio Akiyama, and Samuel Berhanu, "The
Hate Crime Statistics Act of 1990: Develop-
ing a Method for Measuring the Occurrence
of Hate Violence," *American Behavioral Scien-
tist* 46, 1 (2002): 136–53; Gregory M. Herek,
J. Roy Gillis, Jeanine C. Cogan, and Eric K.
Glunt, "Hate Crime Victimization Among

Lesbian, Gay, and Bisexual Adults: Prevalence, Psychological Correlates, and Methodological Issues," *Journal of Interpersonal Violence* 12, 2 (1997): 195–215.

30. Shane Windmeyer, FBI and Education Reporting of Hate Crimes and Bias Incidents, Associations of College Unions International Forum, 2003, http://www.ncjrs.gov/pdffilesl/nij/grants/210300.pdf.

31. *Hate Crimes on Campus*, p. 4. *See also* Robert J. Boeckmann and Carolyn Turpin-Petrosino, "Understanding the Harm of Hate Crimes, *Journal of Social Issues* 58, 2 (2002): 207–25; Brian Levin, "Hate Crimes: Worse by Definition," *Journal of Contemporary Criminal Justice* 15, 1 (1999): 6–21.

32. Cited in American Psychological Association, "Hate Crimes Today: An Age-Old Foe in Modern Dress," http://www.apa.org/pubinfo/hate/#top.

33. *Ibid.*

34. Flowers, *Murder, At the End of the Day and Night*, pp. 105–13.

35. *Ibid.*; Shively, *Study of Literature and Legislation on Hate Crime in America*, pp. 72–73; Dhammika Dharmapala and Nuno Garoupa, "Penalty Enhancement for Hate Crimes: An Economic Analysis," *American Law and Economics Review* 6, 1 (2004): 185–207.

36. American Psychological Association, "Study Finds No Evidence That Economic Downturn Spurs Hate Crimes," 1998, http://www.apa.org/.

37. *Ibid.*

38. CBS News, "Report: Bias Against U.S. Muslims On Rise — While Hate Crimes Are Down Since 9/11 Spike, Prejudice Still A Major Issue, Group Says," December 5, 2008, http://www.cbsnews.com/stories/2008/12/05/national/main4650017.shtml; Deborah Black, "Officials: Hate Crimes Against Muslims in US Increasing," *Voices of America* (May 13, 2005), http://www.voanews.com/english/archive/2005–05/2005–05–13-voa2.cfm; Curt Anderson, "US Sees Drop in Hate Crimes After Post-9/11 Rise: Mass. Officials Report a Significant Decline," *Boston Globe* (November 13, 2003), http://c5.zedo.com//ads2/f/459316/1/0/0/305000449/30500044 9/0/305/149/zz-V1-A-720x300_05–07–

07_CLEAN_BLUE-iiiInteractive.html?a =;l=;p=.

39. "Hate Crimes Today."

40. *Ibid.*; Flowers, *Murder, At the End of the Day and Night*, pp. 112–14.

41. Jack Levin and Jack McDevitt, *Hate Crimes: The Rising Tide of Bigotry and Bloodshed* (New York: Plenum, 1993); Jack McDevitt, Jack Levin, and Susan Bennett, "Hate Crime Offenders: An Expanded Typology," *Journal of Social Issues* 58, 2 (2002): 303–17.

42. McDevitt, Levin, and Bennett, "Hate Crime Offenders," p. 306.

43. Joan C. Weiss, Howard J. Ehrlich, Barbara E. K. Larcom, "Ethnoviolence at Work," *Journal of Intergroup Relations* 18 (Winter, 1991–92): 28–29.

44. *Responding to Hate Crimes and Bias-Motivated Incidences*, pp. 5–6.

45. *Ibid.*, p. 7.

46. Karen Franklin, "Antigay Behaviors Among Young Adults: Prevalence, Patterns, and Motivators in a Noncriminal Population," *Journal of Interpersonal Violence* 15, 4 (2000): 339–62.

47. Crime Awareness and Campus Security Act (1990), 20 U.S.C. §1092.

48. Jeanne Clery Disclosure of Campus Security Policy and Campus Crime Statistics Act (1998), 20 U.S.C. §1092 (f).

49. Hate Crimes Statistics Act (1990), 28 U.S.C. § 534.

50. Violent Crime Control and Law Enforcement Act (1994), P.L. 103–322.

51. *Ibid.*

52. Hate Crime Sentencing Enhancement Act (1994), P.L. 103–322.

53. Church Arson Prevention Act (1996), 18 U.S.C. § 247.

54. Violence Against Women and Department of Justice Reauthorization Act (2005), P.L. 109–162.

55. Local Law Enforcement Hate Crimes Prevention Act (2007), H.R. 1592.

56. Wikipedia, the Free Encyclopedia, "Hate Crime Laws in the United States," http://en.wikipedia.org/wiki/Hate_crime_law s_in_the_United_States.

57. *Ibid.*

58. Seymour, Hook, and Grimes, "Hate and Bias Crime."

BIBLIOGRAPHY

Abbey, Antonia. (1991) "Acquaintance Rape and Alcohol Consumption on College Campuses: How Are They Linked?" *Journal of American College Health* 39: 165–169.

Addiction Treatment Resources for Parents of Teens and Young Adults. Club Drugs: Know the Facts. http://www.drugrehabtreatment.com/club-drugs.html.

ADL: Fighting Anti-Semitism, Bigotry, and Extremism. http://www.adl.org/.

Advocates for Youth. The facts: Dating Violence Among Adolescents. http://www.advocatesforyouth.org/publications/factsheet/fsdating.htm.

Alabama Coalition Against Domestic Violence. Dating Violence. http://www.acadv.org/dating.html.

Alcohol Problems and Solutions. Binge Drinking. http://www2.potsdam.edu/hansondj/BingeDrinking.html.

Aldridge, Andrea. (2000) "Killing Kids: Experts Offer Explanations for School Violence." *Unionite Online: The Union University Magazine* 51, 2. http://www.uu.edu/Unionite/winter00/killingkids.htm.

Alexander, Jamie. (April 2004) "A Look at College Student Victimization." *Front Sight Newsletter.* http://www.frontsight.com/promotion/16/college.htm.

Alexy, Eileen M., Ann W. Burgess, Timothy Baker, and Shirley A. Smoyak. (2005) "Perceptions of Cyberstalking Among College Students." *Brief Treatment and Crisis Intervention* 5, 3: 279–289.

American Association of University Women. (2005) *Drawing the Line: Sexual Harassment on Campus.* Washington, D.C.: AAUW Educational Foundation.

American Psychological Association. Hate Crimes Today: An Age-Old Foe in Modern Dress. http://www.apa.org/pubinfo/hate/#top.

_____. (1998) Study Finds No Evidence That Economic Downturn Spurs Hate Crimes. http://www.apa.org/.

Amethyst Initiative. http://www.amethystinitiative.org/.

Anderson, Curt. (November 13, 2003) "US Sees Drop in Hate Crimes After Post–9/11 Rise: Mass. Officials Report a Significant Decline." *Boston Globe.* http://c5.zedo.com//ads2/f/459316/1/0/0/305000449/305000449/0/305/149/zz-V1-A-720x300_05-07-07_CLEAN_BLUE-iiiInteractive.html?a=;l=;p=.

Anti-Defamation League. Focus on the College Campus. http://www.cbssports.com/nba/scoreboard.

Arias, Ileana, Mary Samios, and K. Daniel O'Leary. (1987) "Prevalence and Correlates of Physical Aggression During Courtship." *Journal of Interpersonal Violence* 2, 1: 82–90.

Arria, Amelia M., Vanessa Kuhn, Kimberly M. Caldeira, Kevin E. O'Grady, Kathryn B. Vincent, and Eric D. Wish. (2008) "High School Drinking Mediates the Relationship Between Parental Monitoring and College Drinking: A Longitudinal Analysis." *Substance Abuse Treatment, Prevention, and Policy* 3: 6.

Ashton, Elizabeth. (2008) "Alcohol Abuse Makes Prescription Drug Abuse More

Likely." *NIDA Notes* 21, 5. http://www.nida.nih.gov/NIDA_notes/NNvol21N5/alcohol.html.

Asian & Pacific Islander Women and Family Safety Center. Informational: Dating Violence Statistics. http://www.apiwfsc.org/apiwfsc/statistics_dating_violence.html.

Avery-Leaf, Sarah, Michele Cascardi, K. Daniel O'Leary, and Annmarie Cano. (1997) "Efficacy of a Dating Violence Prevention Program on Attitudes Justifying Aggression." *Journal of Adolescent Health* 21: 11–7.

Baer, John S., Daniel R. Kivlahan, and G. Alan Marlatt. (2006). "High-Risk Drinking Across the Transition from High School to College." *Alcoholism: Clinical and Experimental Research* 19, 1: 54–58.

Barrett, Sean P., Christine Darredeau, and Robert O. Pihl. (2006) "Patterns of Polysubstance Use in Drug Using University Students." *Human Psychopharmacology Clinical Experience* 21: 225–63.

Basile, Kathleen C., Monica H. Swahn, Jieru Chen, and Linda E. Saltzman. (2006) "Stalking in the United States: Recent National Prevalence Estimates." *American Journal of Preventive Medicine* 31: 172–75.

Berkowitz, Alan. (1992) "College Men as Perpetrators of Acquaintance Rape and Sexual Assault: A Review of Recent Research." *Journal of American College Health* 40: 175–81.

Billingham, Robert E., and Alan R. Sack. (1987) "Conflict Resolution Tactics and the Level of Emotional Commitment Among Unmarrieds." *Human Relations* 40: 59–74.

Bjerregaard, Beth. (2000) "An Empirical Study of Stalking Victimization." *Violence and Victims* 15, 4: 389–406.

Blaauw, Eric, Frans W. Winkel, Ella Arensman, Lorraine Sheridan, and Adriënne Freeve. (2002) "The Toll of Stalking: The Relationship Between Features of Stalking and Psychopathology of Victims." *Journal of Interpersonal Violence* 17, 1: 50–63.

Black, Deborah. (May 13, 2005) "Officials: Hate Crimes Against Muslims in US Increasing." *Voices of America.* http://www.voanews.com/english/archive/2005-05/2005-05-13-voa2.cfm.

Block, Robert I., and Mohamed M. Ghoneim. (1993) "Effects of Chronic Marijuana Use on Human Cognition." *Psychopharmacology* 110: 219–28.

Bocij, Paul. (2002) "Corporate Cyberstalking: An Invitation to Build Theory." *First Monday* 7, 11. http://firstmonday.org/issues/issue7_11/bocij/index.html.

_____. (2004) *Cyberstalking: Harassment in the Internet Age and How to Protect Your Family.* New York: Praeger.

_____, and Leroy McFarlane. (2002) "Online Harassment: Towards a Definition of Cyber Stalking." *Prison Service Journal* 139: 31–38.

Boeckmann, Robert J., and Carolyn Turpin-Petrosino. (2002) "Understanding the Harm of Hate Crimes." *Journal of Social Issues* 58, 2: 207–25.

Boeringer, Scot B. (1999) "Associations of Rape-Supportive Attitudes with Fraternal and Athletic Participation." *Violence Against Women* 5, 1: 81–90.

Bohmer, Carol, and Andrea Parrot. (1993) *Sexual Assault on Campus: The Problem and the Solution.* New York: Lexington.

Bondurant, Barrie. (2001) "University Women's Acknowledgment of Rape: Individual, Situational, and Social Factors." *Violence Against Women: An International and Interdisciplinary Journal* 7, 3: 294–314.

Brady Campaign to Prevent Gun Violence. (June 18, 2008) Brady Blog. http://www.bradycampaign.org/blog/?s=louisiana+campus.

Brent, David. A. (1996) "Risk Factors for Adolescent Suicide and Suicidal Behavior: Mental and Substance Abuse Disorders, Family Environmental Factors, and Life Stress." *Suicide Life Threat Behavior* 25: 52–63.

Briere, John, and Neil M. Malamuth. (1983) "Predicting Self-Reported Likelihood of Sexually Abusive Behavior: Attitudinal Versus Sexual Explanations." *Journal of Research in Personality* 17: 315–23.

Brodbelt, S. (1983) "College Dating and Violence." *College Student Journal* 17: 273–77.

Brodsky, Stanley L., and Susan C. Hobart. (1978) "Blame Models and Assailant Research." *Criminal Justice and Behavior* 5: 379–88.

Brook, Judith S., Elinor B. Balka, and Martin Whiteman. (1999) "Risks for Late Adolescence of Early Adolescent Marijuana Use." *American Journal of Public Health* 89, 10: 1549–54.

Brown, Patricia Q. (2001) *Institution in the United States: 1993–94, 1998–99.* Washington, D.C.: National Center for Education.

Brown, Theresa J., Kenneth E. Sumner, and Romy Nocera. (2002) "Understanding Sexual Aggression Against Women: An Examination of the Role of Men's Athletic Participation and Related Variables." *Journal of Interpersonal Violence* 17, 9: 937–52.

Brownstein, Andrew. (December 8, 2000) "In the Campus Shadows, Women Are Stalkers as Well as the Stalked." *The Chronicle of Higher Education.* http://chronicle.com/free/v47/i15/15a04001.htm.

Bully Online. Issues Related to Bullying. http://www.bullyonline.org/related/stalking.htm.

Burt, Martha R. (1980) "Cultural Myths and Support for Rape." *Journal of Personality and Social Psychology* 38: 217–30.

Caldeira, Kimberly M., Amelia M. Arria, Kevin E. O'Grady, Kathryn B. Vincent, and Eric D. Wish. (2008) "The Occurrence of Cannabis Use Disorders and Other Cannabis-Related Problems Among First-Year College Students." *Addictive Behaviors* 33, 3: 397–411.

California Coalition Against Sexual Assault. (2002) *Campus Stalking.* Washington, D.C.: U.S. Department of Justice.

Campbell, Jacquelyn C., Daniel Webster, Jane Koziol-McLain, Carolyn Block, Doris Campbell, Mary Ann Curry, Faye Gary, Nancy Glass, Judith McFarlane, Carolyn Sachs, Phyllis Sharps, Yvonne Ulrich, Susan A. Wilt, Jennifer Manganello, Xiao Xu, Janet Schollenberger, Victoria Frye, and Kathryn Laughon. (2003) "Risk Factors for Femicide in Abusive Relationships: Results from a Multisite Case Control Study." *American Journal of Public Health* 93, 7: 1089–97.

Campus Sexual Assault Victims' Bill of Rights. (1992) P.L. 102–325.

CampusHealthandSafety.org. Date Rape and Club Drugs. http://www.campushealthandsafety.org/drugs/club-drugs/.

CBS News. (December 5, 2008) Report: Bias Against U.S. Muslims On Rise — While Hate Crimes Are Down Since 9/11 Spike, Prejudice Still A Major Issue, Group Says. http://www.cbsnews.com/stories/2008/12/05/national/main4650017.shtml.

Centers for Disease Control and Prevention. National Center for Injury Prevention and Control. Dating Abuse fact Sheet. http://www.cdc.gov/ncipc/dvp/DatingViolence.htm.

_____. (2006) "Physical Dating Violence Among High School Students-United States, 2003." *Morbidity and Mortality Weekly Report* 55, 19: 532–535.

Chaloupka, Frank J., Michael Grossman, and Henry Saffer. (2002) "The Effects of Price on Alcohol Consumption and Alcohol-Related Problems." *Alcohol Research & Health* 26, 1: 22–34.

Chapman, Matthew. (August 17, 2002) "My Wife Left Me for a Cyber love-Rat." *BBC News.* http://news.bbc.co.uk/1/hi/uk/2197441.stm.

Chase, Kenneth A., Dominique Treboux, and K. Daniel O'Leary. (2002) "Characteristics of High-risk Adolescents' Dating Violence." *Journal of Interpersonal Violence* 17, 1: 33–49.

Choate, Laura Hensley. (2003) "Sexual Assault Prevention Programs for College Men: An Exploratory Evaluation of the Men Against Violence Model." *Journal of College Counseling* 6: 166–76.

Church Arson Prevention Act. (1996) 18 U.S.C. § 247.

Clayton, Mark (January 22, 2002) "Latest Murders Highlight Rise in Campus Crime." *Christian Science Monitor.* http://www.csmonitor.com/2002/0122/p03s01-ussc.html.

Commission on Substance Abuse at Colleges and Universities. (1994) *Rethinking Rites of Passage: Substance Abuse on America's Campuses.* New York: Columbia University, Center on Addiction and Substance Abuse.

Community Epidemiology Work Group. (2004) *Epidemiologic Trends in Drug Abuse, Vol. II, Proceedings of the Community Epidemiology Work Group, December 2003.* Bethesda, MD: National Institute on Drug Abuse.

Consolidated Appropriations Act. (2004) P.L. 108–199.

Copenhaver, Stacey, and Elizabeth Grauerholz. (1991) "Sexual Victimization Among Sorority Women: Exploring the Link Between Sexual Violence and Institutional Practices." *Sex Roles: A Journal of Research* 24: 31–41.

Cornell Law School. Legal Information Institute. U.S. Code Collection. Title 18, Part 1, Chapter 109A. http://www 4.law.cornell.edu/uscode/html/uscode18/usc_sup_01_18_10_I_20_109A.html.

Craig, Kellina M., and Craig R. Waldo. (1996) "'So, What's a Hate Crime Anyway?' Young Adults' Perceptions of Hate Crimes, Victims, and Perpetrators." *Law and Human Behavior* 20, 2: 113–129.

Crime Awareness and Campus Security Act. (1990) Title II of P.L. 101–542.
_____. (1990) 20 U.S.C. §1092.

Cyriaque, Jeanne. (February 1982) "The Chronic Serious Offender: How Illinois Juveniles 'Match Up.'" *Illinois*, pp. 4–5.

D'Ovidio, Robert, and James Doyle. (2003) "A Study on Cyberstalking: Understanding Investigative Hurdles." *FBI Law Enforcement Bulletin* 72, 3: 10–17.

Dating and Domestic Violence on Campus. http://www.thesafespace.org/pdf/handout_dv_on_campus.pdf.

Dating Violence Resource Center. Campus Dating Violence Fact Sheet. http://www.ncvc.org/ncvc/main.aspx?dbID=DB_DatingViolenceResourceCenter101.

Davis, Keith E., and Irene H. Frieze. (2000) "Research on Stalking: What Do We Know and Where Do We Go?" *Violence and Victims* 15, 4: 473–87.

Degenhardt, Louisa, Wayne Hall, and Michael Lynskey. (2003) "Exploring the Association Between Cannabis Use and Depression." *Addiction* 98, 11: 1493–1504.

DeKeseredy, Walter S., and Katharine Kelly. (1993) "The Incidence and Prevalence of Women Abuse in Canadian University and College Dating Relationships." *Canadian Journal of Sociology* 18: 137–59.

Delaney, Chelsey. (February 6, 2009) "Concealed Gun Bill Sparks Debate: Will Allowing College Students to Pack Heat Make Texas Campuses Safer?" ABC News. http://abcnews.go.com/

OnCampus/Story?id=6805680&page=
1.

Department of Criminal Justice Services. (July 2000) Law Enforcement Services Section Sample Directives: Policies in Action. http://www.dcjs.virginia.gov/cple/SampleDirectives/inAction/policy.cfm?&id=2

Dharmapala, Dhammika, and Nuno Garoupa. (2004) "Penalty Enhancement for Hate Crimes: An Economic Analysis." *American Law and Economics Review* 6, 1: 185–207.

Dobash, Rebecca E., and Russell P. Dobash. (1980) *Violence Against Wives: A Case Against the Patriarchy.* London: Open Books.

Douglas, Kathy, Janet L. Collins, Charles Warren, Laura Kann, Robert Gold, Sonia Clayton, James G. Ross, and Lloyd J. Kolbe. (1997) "Results From the 1995 National College Health Risk Behavior Survey." *Journal of the American College Health Association* 46, 2: 55–66.

Dowdall, George W. (2008) *College Drinking: Reframing a Social Problem.* New York: Praeger.

Drug and Alcohol Abuse by College Students: An Issue of Increasing Concern on Campus. http://www.collegedrugabuse.com/.

"Drug Bust Highlights College Students' Rising Drug Use." (July 2008) *Education Reporter* 270. http://www.eaglefo rum.org/educate/2008/july08/rising-drug-use.html.

Drug-Free Schools and Communities Act. (1986) 20 U.S.C. 3181, P.L. 101–226.

Education: Red Orbit. (February 11, 2008) A Dangerous Transition: High School to the First Year of College. http://www.redorbit.com/news/education/125 0094/a_dangerous_transition_high_sch ool_to_the_first_year_of/.

Epstein, Joel, and Stacia Langenbahn. (1994) *The Criminal Justice and Community Response to Rape.* Washington, D.C.: National Institute of Justice.

The Equity Office. (January 11, 2007) Statistics on Dating Violence. http://www.acadiau.ca/president/equity/harass ment_sexual_dating.htm.

The ESPAD Report 2003: Alcohol and Other Drug Use Among Students in 35 European Countries. (2003) http://www.monitoringthefuture.org/pubs/esp adusa2003.pdf.

Federal-Aid Highway Act. (1982) P.L. 97–424.

Fell, James C., Deborah A. Fisher, Robert B. Voas, Kenneth Blackman, and A. Scott Tippetts. (2008) "The Relationship of Underage Drinking Laws to Reductions in Drinking Drivers in Fatal Crashes in the United States." *Accident Analysis and Prevention* 40: 1430–40.

Fiebert, Martin S., and Denise M. Gonzalez. (1997) "College Women Who Initiate Assaults on their Male Partners and the Reasons Offered for Such Behavior." *Psychological Reports* 80: 583–590.

Fisher, Bonnie S. (1995) "Campus Crime and Fear of Victimization: Judicial, Legislative and Administrative Responses." *The Annals of the American Academy of Political and Social Science* 539: 85–101.

_____, Francis T. Cullen, and Michael G. Turner. (2000) *The Sexual Victimization of College Women.* Washington, D.C.: National Institute of Justice, Bureau of Justice Statistics.

_____, Francis T. Cullen, and Michael G. Turner. (2002) "Being Pursued: Stalking Victimization in a National Study of College Women." *Criminology and Public Policy* 1, 2: 257–308.

_____, Leah E. Daigle, Francis T. Cullen, and Michael G. Turner. (2003) "Reporting Sexual Victimization to the Police and Others: Results from a National-Level Study of College

Women." *Criminal Justice and Behavior* 30, 1: 6–38.

Flowers, R. Barri. (1987) *Women and Criminality: The Woman as Victim, Offender, and Practitioner.* Westport, CT: Greenwood Press.

_____. (1994) *The Victimization and Exploitation of Women and Children: A Study of Physical, Mental and Sexual Maltreatment in the United States.* Jefferson, NC: McFarland.

_____. (2000) *Domestic Crimes, Family Violence and Child Abuse: A Study of Contemporary American Society.* Jefferson, NC: McFarland.

_____. (2002) *Kids Who Commit Adult Crimes: A Study of Serious Juvenile Criminality and Delinquency.* Binghamton, NY: Haworth Press.

_____. (2002) *Murder, At the End of the Day and Night: A Study of Criminal Homicide Offenders, Victims, and Circumstances.* Springfield, IL: Charles C Thomas.

_____. (2003) *Male Crime and Deviance: Exploring Its Causes, Dynamics and Nature.* Springfield, IL: Charles C Thomas.

_____. (2006) *Sex Crimes: Perpetrators, Predators, Prostitutes, and Victims,* 2nd ed. Springfield, IL: Charles C Thomas.

_____. (2008) *Drugs, Alcohol and Criminality in American Society.* Jefferson, NC: McFarland.

_____. (2009) *The Adolescent Criminal: An Examination of Today's Juvenile Offender.* Jefferson, NC: McFarland.

_____, and H. Loraine Flowers. (2004) *Murders in the United States: Crimes, Killers and Victims of the Twentieth Century.* Jefferson, NC: McFarland.

Fogg, Piper, and Sharon Walsh. (2002) "The Question of Sex Between Professors and Students." *Chronicle of Higher Education* 48, 30: A8-A9.

Forke, Christine M., Rachel K. Myers, Marina Catallozzi, and Donald F.

Schwarz. (2008) "Relationship Violence Among Female and Male College Undergraduate Students." *Archives Of Pediatrics & Adolescent Medicine* 162, 7: 634–41.

Foshee, Vangie A. (1996) "Gender Differences in Adolescent Dating Abuse Prevalence, Types, and Injuries." *Health Education Research* 11, 3: 275–286.

Franklin, Karen. (2000) "Antigay Behaviors Among Young Adults: Prevalence, Patterns, and Motivators in a Noncriminal Population." *Journal of Interpersonal Violence* 15, 4: 339–62.

Freedner, Naomi, Lorraine H. Freed, Y. Wendy Yang, and S. Bryn Austin. (2002) "Dating Violence Among Gay, Lesbian, and Bisexual Adolescents: Results From a Community Survey." *Journal of Adolescent Health* 31: 469–74.

Freeman-Longo, Robert E., and Geral T. Blanchard. (1998) *Sexual Abuse in America; Epidemic of the 21st Century.* Brandon, VT: Safer Society Press.

Frintner, Mary Pat, and Laura Rubinson. (1993) "Acquaintance Rape: The Influence of Alcohol, Fraternity Membership, and Sports Team Membership." *Journal of Sex Education and Therapy* 12: 272–84.

Fromme, Kim, William R. Corbin, and Marc I. Kruse. (2008) "Behavioral Risks During the Transition from High School to College." *Developmental Psychology* 44, 5: 1497–1504.

Gamache, Denise. (1998) "Domination and Control; The Social Context of Dating Violence." In Barrie Levy, ed. *Dating Violence: Young Women in Danger.* Seattle: Seal Press.

Garrett-Gooding, Joy, and Richard Senter, Jr. (2007) "Attitudes and Acts of Sexual Aggression on a University Campus." *Sociological Inquiry* 57, 4: 348–71.

Gebhard, Paul H., John H. Gagnon, Wardell B. Pomeroy, and Cornelia V. Christenson. (1965) *Sex Offenders: An*

Analysis of Types. New York: Harper & Row.

Gerson, Lowell W. (1978) "Alcohol-Related Acts of Violence: Who Was Drinking and Where the Acts Occurred." *Journal of Studies on Alcohol and Drugs* 39, 7: 1294–96.

Gidycz, Christine A., Kimberly Hanson, and Melissa J. Layman. (1995) "A Prospective Analysis of the Relationships Among Sexual Assault Experiences: An Extension of Previous Findings." *Psychology of Women Quarterly* 19, 1: 5–29.

Goodchilds, J. D., and G. L. Zellman. (1984) "Sexual Signaling and Sexual Aggression in Adolescent Relationships." In Neil Malamuth and E. Donnerstein, eds. *Pornography and Sexual Aggression*. Orlando, FL: Academic Press.

Gover, Angela R. (2004) "Risky Lifestyles and Dating Violence: A Theoretical Test of Violent Victimization." *Journal of Criminal Justice* 32, 1: 171–80.

Grayson, Carla E., and Susan Nolen-Hoeksema. (2005) "Motives to Drink as Mediators Between Childhood Sexual Assault and Alcohol Problems in Adult Women." *Journal of Traumatic Stress* 18, 2: 137–45.

Greenbaum, Paul E., Frances K. Del Boca, Jack Darks, and Mark S. Goldman. (2005) "Variations in the Drinking Trajectories of Freshmen College Students." *Journal of Consulting and Clinical Psychology* 73: 229–38.

Greene, Dennis M., and Rachel L. Navarro. (1998) "Situation-Specific Assertiveness in the Epidemiology of Sexual Victimization Among University Women: A Prospective Path Analysis." *Psychology of Women Quarterly* 22: 589–604.

Groth, A. Nicholas, Ann W. Burgess, and Lynda L. Holmstrom. (1977) "Rape: Power, Anger, and Sexuality." *American Journal of Psychiatry* 34: 1239–43.

_____, and H. Jean Birnbaum. (1979) *Men Who Rape: The Psychology of the Offender*. New York: Plenum.

Halpern, Carolyn T., Mary L. Young, Martha W. Waller, Sandra L. Martin, and Lawrence. L. Kupper. (2004) "Prevalence of Partner Violence in Same-Sex Romantic Relationships in a National Sample of Adolescents." *Journal of Adolescent Health* 35: 124–131.

_____, Selene G. Oslak, Mary L. Young, Sandra L. Martin, and Lawrence L. Kupper. (2001) "Partner Violence Among Adolescents in Opposite-Sex Romantic Relationships: Findings From the National Longitudinal Study of Adolescent Health." *American Journal of Public Health* 91, 10: 1679–85.

Hanson, Kimberly A., and Christine A. Gidcyz. (1993) "Evaluation of a Sexual Assault Program." *Journal of Consulting and Clinical Psychology* 61, 6: 1046–52.

Harkness, Brenda. Portraying a Mass Killer. http://www.mnash.edu.au/pubs/montage/Montage_97_02/killer.html.

Harmon, Ronnie B., Richard Rosner, and Howard Owens. (1995) "Obsessional Harassment and Erotomania in a Criminal Court Population." *Journal of Forensic Sciences* 40, 2: 188–96.

Harrington, Nicole T., and Harold Leitenberg. (1994) "Relationship Between Alcohol Consumption and Victim Behaviors Immediately Preceding Sexual Aggression by an Acquaintance." *Violence and Victims* 9, 4: 315–24.

Hart, Timothy C. (2003) *Violent Victimization of College Students*. Washington, D.C.: U.S. Department of Justice, Bureau of Justice Statistics.

Hate Crime Sentencing Enhancement Act. (1994) P.L. 103–322.

Hate Crimes Statistics Act. (1990) 28 U.S.C. § 534.

Herek, Gregory M., J. Roy Gillis, Jeanine C. Cogan, and Eric K. Glunt. (1997)

"Hate Crime Victimization Among Lesbian, Gay, and Bisexual Adults: Prevalence, Psychological Correlates, and Methodological Issues." *Journal of Interpersonal Violence* 12, 2: 195–215.

Higher Education Amendments. (1998) P.L. 105–244.

Higher Education Opportunity Act. (2008) P.L. 110–315.

Himelein, Melissa J. (2006) "Risk Factors for Sexual Victimization in Dating: A Longitudinal Study of College Women." *Psychology of Women Quarterly* 19, 1: 31–48.

Hingson, Ralph, Timothy Heeren, Michael Winter, and Henry Wechsler. (2005) "Magnitude of Alcohol-Related Mortality and Morbidity Among U.S. College Students Ages 18–24: Changes from 1998 to 2001." *Annual Review of Public Health* 26: 259–279.

Hitti, Miranda. Underage Drinking Hits Grade School. WebMD Health News. http://children.webmd.com/news/2007 0831/underage-drinking-hits-grade-school.

———. (September 28, 2004) Stalkers a Problem For Students. Web MD Health News. http://www.webmd.com/ parenting/news/20040928/stalkers-problem-for-students.

Hoff, Bert H. Battered Men: The Hidden Side of Domestic Violence. MenWeb. http://www.menweb.org/battered/fieber tdate.htm#10.

Holmes, Melissa, Heidi S. Resnick, Dean G. Kilpatrick, and Connie L. Best. (1996) "Rape-Related Pregnancy: Estimates and Descriptive Characteristics from a National Sample of Women." *American Journal of Obstetrics and Gynecology* 175, 2: 320–24.

Human Rights Campaign. http://www. hrc.org/.

Idaho State University. Department of Public Safety. Stalking on Campus. http://www.isu.edu/pubsafe/crime_pre vention/Stalking_On_Campus.shtml.

The Illinois Criminal Sexual Assault Act. (1983) 720 ILCS 5/12–13.

Institute for Social Research. Survey Research Center. Monitoring the Future: A Continuing Study of American Youth. http://www.monitoringthefut ure.org/.

International Survey Associates. (2008) PRIDE Surveys: 2007–08 National Summary — Grades 6 Thru 12. http:// www.pridesurveys.com/.

Interstate Stalking. (1996) 18 U.S.C. § 2261A.

Jaishankar, Karuppannan, and Velmurugan Uma Sankary. Cyber Stalking: A Global Menace in the Information Super Highway. http://www.erces.com/ journal/articles/archives/volume2/v03/v 02.htm.

Jeanne Clery Disclosure of Campus Security Policy and Campus Crime Statistics Act. (1998) 20 U.S.C. §1092 (f).

Johnston, Lloyd. D., Patrick M. O'Malley, Jerald G. Bachman, and John E. Schulenberg. (2008) *Monitoring the Future National Survey Results on Drug Use, 1975–2007*. Vol. I: Secondary School Students. Bethesda, MD: National Institute on Drug Abuse.

Kadison, Richard. (2005) "Getting an Edge: Use of Stimulants and Antidepressants in College." *New England Journal of Medicine* 353: 1089–91.

Kahn, Arnie S., and V. Andreoli Mathie. (2000) "Understanding the Unacknowledged Rape Victim." In C. B. Travis and J. W. White, eds. *Sexuality, Society, and Feminism: Psychological Perspectives on Women*. Washington, D.C.: American Psychological Association.

Kandel, Denise B., and Mark Davies. (1996) "High School Students Who Use Crack and Other Drugs." *Archives of General Psychiatry* 53, 1: 71–80.

Kanin, Eugene J., and Stanley R. Parcell.

(1977) "Sexual Aggression: A Second Look at the Offended Female." *Archives of Sexual Behavior* 6: 67–76.

Karjane, Heather M., Bonnie S. Fisher, and Francis T. Cullen. (2002) *Campus Sexual Assault: How America's Institutions of Higher Education Respond.* Newton, MA: Educational Development Center, Inc.

KCTV News Homepage/Health. (September 3, 2008) Pain Meds Riskier Than Pot, Students Say. http://www.kctv5.com/health/17379322/detail.html.

Kienlen, Kristine K., D. L. Birmingham, Kenneth B. Solberg, J. T. O'Regan, and J. Reid Meloy. (1997) "A Comparative Study of Psychotic and Nonpsychotic Stalking." *Journal of the American Academy of Psychiatry and the Law* 25, 3: 317–34.

Kilpatrick, Dean. (1999) "Sexual Assault." In Grace Coleman, Mario Gaboury, Morna Murray, and Anne Seymour, eds. *National Victim Assistance Academy.* Washington, D.C.: U.S. Office for Victims of Crime. http://www.ojp.usdoj.gov/ovc/assist/nvaa99/welcome.html.

Kimmel, Michael S. (2002) "Gender Symmetry in Domestic Violence: A Substantive and Methodological Research Review." *Violence Against Women* 8: 1332–63.

Kinzie, Susan. (January 25, 2006) "Many Cases Unreported, Survey Finds." *Washington Post,* p. A2.

Koroknay, Alex. Legislative Analysis for the National Minimum Drinking Age Act. http://www.yria.alcade.net/essays/leg-an.htm.

Koss, Mary P. (1988) "Hidden Rape: Sexual Aggression and Victimization in a National Sample of Students in Higher Education." In Ann W. Burgess, ed. *Rape and Sexual Assault II.* New York: Garland.

_____, Christine Gidycz, and Nadine Wisniewski. (1987) "The Scope of Rape: Incidence and Prevalence of Sexual Aggression and Victimization in a National Sample of Higher Education Students." *Journal of Consulting and Clinical Psychology* 55, 2: 162–70.

_____, Thomas E. Dinero, Cynthia A. Seibel, and Susan L. Cox. (2006) "Stranger and Acquaintance Rape: Are There Differences in the Victim's Experience?" *Psychology of Women Quarterly* 12, 1: 1–24.

Krebs, Christopher P., Christine H. Lindquist, Tara D. Warner, Bonnie S. Fisher, and Sandra L. Martin. (2007) *The Campus Sexual Assault (CSA) Study.* Rockville, MD: National Institute of Justice.

Kuehl, Sheila. (1998) "Legal Remedies for Teen Dating Violence." In Barrie Levy, ed. *Dating Violence: Young Women in Danger.* Seattle: Seal Press.

Kuo, Meichun, Henry Wechsler, Patty Greenberg, and Hang Lee. (2003) "The Marketing of Alcohol to College Students: The Role of Low Prices and Special Promotions." *American Journal of Preventive Medicine* 25: 204–211.

LaBrie, Joseph W., Andrea Rodrigues, Jason Schiffman, and Summer Tawalbeh. (2007) "Early Alcohol Initiation Increases Risk Related to Drinking Among College Students." *Journal of Child & Adolescent Substance Abuse* 17, 2: 125–41.

Lackie, Leandra, and Anton F. de Man. (1997) "Correlates of Sexual Aggression Among Male University Students." *Sex Roles: A Journal of Research* 37: 451–57.

LAMBDA GLBT Community Services. http://www.lambda.org/.

Lane, Katherine E., and Patricia A. Gwartney-Gibbs. (1985) "Violence in the Context of Dating and Sex." *Journal of Family Issues* 6, 1: 45–49.

Laner, Mary R. (1989) "Competition and Combativeness in Courtship: Reports From Men." *Journal of Family Violence* 4, 1: 47–62.

Lange, James E., and Robert B. Voas. (2001) "Defining Binge Drinking Quantities Through Resulting Blood Alcohol Concentration." *Psychology of Addictive Behaviors* 84: 508–18.

Langman, Peter. (2009) *Why Kids Kill: Inside the Minds of School Shooters.* New York: Palgrave Macmillan.

Lawrence, Frederick M. (2002) *Punishing Hate: Bias Crimes Under American Law.* Cambridge, MA: Harvard University Press.

Lederman, Douglas. (March 9, 1994) "Weapons on Campus? Officials Warn That Colleges Are Not Immune From the Scourge of Handguns." *Chronicle of Higher Education*: A33–A34.

Lee, Rebecca K. (1988) "Romantic and Electronic Stalking in a College Context." *William & Mary Journal of Women and the Law* 4: 373–466.

Leinwand, Donna. (February 11, 2009) "4 States, Among Last Holdouts, Eye Open-Carry Gun Laws." *USA Today.* http://www.usatoday.com/news/nation/2009–02–11-guns_N.htm.

Lester, David. (1995) *Serial Killers: The Insatiable Passion.* Philadelphia, PA: Charles Press.

Levin, Brian. (1999) "Hate Crimes: Worse by Definition." *Journal of Contemporary Criminal Justice* 15, 1: 6–21.

Levin, Jack, and Jack McDevitt. (1993) *Hate Crimes: The Rising Tide of Bigotry and Bloodshed.* New York: Plenum, 1993.

Levy, Barrie. (1990) "Abusive Teen Dating Relationship: An Emerging Issue for the 90s." *Response to the Victimization of Women and Children* 13, 1: 59.

Local Law Enforcement Hate Crimes Prevention Act. (2007) H.R. 1592.

Lott, Bernice, Mary E. Reilly, and Dale Howard. (1982) "Sexual Assault and Harassment: A Campus Community Study." *Signs: Journal of Women in Culture and Society* 8, 2: 297–319.

Lunde, Donald T. (1979) *Murder and Madness.* New York: Norton.

Luthra, Rohini, and Christine A. Gidycz. (2006) "Dating Violence Among College Men and Women." *Journal of Interpersonal Violence* 21, 6: 717–31.

Malamuth, Neil M. (1981) "Rape Proclivity Among Males." *Journal of Social Issues* 37, 4: 138–57.

Marshall, Linda L., and Patricia Rose. (1987) "Gender, Stress, and Violence in Adult Relationships of a Sample of College Students." *Journal of Social and Personal Relationships* 4: 299–316.

Martin, Patricia Y., and Robert A. Hummer. (1989) "Fraternities and Rape on Campus." *Gender and Society* 3, 4: 457–73.

Martindale, Gayla. Hate Crimes on Campus. StateUniversity.com Blog. http://www.stateuniversity.com/blog/permalink/College-Hate-Crimes.html.

McCabe, Sean Esteban, Brady T. West, and Henry H. Wechsler. (2007) "Alcohol-Use Disorders and Nonmedical Use of Prescription Drugs Among U.S. College Students." *Journal of Studies on Alcohol and Drugs* 68, 4: 543–47.

_____, and Christian J. Teter. (2007) "Drug Use Related Problems Among Nonmedical Users of Prescription Stimulants: A Web-Based Survey of College Students from a Midwestern University." *Drug Alcohol Depend* 91, 1: 69–76.

_____, Christian J. Teter, Carol J. Boyd, John R. Knight, and Henry Wechsler. (2005) "Nonmedical Use of Prescription Opioids Among U.S. College Students." *Addictive Behaviors* 30, 4: 789–805.

_____, John R. Knight, Christian J. Teter, and Henry Wechsler. (2005) "Nonmedical Use of Prescription Stimulants Among U.S. College Students: Prevalence and Correlates From a National Survey." *Addition* 99: 96–106.

McDevitt, Jack, Jack Levin, and Susan Bennett. (2002) "Hate Crime Offenders: An Expanded Typology." *Journal of Social Issues* 58, 2: 303–17.

_____, Jennifer M. Balboni, and Susan Bennett. (2000) *Improving the Quality and Accuracy of Bias Crime Statistics Nationally: An Assessment of the First Ten Years of Bias Crime Data Collection.* Washington, D.C.: Bureau of Justice Statistics.

McEwan, Troy, Paul E. Mullen, and Rosemary Purcell. (2007) "Identifying Risk Factors in Stalking: A Review of Current Research." *International Journal of Law and Psychiatry* 30, 1: 1–9.

McFarlane, Judith M., Jacquelyn C. Campbell, Susan Wilt, Carolyn J. Sachs, Yvonne Ulrich, and Xiao Xu. (1999) "Stalking and Intimate Partner Femicide." *Homicide Studies* 3, 4: 300–16.

McGregor, Margaret J., Ellen Wiebe, Stephen A. Marion, and Cathy Livingstone. (2000) "Why Don't More Women Report Sexual Assault to the Police?" *Canadian Medical Association Journal* 165, 2: 659–60.

Meloy, J. Reid, and Cynthia Boyd. (2003) "Female Stalkers and Their Victims." *Journal of the American Academy of Psychiatry and the Law* 31: 211–19.

Metropolitan Drug Commission. Rave/Club Drugs. http://www.metrodrug.org/drugs/clubdrugs.aspx.

Miller, Jacqueline W., Timothy S. Naimi, Robert D. Brewer, and Sherry Everett Jones. (2007) "Binge Drinking and Associated Health Risk Behaviors Among High School Students." *Pediatrics* 119, 1: 76–85.

Miller, Ted, Mark A. Cohen, and Brian Wiersema. (1996) *Victim Costs and Consequences: A New Look.* Washington, D.C.: National Institute of Justice.

Mohandie, Kris, J. Reid Meloy, Mila Green McGowan, and Jenn Williams.

(2006) "The RECON Typology of Stalking: Reliability and Validity Based upon a Large Sample of North American Stalkers." *Journal of Forensic Sciences* 51, 1: 147–55.

Mohler-Kuo, Meichun, George W. Dowdall, Mary P. Koss, and Henry Wechsler. (2004) "Correlates of Rape While Intoxicated in a National Sample of College Women." *Journal of Studies on Alcohol* 65, 1: 37–45.

Muehlenhard, Charlene L., and Melaney A. Linton. (1987) "Date Rape and Sexual Aggression in Dating Situations: Incidence and Risk Factors." *Journal of Counseling Psychology* 34, 2: 186–96.

Mulford, Carrie, and Peggy C. Giordano. (2008) *Teen Dating Violence: A Closer Look at Adolescent Romantic Relationships.* Washington, D.C.: National Institute of Justice. http://www.ojp.usdoj.gov/nij/journals/261/teen-dating-violence.htm.

Mullen, Paul E., Michele Pathé, and Rosemary Purcell. (2000) *Stalkers and Their Victims*, 2nd ed. Cambridge: Cambridge University Press.

_____, Michele Pathé, Rosemary Purcell, and Geoffrey W. Stuart. (1999) "Study of Stalkers." *American Journal of Psychiatry* 156: 1244–49.

Mustaine, Elizabeth E., and Richard Tewksbury. (1999) "A Routine Activity Theory Explanation of Women's Stalking Victimizations." *Violence Against Women* 5, 1: 43–62.

My Student Health Zone. Personal Safety. http://kidshealth.org/PageManager.jsp?dn=studenthealthzone&article_set=39373&lic=180&cat_id=20305.

Narconon Drug Detox Rehab Program in America. Effects of Heavy Marijuana Use on Learning and Social Behavior. http://www.theroadout.org/drug_information/marijuana/effects_of_heavy_marijuana_use_on_learning_and_social_behavior.html.

National Center for Victims for Crime's Report. Dating Violence on Campus. http://www.ncvc.org/ncvc/AGP.Net/Components/documentViewer/Download.aspxnz?DocumentID=37929.

National Center for Victims of Crime. Minor's Access to Protective Orders. http://www.ncvc.org/ncvc/main.aspx?dbName=DocumentViewer&DocumentID=++32674.

_____. Stalking Resource Center. Criminal Stalking Laws by State/Oregon. http://www.ncvc.org/src/main.aspx?dbID=DB_Oregon179.

_____ and Crime Victims Research and Treatment Center. (1992) *Rape in America: A Report to the Nation.* Arlington, VA: National Center for Victims of Crime.

National Coalition of Anti-Violence Programs. http://www.ncavp.org/.

National Highway Traffic Safety Administration (NHTSA). (2000) "Marijuana and Alcohol Combined Severely Impede Driving Performance." *Annals of Emergency Medicine* 35, 4: 398–99.

National Institutes of Health. National Institute on Drug Abuse. NIDA Info-Facts: Club Drugs (GHB, Ketamine, and Rohypnol). http://www.drugabuse.gov/InfoFacts/clubdrugs.html.

_____. National Institute on Drug Abuse. Research Report Series — Marijuana Abuse. (July 22, 2008) How Does Marijuana Use Affect School, Work, and Social Life? http://www.nida.nih.gov/ResearchReports/Marijuana/Marijuana4.html.

National Minimum Drinking Age Act. (1984) 23 U.S.C. § 158. P.L. 98–363.

National Survey on Drug Use and Health. (2006) "Underage Alcohol Use Among Full-Time College Students." *NSDUH Report* 31. http://oas.samhsa.gov/2k6/college/collegeUnderage.htm.

National Victim Assistance Academy. (2002) Special Topics, Section 2: Stalking. http://www.ojp.usdoj.gov/ovc/assist/nvaa2002/chapter22_2.html.

Neville, Helen A., and Aalece O. Pugh. (1997) "General and Cultural Specific Factors Influencing African-American Women's Reporting Patterns and Perceived Social Support Following Sexual Assault." *Violence Against Women* 3, 4: 361–81.

Newman, Katherine S., Cybelle Fox, Wendy Roth, Jal Mehta, and David Harding. (2005) *Rampage: The Social Roots of School Shootings.* New York: Basic Books.

Nichols, W. David. (1995) "Violence on Campus: The Intruded Sanctuary." *FBI Law Enforcement Bulletin* 64, 6: 1–5.

Nolan, James J. III, Jack McDevitt, Shea Cronin, and Amy Farrell. (2004) "Learning to See Hate Crimes: A Framework for Understanding and Clarifying Ambiguities in Bias Crime Classification." *The Justice Professional* 17, 1: 91–105.

_____, Yoshio Akiyama, and Samuel Berhanu. (2002) "The Hate Crime Statistics Act of 1990: Developing a Method for Measuring the Occurrence of Hate Violence." *American Behavioral Scientist* 46, 1: 136–53.

North Dakota Council on Abused Women's Services. Coalition Against Sexual Assault in North Dakota. What is Stalking? Definitions. http://www.ndcaws.org/harassment/stalkinglaws.asp.

O'Keefe, Maura., K. Brockopp, and E. Chew. (1986) "Teen Dating Violence." *Social Work* 31: 465–68.

_____, and Leah Aldridge. Teen Dating Violence: A Review of Risk Factors and Prevention Efforts. National Online Resource Center on Violence Against Women. http://new.vawnet.org/category/Main_Doc.php?docid=409.

O'Leary, K. Daniel, A. M. Smith Slep, Sarah Avery-Leaf, and Michele Cascardi. (2008) "Gender Differences in

Dating Aggression Among Multiethnic High School Students." *Journal of Adolescent Health* 42: 473–479.

O'Sullivan, Chris. (1991) "Acquaintance Gang Rape on Campus." In Andrea Parrot and Laurie Bechhofer, eds. *Acquaintance Rape: The Hidden Crime.* New York: John Wiley.

Office of National Drug Control Policy. Club Drugs Facts and Figures. http://www.whitehousedrugpolicy.gov/drugfact/club/club_drug_ff.html.

Osterholm, Karen, Deborah E. Horn, and William A. Kritsonis. (2007) "College Professors as Potential Victims of Stalking: Awareness and Prevention: National Implications." *Focus on Colleges, Universities and Schools* 1, 1: 2–4.

Palmer, Carolyn J. (1993) *Violent Crimes and Other Forms of Victimization in Residence Halls.* Asheville, NC: College Administration Publications.

_____. (1996) "Violence and Other Forms of Victimization in Residence Halls: Perspectives of Resident Assistants." *Journal of College Student Development* 37, 3: 268–78.

Paludi, Michele A. (1996) *Sexual Harassment on College Campuses: Abusing the Ivory Power,* 2nd ed. Albany, NY: State University of New York Press.

Partnership for a Drug Free America. Ketamine. http://www.drugfree.org/Portal/Drug_Guide/Ketamine.

Perkins, H. Wesley, William DeJong, and Jeff Linkenbach. (2001) "Estimated Blood Alcohol Levels Reached by 'Binge' and 'Nonbinge' Drinkers: A Survey of Young Adults in Montana." *Psychology of Addictive Behaviors* 15, 4: 317–20.

Perry, Tony. (May 7, 2008) 96 "Arrested in San Diego Drug Bust." *Los Angeles Times.* http://articles.latimes.com/2008/may/07/local/me-drugbust7.

Phillips, Lorraine, Ryan Quirk, Barry Rosenfeld, and Maureen O'Connor. (2004) "Is It Stalking? Perceptions of Stalking Among College Undergraduates." *Criminal Justice and Behavior* 31, 1: 73–96.

Plass, M. S., and J. C. Gessner. (1983) "Violence in Courtship Relations: A Southern Example." *Free Inquiry in Creative Sociology* 11: 198–202.

Pope, Harrison G., Jr. and Deborah Yurgelun-Todd. (1996) "The Residual Cognitive Effects of Heavy Marijuana Use in College Students." *Journal of the American Medical Association* 275, 7: 521–27.

Port, Tami. (August 28, 2007) Stalking Crime Antistalking Laws. Suite101.com. http://personalitydisorders.suite101.com/article.cfm/stalking_law.

Potter, Robert, Jeanne Krider, and Pamela McMahon. (2000) "Examining Elements of Campus Sexual Violence Policies: Is Deterrence or Health Promotion Favored?" *Violence Against Women* 6: 1345–62.

Presley, Cheryl A., Jami S. Leichliter, and Phillip W. Meilman. (1998) *Alcohol and Drugs on American College Campuses: A Report to Colleges Presidents.* Carbondale, IL: Core Institute, Southern Illinois University.

_____, Jami S. Leichliter, and Philip W. Meilman. (1999) *Alcohol and Drugs on American College Campuses: A Report to College Presidents.* Carbondale, IL: Southern Illinois University.

_____, Philip W. Meilman, and Jeffrey R. Cashin. (1996) *Alcohol and Drugs on American College Campuses: Use, Consequences, and Perceptions of the Campus Environment, Volume IV: 1992–94.* Carbondale, IL: Core Institute, Southern Illinois University.

_____, Philip W. Meilman, and Jeffrey R. Cashin. (1997) "Weapon Carrying and Substance Abuse Among College Students." *Journal of American College Health* 46, 1: 3–8.

_____, Philip W. Meilman, and Rob Ly-erla. (1993) *Alcohol and Drugs on College Campuses: Use, Consequence, and Perceptions of the Campus Environment.* Carbondale, IL: Core Institute.

Preventing Underage Drinking: A School-Based Approach. http://www.ed.gov/admins/lead/safety/training/alcohol/prevent.html.

Rape, Abuse and Incest National Network. How Often Does Sexual Assault Occur? http://www.rainn.org/get-information/statistics/frequency-of-sexual-assault.

_____. Who Are the Victims? http://www.rainn.org/get-information/statistics/sexual-assault-victims.

Rayburn, Nadine Recker, Mitchell Earleywine, and Gerald C. Davison. (2003) "Base Rates of Hate Crime Victimization Among College Students." *Journal of Interpersonal Violence* 18, 10: 1209–21.

Reifman, Alan, and Wendy K. Watson. (2003) "Binge Drinking During the First Semester of College: Continuation and Desistance from High School Patterns." *Journal of American College Health* 52, 2: 73–81.

Reilly, Mary E., Bernice Lott, Donna Caldwell, and Luisa DeLuca. (1992) "Tolerance for Sexual Harassment Related to Self-Reported Sexual Victimization." *Gender and Society* 6, 1: 122–38.

Report From Friends of Simon Wiesenthal Center Reveals Internet Hate Sites on the Rise; Center Honours Local Police. (October 20, 2008) Reuters. http://www.reuters.com/article/press Release/idUS135228+20-Oct-2008+M W20081020.

Research Findings on Underage Drinking and the Minimum Legal Drinking Age. http://www.niaaa.nih.gov/AboutNIA AA/NIAAASponsoredPrograms/drinki ngage.htm.

Roberts, Karl A. (2005) "Women's Experience of Violence During Stalking by Former Romantic Partners." *Violence Against Women* 11: 89–114.

Roberts, Timothy A., and Jonathan D. Klein. (2003) "Intimate Partner Abuse and High-Risk Behavior in Adolescents." *Archives of Pediatrics and Adolescent Medicine* 157: 375–80.

Roscoe, Bruce, and Tammy Kelsey. (1986) "Dating Violence Among High School Students." *Psychology* 23, 1: 53–59.

Rosenfeld, Barry. (2004) "Violence Risk Factors in Stalking and Obsessional Harassment." *Criminal Justice and Behavior* 31: 1.

Royakkers, Lambèr. (2000) "The Dutch Approach to Stalking Laws." *California Criminal Law Review* 3: 7.

Russell, Diana E. H. (1986) *The Secret Trauma: Incest in the Lives of Girls and Women.* New York: Basic Books.

Rutledge, Patricia C., Aesoon Park, and Kenneth J. Sher. (2008) "21st Birthday Drinking: Extremely Extreme." *Journal of Consulting and Clinical Psychology* 76, 3: 511–16.

Rymel, Laura. (2004) *What is the Difference Between Rape and Sexual Assault?* Little Rock, AR: School Violence Resource Center.

Sampson, Rana. (2002) *Acquaintance Rape of College Students.* Washington, D.C.: Office of Community Oriented Policing Services.

Sanday, Peggy. (1990) *Fraternity Gang Rape: Sex, Brotherhood, and Privilege on Campus.* New York: New York University Press.

School Violence Resource Center. SVRC Fact Sheet. Murders Involving the College Population. www.svrc.net/Files/Murders.pdf.

Schwartz, Martin D., and Molly S. Leggett. (1999) "Bad Dates or Emotional Trauma? The Aftermath of Campus Sexual Assault." *Violence Against Women: An International and Interdisciplinary Journal* 5, 3: 251–71.

Science Daily. (September 5, 2007) Underage Drinking Starts Before Adolescence. http://www.sciencedaily.com/releases/2007/08/070831093912.htm.

_____. (July 14, 2008) Binge Drinking Tied to Conditions in the College Environment. http://www.sciencedaily.com/releases/2007/08/070831093912.htm.

Scully, Diana, and Joseph Marolla. (1983) "Incarcerated Rapists: Exploring a Sociological Mode." *Final Report for Department of Health and Human Services.* Washington, D.C.: Government Printing Office.

Searles, Patricia, and Ronald J. Berger. (1987) "The Current Status of Rape Reform Legislation: An Examination of State Statutes." *Women's Rights Law Reporter* 10: 25–43.

Security on Campus, Inc. 2008 Clery Act Amendments: Included in Higher Education Opportunity Act (P.L. 110–315) Enacted into Law August 14, 2008; Effective Immediately. http://www.securityoncampus.org/index.php?option=com_content&view=article&id=345%3A2008cleryactamendments&catid=64%3Acleryact&Itemid=60.

_____. Security on Campus, Inc. Major Legislative Accomplishments. http://www.securityoncampus.org/index.php?option=com_content&view=article&id=295:majoraccomplishments&catid=58:federallegislation&Itemid=92.

Sellers, Christine, and Max Bromley. (1996) "Violent Behavior in College Student Dating Relationships: Implications for Campus Providers." *Journal of Contemporary Justice* 12, 1: 1–27.

Sessa, Frances M. (2005) "The Influence of Perceived Parenting on Substance Use During the Transition to College: A Comparison of Male Residential and Commuter Students." *Journal of College Student Development* 46: 62–74.

Seymour, Anne, Melissa Hook, and Carl Grimes. (2002) Hate and Bias Crime. In Anne Seymour, Morna Murray, Jane Sigmon, Melissa Hook, Christine Edmunds, Mario Gaboury, and Grace Coleman, eds. *National Victim Assistance Academy Textbook.* Washington, D.C.: U.S. Department of Justice, Office for Victims of Crime.

_____, Morna Murray, Jane Sigmon, Melissa Hook, Christine Edmunds, Mario Gaboury, and Grace Coleman. (2008) *2000 National Victim Assistance Academy.* Washington, D.C.: U.S. Department of Justice, Office for Victims of Crime.

Sher, Kenneth J., and Patricia C. Rutledge. (2007) "Heavy Drinking Across the Transition to College: Predicting First-Semester Heavy Drinking from Precollege Variables." *Addictive Behaviors* 32, 4: 819–35.

Sheridan, Lorraine P., Eric Blaauw, and Graham M. Davies. (2003) "Stalking: Knowns and Unknowns." *Trauma, Violence, and Abuse* 4, 2: 148–62.

_____, and Graham M. Davies. (2001) "Stalking: The Elusive Crime." *Legal and Criminological Psychology* 6, 2: 133–47.

Shillington, Audrey M., Mark B. Reed, James E. Lange, John D. Clapp, and Susan Henry. (2006) "College Undergraduate Ritalin Abusers in Southwestern California: Protective and Risk Factors." *Journal of Drug Issues* 36, 4: 999–1014.

Shively, Michael. (2005) *Study of Literature and Legislation on Hate Crime in America.* Cambridge, MA: Abt Associates Inc.

Sigelman, Carol K., Carol J. Berry, and Katharine A. Wiles. (1984) "Violence in College Students' Dating Relationships." *Journal of Applied Social Psychology* 14, 6: 530–48.

Silverman, Jay G., Anita Raj, Lorelei A. Mucci, and Jeanne E. Hathaway. (2001)

"Dating Violence Against Adolescent Girls and Associated Substance Use, Unhealthy Weight Control, Sexual Risk Behavior, Pregnancy, and Suicidality." *Journal of the American Medical Association* 286, 5: 572–79.

Simons, Jeffrey S., Raluca M. Gaher, Christopher J. Correia, and Jacqueline A. Bush. (2005) "Club Drug Use Among College Students." *Addictive Behaviors* 30, 8: 1620.

Smith, Paige Hall, Jacquelyn W. White, and Lindsay J. Holland. (2003) "A Longitudinal Perspective on Dating Violence Among Adolescent and College-Age Women." *American Journal of Public Health* 93, 7: 1104–09.

Society for Prevention Research. (September 3, 2008) "First Year College Students Think Using Pain Killers and Stimulants Nonmedically is Less Risky Than Cocaine; More Risky Than Marijuana." http://www.preventionresearch.org/sprnews.php.

Spence-Diehl, Emily. (1999) *Stalking: A Handbook for Victims*. Holmes Beach, FL: Learning Publications.

Spitzberg, Brian H., and G. Hoobler. (2002) "Cyberstalking and the Technologies of Interpersonal Terrorism." *New Media and Society* 4: 71–92.

_____, and William R. Cupach. (2007) "State of the Art of Stalking: Taking Stock of the Emerging Literature." *Aggression and Violent Behavior* 12, 1: 64–86.

Stop Underage Drinking. Portal of Federal Resources. About Us. http://www.stopalcoholabuse.gov/About/.

_____. Portal of Federal Resources. SAMHSA's 2007 National Survey on Drug Use and Health (NSDUH). http://www.stopalcoholabuse.gov/Stats/.

Student Right-to-Know and Campus Security Act. (1990) P.L. 101–452.

_____. (1990) 20 U.S.C. § 1092.

Sugarman, David B., and Gerald T. Ho-

taling. (1998) "Dating Violence: A Review of Contextual and Risk Factors." In Barrie Levy, ed. *Dating Violence: Young Women in Danger*. Seattle: Seal Press.

Surface Transportation and Uniform Relocation Assistance Act. (1987) P.L. 100–17.

Svalastoga, Kaare. (1962) "Rape and Social Structure." *Pacific Sociological Review* 5: 48–53.

Tennessee Victims of Crime State Coordinating Council,. Date Rape Drugs. http://www.tcadsv.org/Websites/vcscc/daterapedrugs.htm.

Testa, Maria, Jennifer A. Livingston, and Kenneth E. Leonard. (2003) "Women's Substance Use and Experiences of Intimate Partner Violence: A Longitudinal Investigation Among A Community Sample." *Addictive Behaviors* 28, 9: 1649–64.

Teter, Christian J., Sean Esteban McCabe, Kristy LaGrange, James A. Cranford, and Carol J. Boyd. (2006) "Illicit Use of Specific Prescription Stimulants Among College Students: Prevalence, Motives, and Routes of Administration." *Pharmacology* 26: 1501–10.

Thisdell, Katie. (September 4, 2008) "JMU May Join Va. Tech in New Gun Policies." *The Breeze*. http://www.thebreeze.org/2008/09–04/news2.html.

Thombs, Dennis L., R. Scott Olds, and Barbara M. Snyder. (2003) "Field Assessment of BAC Data to Study Late-Night College Drinking." *Journal of Studies on Alcohol* 64, 3: 322–30.

Title 18, Part 1, Chapter 109A. (1986) § 2241. Aggravated Sexual Abuse.

_____. (1986) § 2242. Sexual Abuse.

Tjaden, Patricia, and Nancy Thoennes. (1998) *Stalking in America: Findings From the National Violence Against Women Survey*. Washington, D.C.: National Institute of Justice.

_____, and Nancy Thoennes. (2000) *Full*

Report of the Prevalence, Incidence, and Consequences of Violence Against Women: Findings From the National Violence Against Women Survey. Washington, D.C.: National Institute of Justice.

Tyler, Kimberly A., Dan R. Hoyt, and Les B. Whitbeck. (1998) "Coercive Sexual Strategies." *Violence and Victims* 13, 1: 47–61.

Underage Drinking Research. 8th, 10th, and 12th Grade Drinking. http://www.alcoholstats.com/page.aspx?id=135#4.

U.S. Department of Education. Higher Education Center for Alcohol and Other Drug Abuse and Violence Prevention. Drug-Free Schools and Communities Act (DFSCA) and Drug and Alcohol Abuse Prevention Regulations. http://www.higheredcenter.org/mandates/dfsca.

_____. Higher Education Center for Alcohol and Other Drug Abuse and Violence Prevention. GHB. http://www.higheredcenter.org/high-risk/drugs/club-drugs/ghb.

_____. Higher Education Center for Alcohol and Other Drug Abuse and Violence Prevention. Other Drugs. http://www.higheredcenter.org/high-risk/drugs/.

_____. Higher Education Center for Alcohol and Other Drug Abuse and Violence Prevention. Prescription Abuse Among College Students. http://www.higheredcenter.org/services/assistance/topics/prescription-drug-abuse-among-college-students.

_____. Higher Education Center for Alcohol and Other Drug Abuse and Violence Prevention. Rohypnol. http://www.higheredcenter.org/high-risk/drugs/club-drugs/rohypnol.

_____. National Center for Education Statistics. (2005) *Indicators of School Crime and Safety: 2005*. Washington, D.C.: Institute of Education Sciences.

_____. National Center for Education Statistics. (2007) *Indicators of School Crime and Safety: 2007*. Washington, D.C.: Institute of Education Sciences.

_____. Preventing Underage Drinking: A School-Based Approach. http://www.ed.gov/admins/lead/safety/training/alcohol/prevent.html.

U.S. Department of Health and Human Services. Centers for Disease Control and Prevention. Quick Stats: Underage Drinking. http://www.cdc.gov/Alcohol/quickstats/underage_drinking.htm.

_____. (2008) *Monitoring the Future National Survey Results on Drug Use, 1975–2007: Volume I, Secondary School Students, 2007*. Bethesda, MD: National Institute on Drug Abuse.

_____. (2008) *Monitoring the Future National Survey Results on Drug Use, 1975–2007: Volume II, College Students and Adults Age 19–45, 2007*. Bethesda, MD: National Institute on Drug Abuse.

_____. (2009) *Monitoring the Future National Survey Results on Adolescent Drug Use: Overview of Key Findings, 2008*. Bethesda, MD: National Institute on Drug Abuse.

_____. National Institute on Alcohol Abuse and Alcoholism. (October 2002) *Alcohol Alert* 58. http://pubs.niaaa.nih.gov/publications/aa58.htm.

_____. National Institute on Alcohol Abuse and Alcoholism. (April 2006) *Alcohol Alert* 68. http://pubs.niaaa.nih.gov/publications/aa68/aa68.htm.

_____. National Institute on Alcohol Abuse and Alcoholism. (November 2007) College Drinking and its Consequences: New Data. http://www.collegedrinkingprevention.gov/1College_Bulletin-508_361C4E.pdf.

_____. National Institute on Alcohol Abuse and Alcoholism. Research Findings on College Drinking and the Minimum Legal Drinking Age. http://www.niaaa.nih.gov/AboutNIAAA/NIAAASponsoredPrograms/CollegeDrinkingMLDA.htm.

_____. National Institute on Alcohol Abuse and Alcoholism. Statistical Snapshot of College Drinking. http://www.niaaa.nih.gov/AboutNIAAA/NIAAA SponsoredPrograms/StatisticalSnap shotCollegeDrinking.htm.

_____. National Institute on Alcohol Abuse and Alcoholism. Statistical Snapshot of Underage Drinking. http://www.niaaa.nih.gov/AboutNIAAA/NI AAASponsoredPrograms/Statistical SnapshotUnderageDrinking.htm.

_____. National Survey on Drug Use and Health. (2005) *The NSDUH Report: College Enrollment Status and Past Year Illicit Drug Use Among Young Adults: 2002, 2003, and 2004.* Rockville, MD: Office of Applied Studies.

_____. SAMHSA's National Clearinghouse for Alcohol and Drug Information. Binge Drinking in Adolescents and College Students. http://ncadi.sam hsa.gov/govpubs/rpo995/.

_____. Substance Abuse and Mental Health Services Administration. (2008) *Results from the 2007 National Survey on Drug Use and Health: National Findings.* http://oas.samhsa.gov/NSDUH/2k7NSDUH/2k7results.cfm#2.2.

_____. The Surgeon General's Call to Action to Prevent and Reduce Underage Drinking. (2007) Rockville, MD. http://www.surgeongeneral.gov/top ics/underagedrinking.

U.S. Department of Justice. (1999) *1999 Report on Cyberstalking: a New Challenge for Law Enforcement Industry.* A Report from the Attorney General to the Vice President, August 1999. http://www.usdoj.gov/criminal/cybercrime/cy berstalking.htm.

_____. (2000) *Responding to Hate Crimes and Bias-Motivated Incidences on College/University Campuses.* Washington, D.C.: Community Relations Service.

_____. (2001) *Hate Crimes on Campus: The Problem and Efforts to Confront It.*

Washington, D.C.: Bureau of Justice Assistance.

_____. (2005) *Drinking in America: Myths, Realities, and Prevention Policy.* Washington, D.C.: Office of Juvenile Justice and Delinquency Prevention. http://www.udetc.org/documents/Drinking_i n_America.pdf.

_____. Bureau of Justice Statistics. Crime Victimization in the United States–Statistical Tables Index. http://www.ojp.usdoj.gov/bjs/abstract/cvus/defini tions.htm#rape_sexual_assault.

_____. Bureau of Justice Statistics. Intimate Partner Violence in the United States. http://www.ojp.usdoj.gov/bjs/intimate/ipv.htm.

_____. Bureau of Justice Statistics Special Report. (2005) *Hate Crime Reported by Victims and Police.* Washington, D.C.: Office of Justice Programs.

_____. Bureau of Justice Statistics Special Report. (2005) *Violent Victimization of College Students, 1995–2002.* Washington, D.C.: Office of Justice Programs.

_____. Bureau of Justice Statistics Special Report. (2008) *Campus Law Enforcement, 2004–05.* Washington, D.C.: Office of Justice Programs.

_____. Bureau of Justice Statistics Special Report. (2009) *National Crime Victimization Survey: Stalking Victimization in the United States.* Washington, D.C.: Office of Justice Programs.

_____. Federal Bureau of Investigation. *Uniform Crime Reports.* http://www.fbi.gov/ucr/ucr.htm.

_____. Federal Bureau of Investigation. (2004) *Crime in the United States 2004.* Hate Crime. http://www.fbi.gov/ucr/cius_04/offenses_reported/hate_crime/i ndex.html.

_____. Federal Bureau of Investigation. (October 2007) *School Violence, Crime in Schools and Colleges: A Study of Offenders and Arrestees Reported via National Incident-Based Reporting System*

Data. http://www.fbi.gov/ucr/schoolviolence/2007/index.html.

_____. Federal Bureau of Investigation. (2008) *Crime in the United States 2007*. Washington, D.C.: Criminal Justice Information Services Division. http://www.fbi.gov/ucr/cius2007/offenses/expanded_information/data/shrtable_02.html.

_____. Federal Bureau of Investigation. (January 12, 2009) *Crime in the United States: Preliminary Semiannual Uniform Crime Report, January to June 2008*. http://www.fbi.gov/ucr/2008prelim/index.html.

_____. National Institute of Justice. (October 1, 2008) Laws to Make Campuses Safer. http://www.ojp.usdoj.gov/nij/topics/crime/rape-sexual-violence/campus/laws.htm.

_____. Office of Justice Programs. Stalking. http://www.ojp.usdoj.gov/nij/topics/crime/stalking/welcome.htm#tja.

U.S. Secret Service. National Threat Assessment Center. (2002) "Preventing School Shootings: A Summary of a U.S. Secret Service Safe School Initiative Report." *National Institute of Justice Journal* 248: 10–15. http://www.ncjrs.gov/rr/vol4_2/38.html; Sam Houston University, "Right to Know and Campus Security Act of 1990," http://www.shsu.edu/students/righttoknow.html.

United Way of King County. Teen Dating Violence. http://www.uwkc.org/kcca/impact/DVSA/teen.asp.

University of Arkansas for Medical Sciences. (March 21, 2002) "Club Drugs" Are Dangerous, Psychologist Warns Teens. http://www.uams.edu/today/2002/032102/club.htm.

University of Chicago. Vice President for Campus Life and Dean of Students. Sexual Violence: Acquaintance/Date Rape. http://sexualviolence.uchicago.edu/daterape.shtml.

University of Michigan News Service.

(December 11, 2008) Various Stimulant Drugs Show Continuing Gradual Declines Among Teens in 2008, Most Illicit Drugs Hold Steady. http://monitoringthefuture.org/data/08data.html#2008data-drugs.

Vice President For Campus Life and Dean of Students in the University. Sexual Assault and Sexual Abuse. http://sexualviolence.uchicago.edu/assault.shtml.

Violence Against Women and Department of Justice Reauthorization Act. (2005) H.R. 3042.

_____. (2005) P.L. 109–162.

Violent Crime Control and Law Enforcement Act. (1994) P.L. 103–322.

Voas, Robert B., A. Scott Tippetts, and James C. Fell. (2003) "Assessing the Effectiveness of Minimum Legal Drinking Age and Zero Tolerance Laws in the United States." *Accident Analysis and Prevention* 35, 4: 579–87.

Waiping, Alice Lo, and Michael J. Sporakowski. (1989) "The Continuation of Violent Dating Relationships Among College Students." *Journal of College Student Development* 30: 432–39.

Walch, Anne G., and W. Eugene Broadhead. (1992) "Prevalence of Lifetime Sexual Victimization Among Women Patients." *Journal of Family Practice* 35: 511–16.

Wasserman, Cressida. Dating Violence on Campus: A Fact of Life. U.S. Department of Education's Higher Education Center for Alcohol and Other Drug Abuse and Violence Prevention, pp. 16–21. http://www.higheredcenter.org/resources/dating-violence-campus-fact-life.

Watts, W. David, and Anne Marie Ellis. (1993) "Sexual Abuse, Drinking and Drug Use: Implications for Prevention." *Journal of Drug Education* 23: 183–200.

Wechsler, Henry, Andrea Davenport, George W. Dowdall, Barbara Moeykens, and Sonia Castillo. (1994) "Health and Behavioral Consequences of Binge Drinking in College: A National Survey of Students at 140 Campuses." *Journal of the American Medical Association* 272: 1672–77.

_____, Jae Eun Lee, Jeana Gledhill-Hoyt, and Toben F. Nelson. (2001) "Alcohol Use and Problems at Colleges Banning Alcohol: Results of a National Survey." *Journal of Studies on Alcohol* 62: 133–41.

_____, Jae Eun Lee, Meichun Kuo, Mark Seibring, Toben F. Nelson, and Hang P. Lee. (2002) "Trends in College Binge Drinking During a Period of Increased Prevention Efforts: Findings From Four Harvard School of Public Health Study Surveys, 1993–2001." *Journal of American College Health* 50, 5: 203–217.

_____, Jae Eun Lee, Toben F. Nelson, and Hang P. Lee. (2001) "Drinking Levels, Alcohol Problems and Secondhand Effects in Substance-Free College Residences: Results of a National Study." *Journal of Studies on Alcohol* 62: 23–31.

_____, Jae Eun Lee, Toben F. Nelson, and Meichun Kuo. (2002) "Underage College Students' Drinking Behavior, Access to Alcohol, and the Influence of Deterrence Policies: Findings From the Harvard School of Public Health College Alcohol Study." *Journal of American College Health* 50, 5: 228.

_____, Matthew Miller, and David Hemenway. (2005) "College Alcohol Study: Guns at College. Harvard School of Public Health." http://www.h sph.harvard.edu/cas/Documents/guns.

Weiss, Joan C., Howard J. Ehrlich, Barbara E. K. Larcom. (Winter, 1991–92) "Ethnoviolence at Work." *Journal of Intergroup Relations* 18: 28–29.

Wekerle, Christine, and David A. Wolfe. (1999) "Dating Violence in Mid-Adolescence: Theory, Significance, and Emerging Prevention Initiatives." *Clinical Psychology Review* 19: 435–56.

White, Barbara P., Kathryn A. Becker-Blease, Kathleen Grace-Bishop. (2006) "Stimulant Medication Use, Misuse, and Abuse in an Undergraduate and Graduate Student Sample." *Journal of American College Health* 54: 261–68.

Whitten, Lori. (2006) "Studies Identify Factors Surrounding Rise in Abuse of Prescription Drugs by College Students." *NIDA Notes* 20, 4. http://www. drugabuse.gov/NIDA_notes/NNvol20 N4/Studies.html.

Wiehe, Vernon R., and Ann Richards. (1995) *Intimate Betrayal: Understanding and Responding to the Trauma of Acquaintance Rape.* Thousand Oaks, CA: Sage.

Wikipedia, the Free Encyclopedia. Clery Act. http://en.wikipedia.org/wiki/Clery _Act.

_____. Cyberstalking. http://en.wikiped ia.org/wiki/Cyberstalking.

_____. Hate Crime Laws in the United States. http://en.wikipedia.org/wiki/Ha te_crime_laws_in_the_United_States.

_____. List of School-Related Attacks. http://en.wikipedia.org/wiki/List_of_ school-related_attacks.

_____. School Shooting. http://en.wiki pedia.org/wiki/School_massacre.

_____. Stalking. http://en.wikipedia.org/ wiki/Stalking.

Williams, Jenny, Frank J. Chaloupka, and Henry Wechsler. (2005) "Are There Differential Effects of Price and Policy on College Students' Drinking Intensity?" *Contemporary Economic Policy* 23: 78–90.

Windmeyer, Shane. (2003) FBI and Education Reporting of Hate Crimes and Bias Incidents, Associations of College Unions International Forum. http:// www.ncjrs.gov/pdffiles1/nij/grants/2103 00.pdf.

Wolfe, David A., Christine Wekerle, Katreena Scott, Anna-Lee Straatman, and Carolyn Grasley. (2004) "Predicting

Abuse in Adolescent Dating Relationships Over 1 Year: The Role of Child Maltreatment and Trauma." *Journal of Abnormal Psychology* 113, 3: 406–15.

Women's Resource Center. Stop Dating Violence. http://www.uh.edu/wrc/DatingViolence.html.

Wood, Robert A., and Nona L. Wood. (2002) "Stalking the Stalker: A Profile of Offenders." *FBI Law Enforcement Bulletin* 71, 12: 1–7.

Yacoubian, George S., Jr., Meghan K. Green, and Ronald J. Peters. (2003) "Identifying the Prevalence and Correlates of Ecstasy and Other Club Drug (EOCD) Use Among High School Se-niors." *Journal of Ethnicity in Substance Abuse* 2, 2: 53–66.

Yanowitz, Karen L. (2006) "Influence of Gender and Experience on College Students' Stalking Schemas." *Violence and Victims* 21, 1: 91–100.

Your Total Health. (June 1, 2006) "Drug Use a Factor in Two-Thirds of Sexual Assaults." *Health Day News.* http://yourtotalhealth.ivillage.com/drug-use-factor-in-twothirds-sexual-assaults.html.

Zona, Michael A., Kaushal K. Sharma, and John Lane. (1993) "A Comparative Study of Erotomanic and Obsessional Subjects in a Forensic Sample." *Journal of Forensic Sciences* 38, 4: 894–903.

INDEX

175